The Hunter writing System

Sentence
Sense

Red Level

The Hunter Writing System

Sentence Sense

Red Level

Anthony Devereux Hunter, Sr.

Hunter & Joyce Publishing Company
Delhi, New York

THE SERIES:

THE HUNTER WRITING SYSTEM: SENTENCE SENSE,
RED LEVEL [The "Red Level" is the INTRODUCTORY LEVEL.]
The Hunter Writing System: Sentence Sense, Green Level
(September 1991) [The "Green Level" is the INTERMEDIATE LEVEL.]
The Hunter Writing System: Sentence Sense, Blue Level
(September 1992) [The "Blue Level" is the ADVANCED LEVEL.]

An accompanying *Skills Practice Book* and teacher's manual are
(or will be) available for each of these levels.

ORDERING INFORMATION:

CALL: 607-746-3196 or 800-462-7483 (800-INC-RITE)
WRITE: Hunter & Joyce Publishing Company
R.D. 2, Box 54
Delhi, NY 13753

ANTHONY DEVEREUX HUNTER, SR. has taught English for twenty-
nine years and Latin for one year in junior and senior high schools and
in colleges in the United States. In addition, he has taught English as
a second language overseas for three years. He has conducted many
workshops in the area of grammar and writing. His degrees include a
Ph.L. from St. Louis University and an M.A. and Ed.D—in the Teaching
of High School English—from Teachers College, Columbia University.

COVER: The layout for the cover is the work of Scott Jensen.

Printed in the United States of America
ISBN: 0-9625839-4-4

Preface

This is a *two*-volume work. This book contains all of the instruction. Its companion book, *The Hunter Writing System: Sentence Sense* SKILLS PRACTICE BOOK *(Red Level)*, contains all of the practice material.

Note that, ideally, each student will have his or her own copy of this book *to study from* because its graphic material and multitude of examples have been designed to give *visual* reinforcement to its instructional content.

Ideally too, all students will have their own copy of the companion volume, the *Skills Practice Book, to write in*. Their freedom to write in that book will enable them to devote their undivided attention to achieving the goals of the exercises as they carry them out.

As you can imagine, a work like this is the fruit of continual creation, experimentation, revision, and reaction to advice. I wish to pay tribute here to those who have most helped in this process.

I am indebted most of all to the late Robert L. Allen for his system of sector analysis, which he encouraged me to use and whose simplest elements have become one of the cornerstones of this work.

I am also indebted to the hundreds of students on Long Island and at the State University of New York at Delhi who have used my materials and in turn have helped me to improve them.

I am indebted, besides, to my wife Kathy—for her forbearance with my absorption in my work, for her encouragement throughout the project, for her insightful suggestions for its improvement, and for the numberless hours she has spent helping with the keyboarding.

I am also indebted to Richard A. Mitchell whose encouragement and critiquing of an important chapter of the work came at a critical time in its evolution.

I am indebted, too, to my sons Joseph, Philip, and Andrew who have taken the time to read significant parts of the text and whose insights have helped me improve it in important ways; to my daughter Julia for the extensive editing she has done; and to my daughter Rosemary for her help with the keyboarding.

I am indebted also to Eileen Scholl, Diane Meredith, and Edith Lacey, who have taught my most recent version(s) of the text and who have shared their reactions and offered valuable advice.

Finally, I am especially indebted to Denis M. Hennessy who has coached my every step in the last phase of this enormous undertaking.

A.H.

To the Student

The goal of this text is to help you *experience* how the structure of a sentence influences its meaning. This should benefit you in all the areas in which you use language. You should find yourself writing more spontaneously and effectively; reading with quicker and surer comprehension; speaking with greater confidence and correctness; and comprehending more surely and completely as you listen to others.

Though this text concerns itself with "grammar," it has discarded the inexact definitions in current use. It has replaced them with strategies that are easy, familiar, and fun.

This text has other unique features. It teaches the verb first and to 100% accuracy. It teaches a sense of structure by involving you in the rearranging of sentence parts and in the carrying out of substitutions. As a result, you learn by experience how groups of words can perform the important jobs in a sentence.

It has still more helpful features. It teaches the right order in which to unravel longer sentences. It has a superabundance of examples and practice material. Lastly, it has a handful of simpler terms and of new ones, but the changes should make learning easier and more enjoyable.

For those of you who already know some "school" grammar, you will find no conflict in terminology. However, the strategies used here are more accurate, more helpful, and (often) easier. You would be well advised to adopt these new strategies **in their entirety** if you wish to enjoy all the benefits that this new approach offers.

Here is some final advice. Learn the terms and strategies so well that you will not forget them. Then do the practice work **with utmost care**. You will find that your writing and reading will benefit exactly in proportion to the amount of effort you put in.

A.H.

Contents

Preface   v

To the Student   vii

1. **Background for Understanding Verbs**   1

   Background Terms   1
   What a Verb Is   3
   Jobs That Verbs Do   3
   Two Important Terms   4
   Verb Phrases and Their Ingredients   5
   Two Kinds of Helpers   8
   Components of a Main Verb   9
   Endnotes   12
   Review   13

2. **Nouns and Their Replacers**   15

   Nouns and Their Jobs   15
   The Noun Replacers   18
   Review   31

3. **Introduction to Agreement of Verbs with Their Subjects**   34

   Background Terms   34
   Agreement of a Verb with Its Subject   40
   Review   45

4. **More Information about Verbs**   46

   Spelling Patterns for Components of Main Verbs   46
   Importance of Verbs   52
   Misconceptions about Ways to Find Verbs   58
   Best Ways to Find Verbs   59
   Review   60

5. Helping Verbs   61

Starter Helping Verbs   61
Follower Helping Verbs   71
Review   76

6. Helping Verbs as Markers   77
   of Main Verbs

Truths about the Words That Make up   77
   Verb Phrases
Introduction to the "Tests to Follow   80
   to Succeed"
The Helpers plus WHAT/ING Word Verb Test   81
Endnotes about *WHAT*-Answering Wording   96
Review   97

7. Remaining Main Verbs   99

Truths about Remaining Verbs   99
The Do/does/did Test (to Find Remaining   105
   Main Verbs)
Endnote   123
Review   123

8. Simpler Questions   125

Truths about the Chief Parts of a Sentence   125
Terms to Know   131
The Main Subject Test—for Questions   132
Endnotes   141
Review   142

9. The Helper That Shifts   144
   —in Statements

Truths about the Ways to Find Main   145
   Subjects
More Truths about the Chief   147
   Parts of a Sentence
The Movable Starter Test   149
Review   165

10. Finding Main Subjects in Statements 167
The Main Subject Test—for Statements 167
Writing Tips for Using Space-filler *There* 174
Review 177

11. Front Wording **178**
Truths about Wording in the Front Position 178
The Comma Test (to Find Front Adverbials) 183
Changes Required for Other Tests 190
Changes You Must Make as an Editor 197
Identifying Front Adverbials 200
  inside Paragraphs
Final Truth about Front Adverbials 201
Writing Tips for Using Front Adverbials 201
Endnote 204
Review 204

12. Introduction to Conjunctions and **206**
  Punctuation
The Punctuation Marks of Greatest Importance 206
Terms to Know 210
The Job of Coordinating Conjunctions 213
Special Sentence Combining Strategies 217
Remedying Punctuation Faults 219
Endnote 223
Review 223

13. Questions That Start with a **225**
  Question Word
Truths about Question Words and 225
  Question Word Questions
The Main Subject Test—for Questions 236
  (Expanded) 236
Endnote 242
Review 243

14. Subjects versus Objects   245

Truths about Noun Jobs in Common   245
The Noun Job Tests   252
Truths about Subjects   253
Truths about Objects of Verbs   255
Truths about Prepositions and Their Objects   259
Writing Tips for Correct Choice of Pronoun   265
    Spelling
Endnotes   267
Review   269

15. Adjectives   271

Truths about Adjectives   271
Truths about Noun Clusters   278
The Adjective Test   281
Spelling Rules   289
Endnotes   293
Review   295

16. Adverbs   298

Truths about Adverbs That Modify Verbs   298
Truths about Adverbs That Modify   304
    Adjectives or Other Adverbs
The Adverb Test   307
Spelling Rules   307
Endnotes   310
Review   311

17. Introduction to Dependent Clauses   313

Truths about Dependent Clauses   313
The Dependent Clause Test   323
Endnotes   324
Review   325

Appendix: Rules for Agreement   327
    of a Verb with Its Subject

Index   330

Chapter 1

Background for Understanding Verbs

Verbs and nouns are the core components of English.
This chapter serves as an introduction to verbs. It stresses the primary jobs that they do, their component parts and spellings, and how they relate to sentences and dependent clauses.

You will find an introduction to nouns in the next chapter.

Background Terms

You must have a clear understanding of what a SENTENCE is and, in contrast, of what a DEPENDENT CLAUSE is.

Sentence

Most simply, a SENTENCE is wording that you may place a period or question mark after.

However, you may **not** place a period or question mark just anywhere. There are three sorts of arrangements of words that are acceptable sentences and that you may punctuate with a period or question mark.

The **first** of these is WORDING THAT ASKS A FULLY WORDED QUESTION.

Has Ed arrived?

Notice that these words ask a question even if you keep the question mark covered.

The **second** of these is WORDING THAT YOU CAN TURN INTO A QUESTION. (Such wording is called a STATE-MENT.)

A truck IS coming. ➡ *Is a truck i̶s̶ coming?*
[The second *is* has a line through it to indicate that
you should cover it AS YOU ASK THE QUESTION.]

Notice how you turn statements into questions. You take the word *IS* from **inside** the sentence and place it at the **start** of the sentence. NOTE THAT YOU CAN **NOT** LEAVE *IS* IN ITS OLD PLACE IN THE SENTENCE AT THE SAME TIME.

The **third** sort of arrangement of words is WORDING THAT INDICATES A COMMAND.

Drive carefully.

Notice how such a sentence is **neither** a question **nor** a statement.

● Do *PRACTICE A* (IDENTIFYING TYPES OF SENTENC-ES) in your *Skills Practice Book.*

Dependent Clause

A DEPENDENT CLAUSE is wording that looks as if it is a sentence. However, you may not punctuate such wording with a period or question mark because you cannot turn it into a question. Note this example.

if Ed has arrived

This is a clause (and **not** a sentence) because you cannot say H̶a̶s̶ ̶i̶f̶ ̶E̶d̶ ̶a̶r̶r̶i̶v̶e̶d̶ (note that this text uses a **strike-**

through line to indicate **incorrect** English).

If you want to make the wording *if Ed has arrived* a sentence, you must add more wording. See the example.

Everyone is here if Ed has arrived.

You know that this is a sentence because you can create the question *Is everyone here if Ed has arrived?* See below and Chapter 17 for more complete explanations.

● Do *PRACTICE B* (DISTINGUISHING BETWEEN SENTENCES AND DEPENDENT CLAUSES) in your *Skills Practice Book.*

What a Verb Is

The word VERB is the name given to wording whose **primary role** is to serve as the CORE OR NUCLEUS OF A SENTENCE OR DEPENDENT CLAUSE. Here are examples (the verbs are in darker lettering).

*Many birds **live** near a brook.*
*Cars **have made** traveling fun.*
*Businesses **must advertise** their goods.*

Notice that in these examples the verb is sometimes a **single word** while at other times it is a **set of words**. Notice also that when a verb is a set of words—as in *have made* above—the final word (*made*) is the word that carries the verb's main dictionary meaning.

The **secondary role** of the verb is to serve as **core of a group of words called a "verbal phrase."** See Chapters 2 and 4 for a fuller explanation of these.

Jobs That Verbs Do

In their primary role as the core of sentences or dependent clauses, verbs actually do at least **two jobs** at once. First, they **add information** about people, places, things, events, and so forth. Second, they indicate the time of the truth of the message.

When you say *Everyone UNDERSTANDS*, you are adding the information about *everyone* that they DO UNDERSTAND.

When you say *Everyone UNDERSTANDS*, you are also indicating that the TIME OF UNDERSTANDING IS NOW.

Two Important Terms

This should help you understand two new and important terms.

Subject

The first of these new terms is the word SUBJECT. Grammarians use the word SUBJECT to mean THE WORDING THAT THE VERB ADDS INFORMATION ABOUT. For example, in the sentence *EVERYONE understands*, the subject is *EVERYONE*.

Subject:
Wording (usually before the verb) that a verb adds information about.

Important Note: This text will use SHADING INSIDE BOXES to indicate MATERIAL THAT YOU SHOULD LEARN SO WELL THAT YOU WILL NOT FORGET IT.

Tense

The second new term is the word TENSE. Grammarians use the word TENSE to mean THE WAY OF WRITING A VERB TO INDICATE THE TIME OF HAPPENING OF THE MESSAGE. The three most important times (each has a corresponding tense) are these: TIME NOW or in the PRESENT, TIME EARLIER THAN NOW or in the PAST,

4

and TIME LATER THAN NOW or in the FUTURE. Note the examples.

*Beth **understands**. / We **understand**.*
[Time is **now**; tense is **present**]

*Everyone **understood**.*
[Time is **earlier than now**; tense is **past**]

*Everyone **will understand**.* [Time is **later than now**; tense is **future**]

Notice, in the last example, the use of the **two words** *WILL UNDERSTAND* to indicate **future tense.**

Tense:
Way of writing a verb to indicate the time of happening of the message.

Verb Phrases and Their Ingredients

As you just saw for the future tense, it often takes two or more words to enable a verb to carry all the information that it must.

Verb Phrases

There is a special name for A VERB THAT IS MADE UP OF TWO OR MORE VERB WORDS. Grammarians use the name VERB PHRASE for such verbs. As you have seen, the future tense (*will understand*) uses a verb phrase.

Here are more examples of verb phrases (the verb phrases are in darker lettering).

*Ignored potholes **will grow** in size.*
*Man-made lakes **must be drained** to be cleaned.*
*Students who **have prepared** well **can find** tests to be easy.*

Grammarians have a name for each of the words in a verb phrase. The beginning words have the name HELPING VERBS. The last word always has the name MAIN VERB. See below for some important things to know about each of these terms.

Helping Verbs

Grammarians have a name for the BEGINNING WORDS OF A VERB PHRASE. They call these words HELPING VERBS. This text calls them HELPERS (for short). In the verb phrase *will be* coming, the words *will* and *be* are both helping verbs or helpers. Here is a display of this.

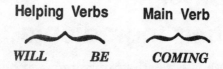

Important Note: HELPING VERBS **are just as TRULY VERB WORDS as a main verb word.** Sometimes (see below), they **serve as a main verb** instead of as a helping verb.

Note Again: When helping verbs have a companion main verb, the main verb ALWAYS **FOLLOWS** THE HELPING VERB(S).

Main Verb

Grammarians use the term MAIN VERB to mean the LAST WORD IN A VERB PHRASE—for example, the word *coming* in the verb phrase *will be coming.*

Grammarians **also** use the term MAIN VERB to mean a ONE-WORD VERB—for example, the **one word** *KNEW* in the sentence *Everyone knew the answer.*

Grammarians call the last word in a verb phrase the main verb because it alone carries the verb's main dictionary meaning. A one-word verb is also a main verb because it too carries the (verb's) main dictionary meaning.

Main Verb:
Last word in a verb phrase OR a stand-alone verb.

● **Do *Practice C*** (IDENTIFYING MAIN VERBS IN A VERB PHRASE) in your *Skills Practice Book.*

● **Do *Practice D*** (IDENTIFYING HELPING VERBS IN A VERB PHRASE) in your *Skills Practice Book.*

● **Do Practice E** (IDENTIFYING ONE-WORD MAIN VERBS) in your *Skills Practice Book.*

● **Do Practice F** (IDENTIFYING MAIN VERBS AND HELPING VERBS) in your *Skills Practice Book.*

Length of Verb Phrases

There is a limit to the number of words that a verb phrase can contain. The limit is **five** words altogether. Here are examples of verb phrases with an ever increasing number of verb words.

Al ***will carry*** *everything.*
[**two**-word phrase]

Al ***will have carried*** *everthing.*
[**three**-word phrase]

Bags ***will have been carried*** *aboard.*
[**four**-word phrase]

The Olympic torch ***will have been being carried*** *uninterruptedly for an entire week.*
[**five**-word phrase]

The five-word verb phrase looks strange because people rarely need to use it, but it does exist. You see it used in a sentence like *Our spy* ***could have been being watched*** *all that time.*

Two Kinds of Helpers

In this text, you will learn that there are two kinds of helpers.

Starter Helping Verbs

One kind of helper has the JOB OF MARKING THE PRESENCE OF A VERB. Most commonly, it MARKS THE START OF A VERB PHRASE as well. This text calls these STARTER HELPING VERBS or STARTERS (for short). There are twenty starters that are probably the most important words in English. See Chapter 5 for a complete list.

Follower Helping Verbs

The other kind of helper has the JOB OF FOLLOWING A STARTER. This text calls these helping verbs FOLLOWER HELPING VERBS or FOLLOWERS (for short). There are only four of these in English. See Chapter 5 for the list and further explanation.

Helping Verbs

Starter   Followers   Main Verb

COULD   *HAVE*   *BEEN*   *CARRIED*

Verb Phrase

Explanation: In this example, the word *could* is the starter helping verb (starter). The words *have* and *been* are the follower helpers (followers).

Components of a Main Verb

You have already learned that verbs have more than one job. The job to be done determines which component of the main verb you can use. For example, you cannot use the spelling *agree* when the time of the message is earlier than now and requires *agreed*. Note.

Last year, her parents ~~agree~~ *to give Sue a cat.*

Each of these spellings carries a different tense. Therefore, they are **not** interchangeable.

Almost without exception, the COMPONENTS of a main verb are its FIVE FIXED AND (USUALLY) CHARACTERISTIC SPELLINGS, EACH OF WHICH HAS ONE OR MORE JOBS THAT IT ALONE CAN PERFORM. (The verb *be* **alone** has EIGHT component parts.) Here is a list of the components of the verb break.

break   breaks   breaking   broke   broken

Jobs of Components

Most of a verb's five components have more than one job to do. For example, we use the basic component *agree* not only to indicate present tense but also as a partial indicator of future tense. You remember that we combine the helper *will* with the component *agree* to form the future tense *will agree.*

Therefore, a COMPONENT has both a fixed spelling and a specific set of uses or jobs for which this component— and no other—is to be used. For example, no writer can correctly write ~~will agreed~~.

You will learn more about these jobs as you proceed through the text.

Names for the Five Components

Schoolbooks have traditional names for each of the five components, but these are hard to understand and remember. This text has supplied simpler, DESCRIPTIVE NAMES (see below) that should be easier to remember.

YOU MUST LEARN THESE **DESCRIPTIVE NAMES** AND THEIR **MEANINGS** SO WELL THAT YOU WILL NOT FORGET THEM.

COMPONENTS OF A MAIN VERB

Traditional Name	DESCRIPTIVE NAME	DEFINITION
Infinitive	**Basic**	SPELLING TO WHICH YOU CAN ADD *ING.*
Third person singular, present tense	**S/es**	BASIC COMPONENT + S/ES. The verb *be* uses *is.* The verb *have* uses *has.*
Present participle	**Ing**	BASIC COMPONENT + ING. Every (main) verb in English has an *ING* component.
Past tense	**Past Tense**	**The component that "fits" when you say the verb with *yesterday* and without helpers**—it indicates time earlier than now.
Past participle	**After-Had**	**This is the component that "fits" when you say the verb after the helper *had.***

Examples				
Basic	S/es	Ing	Past Tense	After-Had
break *want*	*breaks* *wants*	*breaking* *wanting*	*BROKE* *WANTED*	*BROKEN* *WANTED*

Notice the difference in spelling of the **past tense** and **after-had** components of these two verbs. For the verb *break*, BROKE and BROKEN are different from each other and both are quite different from **break**. In contrast, for the verb *want*, WANTED and WANTED are both the same because both have **want** for their root spelling and both end in *ed*.

Most verbs have spellings like the verb *want* and have the name REGULAR VERBS. All those that have spellings UNLIKE the verb *want* have the name IRREGULAR VERBS. The verb *break* is one example of an irregular verb. See Chapter 4 for a fuller explanation of these two types of verbs.

● Do *PRACTICE G* (SUPPLYING COMPONENT SPELL-INGS FOR SIMPLER VERBS) in your *Skills Practice Book*.

Endnotes

Principal Parts of a Verb: Schoolbooks use the name "THE PRINCIPAL PARTS OF A VERB" to mean the four major components of the verb—its BASIC, ING, PAST TENSE, and AFTER-HAD COMPONENTS. This text will not use this terminology.

Starters as Main Verbs: Sometimes the JOB OF A STARTER is TO MARK THE PRESENCE OF A VERB BUT **NOT** OF A VERB PHRASE because it functions as the main verb all by itself. The starters from the *DO, HAVE,* and *BE*

SETS can have such a role. Note these examples.

Everyone DID well.
Bill HAS enough money.
Maria IS the captain.

Followers as Main Verbs: Sometimes the JOB OF A FOLLOWER is to follow a starter AND SERVE AS MAIN VERB (instead of just serving as a bridge to a main verb). Note these examples.

We SHOULD HAVE more scrap paper.
Three pages WILL BE enough.
Joanne HAS BEEN captain for two years.

Definition of a Verb: By the name VERB, grammarians mean a word in a sentence that carries an *-ing* way it can be spelled or a set of words whose last word carries an *-ing* way it can be spelled. This "word" must be "sayable"—that is, must be an acceptable English word—outside the sentence with or without an *-ing* ending **and** must retain the meaning it has in the sentence.

Review

DEFINITIONS IN DARKER LETTERING
MUST BE REMEMBERED.

Subject: Wording (usually before the verb) that a verb adds information about.

Tense: Way of writing a verb to indicate the time of happening of the message.

Present Tense: The time of happening is now.

Past Tense: The time of happening is earlier than now.

Future Tense: The time of happening is later than now.

Verb Phrase: Verbs made up of two or more verb words.

Starter Helper (Starter): A verb word that can start a verb phrase.

Follower Helper (Follower): A verb word that follows a starter helper.

Helping Verbs (Helpers): Starters and followers.

Main Verb: Last word in a verb phrase OR a stand-alone verb.

Components of a Main Verb: The five (eight for the verb *be*) fixed spellings that have one or more jobs that they alone can perform.

Basic Component: Spelling to which ING can be added.

S/es Component: BASIC COMPONENT PLUS S/ES.

Ing Component: BASIC COMPONENT PLUS ING.

Past Tense Component: Component sayable with *yesterday* when there is no helper.

After-Had Component: Component sayable after helper HAD.

Chapter 2

Nouns and
Their Replacers

This chapter serves as an introduction to nouns and their replacers.

Nouns and Their Jobs

THE IMPORTANCE OF THE JOBS OF NOUNS IS SECOND ONLY TO THE IMPORTANCE OF THE JOBS OF VERBS.

Nouns

Because nouns are one of the chief building blocks of English, you need a short-cut way of identifying one. There is such a way. It has the name the THE TEST (for finding nouns).

The THE TEST works this way: **You say** *THE* **before each word outside the sentence. If it "fits"—that is, if the two words sound right together—AND if the word's meaning does not change, the word is a noun.**

*A **horse** is an **animal** that will obey its **owner**.*

In this sentence, the nouns are *horse, animal,* and *owner* BECAUSE—**outside the sentence**—you can say THE *horse,* THE *animal,* and THE *owner.*

THIS IS AN INCOMPLETE VERSION OF THIS TEST. You will find the complete test in Chapter 15.

● Do *PRACTICE A* (USING THE THE TEST—TO FIND NOUNS) **in your** *Skills Practice Book.*

The THE Test for nouns fails to identify nouns that require capital letters. To find these other nouns, you simply look for their capital letter(s). (See the Capital Letter Test below.)

Noun:

A word you find by the THE Test and the Capital Letter Test and that serves as chief word in a noun territory.

The Job of Subject

You already know that a subject is the wording (usually) before a verb that the verb adds information about. You know, then, that the subject has an expected location or "territory." In this territory, the subject has one more job—namely, to answer WHO or WHAT there (sometimes it **asks** one of these questions instead).

The JOB OF SUBJECT is TO OCCUPY THE "TERRITORY" BEFORE A VERB AND ANSWER (OR ASK) *WHO* OR *WHAT* THERE.

Here is an example.

Trees sway.

In this sentence, the word *trees* does the job of a subject because it both fills the territory before the verb *sway* and answers the question *WHAT* when you ask *WHAT sway?* Here are more examples (the subjects are in darker lettering).

Ice melts.
Echoes reverberate.

Job of Subject:

To occupy the territory before a verb and answer (or ask) WHO or WHAT there.

The Term Noun Job

Notice that in *Trees sway* the subject *trees* is a **noun**. It is common that a noun will be either the only occupant or the chief occupant of such a territory. Since this is so, the job of occupying such a territory has the name NOUN JOB in this text. The term NOUN JOB means THE JOB THAT A NOUN (OR ITS REPLACER) DOES WHEN IT OCCUPIES A NOUN TERRITORY (LIKE THAT OF SUBJECT).

Noun Job:

The job that a noun (or its replacer) does when it occupies a noun territory.

All the jobs that nouns do have specific territories (like a subject does), and the words that fill the territory answer (or ask) *WHO, WHOM,* or *WHAT* there.

Three Noun Jobs

The job of subject is one of three especially important noun jobs.

The other two are to occupy two other noun-job territories—one **after a VERB** and the other **after a PREPOSITION**—and answer the questions *WHOM* or *WHAT* after the verb and preposition respectively. These jobs have the names OBJECT OF VERB and OBJECT OF PREPOSITION. Here are examples.

Sunshine HAS **warmth.**
Jan came WITH **friends.**

The word **warmth** does the (noun) job of OBJECT OF VERB, and the word **friends** does the (noun) job of OBJECT OF PREPOSITION. A PREPOSITION is a word like the word *WITH* in this sentence. It requires noun-job wording to complete its sense. See Chapter 14 for further explanation.

Here is a diagram to show the three noun-job territories as if in a picture (notice the use of the double underline to represent the location of a verb and the use of the right-angle symbol or "chair" to represent the location of a preposition).

Diagram to Show the Territories of Noun Jobs

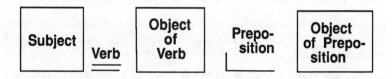

The preposition and its noun-job object have the name PREPOSITIONAL PHRASE and can appear almost anywhere in a sentence. Such a phrase is a tight-knit unit that is often only two or three words long.

Here is a sentence with its parts labeled to illustrate this.

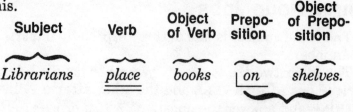

The Noun Replacers

Besides the noun, there can be other one-word or many-word occupants of a noun territory. These have the names **proper nouns, noun clusters, pronouns, phrases that can do the job of nouns, and noun clauses**. Because these occupants have the **same trait in common**—namely, TO OCCUPY A NOUN TERRITORY AND DO THE JOB OF A NOUN THERE—they have the name NOUN REPLACERS in this text.

Noun Replacer:

Wording that can occupy a noun territory and answer (or ask) the questions of a noun there.

Proper Nouns

There is one type of noun replacer that can be either one word long or many words long. This is another sort of noun. These nouns **start with capital letters** and have the special name PROPER NOUNS. Grammarians use the name PROPER NOUN to mean THE NAME OF A PARTICULAR PERSON, PLACE, OR "THING." Here is a sentence with examples.

*One of the theaters in **New York City** is **Radio City Music Hall**.*

[Remember that the **first word** of a sentence **always** starts with a capital letter, whether it is a proper noun or not.]

The proper nouns, of course, are **New York City** and **Radio City Music Hall**. NOTICE THAT EACH IMPORTANT WORD IN A PROPER NOUN BEGINS WITH A CAPITAL LETTER. Here are more examples.

*My friend **Jim Baxter** lives in **Dallas, Texas**.*

Note that a person's name is often a two- or three-word proper noun. On the other hand, a city or town has a name that is different from the name of its state, though the name of the state often accompanies it. Notice the COMMA that separates a city from its state.

Proper Nouns:
The name of a particular person, place, or "thing."

The capital letter at the start of important words in proper nouns is a MARKER of this kind of noun. It forms the basis for our **second test** to find nouns, the capital letter test. (We need this test because the THE TEST—FOR FINDING NOUNS does not work for proper nouns.)

The CAPITAL LETTER TEST works like this: YOU LABEL AS NOUNS THOSE WORDS THAT START WITH CAPITAL LETTERS (AND ARE DOING THE JOB OF A NOUN).

To find all nouns, you must use the CAPITAL LETTER TEST as a companion to the THE TEST. See Chapter 15.

Here are examples of proper nouns doing the job of subject.

Dorothy Hamill skates.
General Motors Company thrives.

● Do **PRACTICE B** (IDENTIFYING PROPER NOUNS) in your *Skills Practice Book*.

● Do **PRACTICE C** (IDENTIFYING MORE NOUNS) in your *Skills Practice Book*.

Noun Clusters

There is a many-word noun replacer that has the name NOUN CLUSTER. Grammarians use the name NOUN CLUSTER to mean ALL THE WORDS IN A NOUN TERRITORY WHEN THE CHIEF WORD IS A NOUN, PROPER NOUN, OR PRONOUN.

Here is an example.

The rather old TREE has lost a diseased LIMB.

In this sentence, the noun clusters are *the rather old TREE* and *a diseased LIMB*. The words *the rather old tree* are in the subject territory (*WHAT has lost a diseased limb?*). The words *a diseased limb* are in the object of verb territory (*has lost WHAT?*).

Notice the words *THE* and *A* that begin the clusters. These two words and a third word *AN*—called ARTICLES—are words that often begin a noun cluster and act as a marker of one when they do.

Here are examples of noun clusters doing the job of subject.

The oldest BOY works.
Well-prepared STUDENTS excel.

The chief word in a noun cluster, grammatically speaking, is the NOUN or PRONOUN (see below) that the surrounding words accompany. In the two sentences just given, the words of most grammatical importance in the two subjects are the nouns *BOY* and *STUDENTS*. The grammatical essence of these two sentences would be *...BOY works* and *...STUDENTS excel*.

Pronouns

PRONOUNS are WORDS THAT ARE NOT NOUNS BUT THAT CARRY THE MEANING OF A NOUN OR NOUN CLUSTER AND

TAKE THE PLACE OF THE NOUN AS THE CHIEF WORD IN A NOUN TERRITORY. Here are examples.

> *The boy beside **me** said that **he** had placed*
> ***his** beside **mine**.*

In this sentence, the pronouns are the words **me, he, his,** and **mine.** Notice that you cannot say *the* before these words outside the sentence **and** that each fills a noun territory (the word *beside* is a preposition).

Pronoun:

Words that are not nouns but that carry the meaning of a noun or noun cluster and take the place of the noun as the chief word in a noun territory.

Notice that the coming sections discuss several types of pronouns. IT WILL HELP YOU IF YOU CAN RECOGNIZE THESE PRONOUNS ON SIGHT whenever you see them.

Personal Pronouns

The PERSONAL PRONOUNS are the most commonly used of all pronouns in English. There are **seven** of them—each with a basic spelling. Note these.

BASIC SPELLING FOR THE SEVEN PERSONAL PRONOUNS

I	*it*
you	*we*
he	*they*
she	

22

This memory aid may be of help.

**MEMORY AID
FOR THE BASIC PERSONAL PRONOUNS**

YOU·HE IT·SHE [from] THEY I·WE —
(Say: "Hughey itchy from the ivy.")
[Note that "Hugh" or "Hughey" is a boy's name.]

Note that EACH OF THE SEVEN HAS SEVERAL COMPO-
NENTS AND EACH OF THESE COMPONENTS HAS A FIXED
SPELLING AND ONE OR MORE SPECIFIC JOBS THAT IT
ALONE PERFORMS. SOME HAVE THE **SAME** SPELLING FOR
MORE THAN ONE COMPONENT.

Note, too, that "personal" pronouns do not always
refer to human beings. See Chapter 3 for an explanation of their relationship to the verbs that accompany
them.

As Subjects

The **"BASIC" SPELLINGS** for the personal pronouns are
I, you, he, she, it, we, and *they* (see the Memory Aid
above). ONE OF THE JOBS OF THESE PRONOUNS IN
THEIR BASIC SPELLING IS TO SERVE AS SUBJECTS.
THEY CAN FILL THE SUBJECT TERRITORY AND ANSWER
WHO OR *WHAT* WHEN ASKED BEFORE THE VERB. Here is
an example.

*We are on one side, but **they** are on the other.*

The personal pronoun *we* is subject of the first *are* (*WHO
are on one side?*) while the personal pronoun *they* is
subject of the second *are* (*WHO are on the other?*).

THIS TEXT USES EACH BASIC ("SUBJECT") SPELLING AS
THE NAME FOR THE SET OF PRONOUNS THAT ARE TIED TO
THEM IN MEANING AND SPELLING. For example, there is
the *I* GROUP of personal pronouns that consist of the four
pronouns *I, me, mine,* and *myself.*

● Do **_PRACTICE D_** (IDENTIFYING PERSONAL PRO-
NOUNS IN THEIR BASIC/"SUBJECT" SPELLING) in
your **_Skills Practice Book._**

As Objects

There is another component, usually with a different
spelling, for the personal pronouns. THESE SERVE AS
OBJECTS. YOU USE THESE IN THE OBJECT OF VERB OR
OBJECT OF PREPOSITION TERRITORIES, WHERE THEY
ANSWER *WHOM* OR *WHAT* WHEN ASKED AFTER THE VERB
OR PREPOSITION. Here is an example sentence.

*Mary took **them** with **her**.*

The pronoun **them** from the *THEY* GROUP is object of the
verb *took* (*Mary took WHAT?*). The pronoun **her** from the
SHE GROUP is object of the preposition *with* (*with
WHOM?*).

Here is a chart of the two sets of spellings in contrast.

SPELLINGS FOR PERSONAL PRONOUN GROUPS BY TYPE	
As Subject	**As Object**
I	*me*
you	*you*
he	*him*
she	*her*
it	*it*
we	*us*
they	*them*

● Do **_PRACTICE E_** (IDENTIFYING PERSONAL PRO-
NOUNS IN THEIR SPELLINGS AS "OBJECTS") **in your**
Skills Practice Book.

As Adjectives

ANOTHER SET OF SPELLINGS RELATED TO THE SEVEN
PERSONAL PRONOUNS DO NOT SERVE AS PRONOUNS BUT AS
ADJECTIVES. When these pronouns (called POSSESSIVE
PRONOUNS) do the job of an adjective, they **appear**
inside any of the three noun territories, **stand before**
their chief noun—but not always right before it—and are
sayable with it. They answer the question WHOSE
when asked before the noun. Note this example.

Their _horse won_ **_his_** _first race with_ **_its_** _purse._

In this sentence, the words **_their, his,_** and **_its_** are all
doing the job of an adjective and **not** of a noun. They
answer respectively WHOSE _horse,_ WHOSE _race,_ and
WHOSE _purse._ The seven spellings for this job are: _my,_
your, his, her, its, our, and _their._

Explanation: You can **not** use the word _their_ in a
noun position because it is a substitute for the (prepositional) phrase _of them_—that also does the job of an
adjective. Note.

THEIR _plans changed._ [_The plans_ OF THEM _changed._]

As Indicators of Ownership

There is another component for these personal pronoun groups. THESE CAN FILL ANY NOUN TERRITORY
AND INDICATE "OWNERSHIP." Note these examples.

His _is with_ **_mine,_** _but_ **_yours_** _is on the chair._

The pronouns **_his_** and **_yours_** serve as subjects. The
pronoun **_mine_** is doing the job of object of preposition.

This chart shows these spellings in contrast with the
earlier ones.

SPELLINGS FOR PERSONAL PRONOUN GROUPS BY TYPE		
AS SUBJECT	AS OBJECT	INDICATING OWNERSHIP
I	*me*	*mine*
you	*you*	*yours*
he	*him*	*his*
she	*her*	*hers*
it	*it*	*its*
we	*us*	*ours*
they	*them*	*theirs*

● Do *PRACTICE F* (IDENTIFYING PERSONAL PRO-
NOUNS IN THEIR SPELLINGS THAT INDICATE OWN-
ERSHIP) in your *Skills Practice Book*.

As Indicators of "Self"

There is one last component of these personal pronoun
groups. THESE CAN FILL THE OBJECT OF VERB TERRI-
TORY AND INDICATE "SELF"—THAT IS, THE SAME
PERSON OR "THING" AS THE SUBJECT. Here is an
example.

*George could picture **himself** as a catcher.*

The pronoun *himself* serves as object of verb (*could
picture* WHOM?) and identifies as object of verb the
person who is the subject—namely, *George*.

These pronouns also have the more technical names
REFLEXIVE or INTENSIVE pronouns.

Here is a chart listing all the personal pronoun
spellings in contrast with each other.

SPELLINGS FOR PERSONAL PRONOUN GROUPS BY TYPE			
AS SUBJECT	AS OBJECT	INDICATING OWNERSHIP	INDICATING SELF
I	*me*	*mine*	*myself*
you	*you*	*yours*	*yourself* *yourselves*
he	*him*	*his*	*himself*
she	*her*	*hers*	*herself*
it	*it*	*its*	*itself*
we	*us*	*ours*	*ourselves*
they	*them*	*theirs*	*themselves*

● Do *PRACTICE G* (IDENTIFYING PERSONAL PRO-
NOUNS IN THEIR SPELLINGS THAT "SELF-NAME") in
your *Skills Practice Book.*

● Do *PRACTICE H* (IDENTIFYING ALL PERSONAL
PRONOUNS) in your *Skills Practice Book.*

Indefinite Pronouns

The INDEFINITE PRONOUNS are the next most com-
monly used type of pronoun in English. These are THE
PRONOUNS THAT REFER TO AN UNIDENTIFIED, SOME-
TIMES NONEXISTENT, AND THEREFORE "INDEFINITE"
PERSON OR "THING." Here are examples.

Someone with *nothing* cannot easily impress
anybody.

The indefinite pronouns are the darkened words *someone, nothing,* and *anybody.*

The groupings of indefinite pronouns that follow may help you remember them better. The first list shows three sets with **identical beginning letters OR ending letters.** The other lists are first of **pairs** of indefinite pronouns and then of **miscellaneous** ones.

INDEFINITE PRONOUNS BY GROUP			
Base word	-One Group	-Thing Group	-Body Group
(any)	*anyone*	*anything*	*anybody*
(every)	*everyone*	*everything*	*everybody*
(some)	*someone*	*something*	*somebody*
(no)	*none*	*nothing*	*nobody*

MEMORY AID
FOR *-ONE,-THING,-BODY* INDEFINITE PRONOUNS

-One/-thin'/-body Group

Explanation: The hyphen (-) indicates that this is an ending or suffix.

● Do *PRACTICE J* (IDENTIFYING PRONOUNS, ESPE-CIALLY INDEFINITE PRONOUNS IN THEIR -ONE/-THING/ -BODY FORMS) in your *Skills Practice Book.*

INDEFINITE PRONOUNS IN ASSORTED GROUPS	
Opposites	Miscellaneous
many, few *either, neither* *all, (none)*	*one(s)* *both* *other(s)* *several* *another* *some* *each* *most*

● Do *PRACTICE K* (IDENTIFYING PRONOUNS, ESPE-
CIALLY THE INDEFINITE PRONOUNS IN THE "OPPO-
SITES" AND "MISCELLANEOUS" GROUPS) in your
Skills Practice Book.

● Do *PRACTICE L* (IDENTIFYING PRONOUNS, ESPE-
CIALLY INDEFINITE PRONOUNS) in your *Skills
Practice Book.*

Demonstrative Pronouns

There is a final kind of pronoun for you to know. This
kind has the name DEMONSTRATIVE (POINTING) PRONOUN.
A DEMONSTRATIVE PRONOUN is a PRONOUN ACCOMPA-
NIED BY A "POINTING" OR "NODDING"—WHETHER
PHYSICAL OR DUE TO REFERENCE TO SOMETHING SAID
EARLIER. There are only **four** such pronouns—namely:
this, that, these, and *those.* Here are examples.

This is my hat; that is yours; and those are theirs.

Notice that in this sentence the demonstrative pronouns
this, that, and *those* are all doing the job of subject.

Demonstrative Pronouns	
Referring to ONE	Referring to MORE THAN ONE
this	*these*
that	*those*

● Do *PRACTICE M* (IDENTIFYING PRONOUNS, ESPE-CIALLY DEMONSTRATIVE PRONOUNS) in your *Skills Practice Book.*

● Do *PRACTICE N* (IDENTIFYING MORE NOUNS AND PRONOUNS) in your *Skills Practice Book.*

Phrases That Do Noun Jobs

Another many-word noun replacer is a *PHRASE THAT DOES THE JOB OF A NOUN.* Such a phrase has no noun or pronoun that alone serves as its chief word. Instead, ALL the words of the phrase do the noun job—as a unit. Note these examples (the phrases are in darker lettering).

To catch fish is fun.
Catching fish is fun.

Notice that when you ask *WHAT is fun*, the answer in each case is the wording before the verb as a unit—*to catch fish* and *catching fish*.

This sort of the phrase has the name verbAL phrase. You will be learning more about such phrases in later works in this series. You are not responsible for them until then.

Noun Clauses

The last sort of many-word noun replacer is the noun clause. Grammarians use the name NOUN CLAUSE to mean **A DEPENDENT CLAUSE WHOSE WORDS DO THE JOB OF A NOUN AS A UNIT.**

Note that the chief difference between a NOUN *CLAUSE* and a NOUN *CLUSTER* is that the **chief wording in the CLAUSE** is **not** a single noun or pronoun. Instead, the CHIEF WORDING IS THE WHOLE CLAUSE because all the words of the clause—which always include at least a verb and its subject—do their (noun) job AS A UNIT.

Here are example sentences (the noun clauses are in darker lettering).

__When we should leave__ has not been decided.
Everyone wondered __how the gadget worked.__

In the first sentence, the clause *__when we should leave__* is doing the job of subject of the verb *has been decided* (***WHAT** has not been decided?*).

Notice for this first sentence that there is no single noun or pronoun inside the wording *when we should leave* that serves as "chief wording." Instead, **all the words of this clause work as a unit to answer WHAT** when you ask *WHAT* before the words *has not been decided.*

In the second sentence, **all the words** of the noun clause *__how the gadget worked__* are doing the noun job of object of verb **as a unit** (*wondered WHAT?*).

See Chapter 17 for a fuller explanation of noun clauses. You will not be responsible for these until you reach that chapter.

Review

DEFINITIONS IN DARKER LETTERING MUST BE REMEMBERED.

Noun: A word you find by the THE Test and the Capital Letter Test and that serves as chief word in a noun territory.

THE Test: Say *the* before each word outside the sentence to see if it "fits" and if the word's meaning does not change.

Capital Letter Test: You identify as nouns those words that start with capital letters and are doing the job of chief wording in a noun cluster.

Noun Job: The job done by a noun (or its replacer) when it occupies a noun territory.

Subject Job: To occupy a territory (usually) before a verb and answer the questions WHO or WHAT when asked before the verb.

Object of Verb Job: To occupy a territory (usually) after a verb and answer the questions WHOM or WHAT when asked after the verb.

Object of Preposition Job: To occupy a territory (usually) after a preposition and answer the questions WHOM or WHAT when asked after the preposition.

Preposition: A word, such as *with*, that requires a noun or noun replacer after it to complete its sense.

Noun Replacer: Wording that can occupy a noun territory and answer (or ask) the questions of a noun there.

Proper Noun: The name of a particular person, place, or "thing."

Noun Cluster: All the words in a noun territory when the chief word(ing) is a noun, proper noun, or pronoun.

Articles: The words AN, A, and THE.

Pronoun: Words that are not nouns but that carry the meaning of a noun or noun cluster and take the place of the noun as the chief word in a noun territory.

Personal Pronouns: The pronouns whose job is to carry grammatical "person"—the pronouns whose basic components are *I, you, he, she, it, we,* and *they.*

Components as Subjects: *I, you, he, she, it, we,* and *they.*

Components as Objects: *me, you, him, her, it, us,* and *them.*

Components as Indicators of Ownership: *mine, yours, his, hers, its, ours,* and *theirs.*

Components as Indicators of "Self": *myself, yourself, yourselves, himself, herself, itself, ourselves,* and *themselves.*

Indefinite Pronouns: Pronouns that refer to an unidentified person, place, or "thing."

List of (Selected) Indefinite Pronouns: anyone, everyone, someone, none; anything, everything, something, nothing; anybody, everybody, somebody, nobody; many, few; either, neither; much, little; one/ones; other/others; another, both, several, all, each some.

Demonstrative Pronoun: A pronoun accompanied by a pointing—whether physical or of reference to something said earlier.

List of Demonstrative Pronouns: *this, that, these, those.*

Noun Clause: A dependent clause that does the job of a noun as a unit.

Chapter 3

Introduction
to Agreement
of Verbs
with Their Subjects

Writers are **not** free to choose any component of a verb to follow any subject. They must, rather, choose the spelling that "matches" the subject—that is, that AGREES with it—in both NUMBER and PERSON. See below for an explanation of all these new terms.

Background Terms

The terms explained in this section are of great importance. Learn them well.

Number

Grammarians use the word NUMBER to mean the WAY OF WRITING A WORD TO INDICATE WHETHER IT REFERS TO ONE OR MORE THAN ONE.

One kind of word that carries NUMBER in English is a noun. When nouns carry an *s/es* ending—like *trees*—you know that the writer is referring to **more than one** *tree*. When they **lack** an **s/es** ending—like *tree_*—you know that the writer is referring to **only one** *tree*.

Number:

The way of writing a word to indicate whether it refers to one or more than one.

There are only two NUMBERS in grammar then—ONE and MORE THAN ONE. When the **number is** ONE, it has the name SINGULAR. When the **number is** MORE THAN ONE, it has the name PLURAL.

Singular in Number:

When wording refers to one or less than one.

Plural in Number:

When wording refers to more than one.

Here is a chart to show this more graphically.

TYPES OF NUMBER WITH THEIR NAMES, MEANINGS, AND EXAMPLES		
Name	Meaning	Example
SINGULAR	ONE	*tree_*
PLURAL	MORE THAN ONE	*trees*

A NOUN IS SINGULAR OR PLURAL ACCORDING TO ITS
MEANING, NOT WHETHER IT HAS AN S/ES SPELLING. Some
examples of **plural** nouns that do **not** end in s/es are
children, teeth, and *mice.*

As you would expect, (usually) both nouns and pronouns change their spellings to indicate their NUMBER.
These charts give examples.

Examples of Number in the Spellings of NOUNS	
Singular (ONE)	**Plural** (MORE THAN ONE)
house	*houses*
foot	*feet*
woman	*women*

Examples of Number in the Spellings of PRONOUNS	
Singular (ONE)	**Plural** (MORE THAN ONE)
she *he* *it*	*they*
this	*these*
one	*ones*

● Do _**PRACTICE A**_ (IDENTIFYING SINGULAR AND
PLURAL NOUNS AND PRONOUNS) in your *Skills
Practice Book.*

Verbs too change their spelling to AGREE with the
number of their subjects, as you will see shortly.

Person

The most important of the words that carry PERSON in English are the PERSONAL (that is, "PERSON"-carrying) PRONOUNS. Grammarians use the word PERSON to mean RELATIONSHIP TO THE SENDER OF A MESSAGE OF WHOEVER OR WHATEVER IS TALKED ABOUT.

> ## Person:
> ### The relationship to the sender of the message of whoever or whatever is talked about.

If the RELATIONSHIP is that of SENDER (OR SENDERS) OF THE MESSAGE—that is, the writer (or writers) is talking **about** himself or herself (or themselves)—the writer(s) must use a FIRST-PERSON PERSONAL PRONOUN GROUP.

You probably remember these two FIRST-PERSON PERSONAL PRONOUN GROUPS.

I group: *I, me, mine, myself*
WE group: *we, us, ours, ourselves*

> ## First Person:
> ### The sender(s) of the message himself/herself/themselves (use only the *I* and *WE* groups of personal pronouns).

If the RELATIONSHIP is that of AUDIENCE—that is, the writer is talking **about** his readers (the receivers of the message)—the writer must use the SECOND-PERSON PERSONAL PRONOUN GROUP.

Here is the list of the SECOND-PERSON PERSONAL PRONOUNS.

YOU group: *you, yours, yourself, yourselves*

Second Person:

The audience (use only the *YOU* group of personal pronouns).

If the RELATIONSHIP is that of NEITHER SENDER NOR RECEIVER OF THE MESSAGE—that is, the writer is talking **about** someone or something other than himself/herself and his/her reader—the writer must use ANY OTHER WORD (PRONOUN OR NOUN) THAN THOSE LISTED AS BELONGING TO THE FIRST AND SECOND PERSON. **The writer must use only THIRD PERSON words.**

These are the THIRD PERSON words in English.

The THIRD-PERSON PERSONAL PRONOUN GROUPS:
HE group: *he, him, his, himself*
SHE group: *she, her, hers, herself*
IT group: *it, its, itself*
THEY group: *they, them, theirs, themselves*
ALL NON-"PERSONAL" PRONOUNS
ALL NOUNS

The **only FIRST PERSON** words in English are the *I* and *WE* groups, and the **only SECOND PERSON** words are the *YOU* group. **All other words in English belong to the THIRD PERSON.**

Third Person:

Neither the sender of the message nor the audience but someone or something else (use ANY NOUN or ANY PRONOUN <u>other than</u> those in the *I*, *WE*, and *YOU* groups of personal pronouns).

Here is a chart to demonstrate this.

TYPES OF PERSON WITH THEIR NAMES, MEANINGS, AND EXAMPLES		
Person	**Meaning**	**Example**
FIRST	WRITER (OR WRITERS) TALKS ABOUT SELF (SELVES)	*I* GROUP *WE* GROUP
SECOND	WRITER TALKS TO OR ABOUT THE AUDIENCE	*YOU* GROUP
THIRD	WRITER TALKS ABOUT ANYONE OR ANYTHING OTHER THAN SELF OR AUDIENCE	ALL NOUNS ALL OTHER PRONOUNS

This chart demonstrates the person and number of selected pronouns.

PERSON AND NUMBER FOR SELECTED PRONOUNS		
PERSON	**NUMBER**	
	Singular	**Plural**
FIRST	*I*	*we*
SECOND	*you*	*you/(you all)*
THIRD	*he, she, it something this*	*they all some*

This chart demonstrates person and number for selected nouns.

PERSON AND NUMBER FOR SELECTED NOUNS		
PERSON	**NUMBER**	
	Singular	**Plural**
FIRST	[none]	[none]
SECOND	[none]	[none]
THIRD	ALL SINGULAR NOUNS—*Jane, land, thought*	ALL PLURAL NOUNS—*ideas, Smiths, places*

● Do *PRACTICE B* (IDENTIFYING THE PERSON OF NOUNS AND PRONOUNS) in your *Skills Practice Book.*

● Do *PRACTICE C* (MORE IDENTIFYING OF SINGULAR AND PLURAL NOUNS AND PRONOUNS) in your *Skills Practice Book.*

Agreement of a Verb with Its Subject

Verbs commonly follow the subjects they accompany. Sometimes they carry their BASIC SPELLING as in *Buildings WEAKEN.* Other times they carry their S/ES SPELLING as in *Water EVAPORATES.*

Notice how these spellings contrast with each other.

Water_   evaporateS.

BuildingS   weaken_.

Writers **must choose the correct spelling for a verb** so that the reader can know which verb goes with which subject, especially in more complicated sentences.

The **RULE** is that **PLURAL NOUNS** (that often END IN

S/ES) **REQUIRE VERBS WITHOUT** S/ES and that **SINGULAR NOUNS** (that often END WITHOUT S/ES) **REQUIRE VERBS THAT END IN S/ES.** This is especially important in the present tense—that is, when the happening is true now.

As a rule of thumb—for those nouns whose plurals are formed by adding s/es—a **word with s/es must accompany a word without s/es.** See this graphically.

NOUN **+ S** ➡ VERB **– S** [Basic spelling]

NOUN **– S** ➡ VERB **+ S** [S/es spelling]

When a writer chooses the spelling for a verb that "matches" the number of its subject in this way, grammarians say that the verb AGREES WITH ITS SUBJECT IN NUMBER. They also speak of this as AGREEMENT (IN NUMBER) BETWEEN A VERB AND ITS SUBJECT.

Agreement:
The way of writing a word to achieve a grammatically required "match" with a related word.

Agreement in Number:
A match in number.

When your focus changes from nouns to PRONOUNS, you must make sure that the verb agrees with its subject **both** in NUMBER **and** in PERSON. In other words, you use the BASIC—**not** the S/ES—spelling of a verb **for the first and second person** SINGULAR **pronouns** *I* **and** *you* in the present tense. You write *I agree* and *You agree*—not ~~I agrees~~ nor ~~You agrees~~. The only verb for which this is not true is the verb *be* (see below).

To explain this another way, in the present tense the S/ES agreement is only for the THIRD PERSON WORDS in the singular and **not** for the FIRST OR SECOND PERSON WORDS.

Agreement in Person:
A match in person.

This chart (below) shows how most verbs change as they **agree with** PRONOUNS **in person and number**. Notice that this is a chart of the **present tense** (the time of happening is **now**) for the verb *want*.

SPELLINGS OF THE VERB *WANT* IN THE PRESENT TENSE THAT MATCH CHANGES IN PERSON AND NUMBER OF SUBJECTS		
PERSON	NUMBER	
	Singular	Plural
FIRST	*I* ***want_***	*we* ***want_***
SECOND	*you* ***want_***	*you* ***want_***
THIRD	*he she it* ***wantS***	*they* ***want_***

THIS AGREEMENT OF A VERB WITH ITS SUBJECT IS A FUNDAMENTAL REQUIREMENT OF ENGLISH.

Here are examples of correct agreement.

*Fred **enjoyS** soccer.*
*Tomato **plantS need** fertilizer.*
*Strenuous **exercise improveS** health.*
*Most **birdS fly** south in winter.*

● Do **_PRACTICE D_** (MAKING VERBS AGREE WITH THEIR SUBJECTS) in your *Skills Practice Book.*

● Do **_PRACTICE E_** (REWRITING A PARAGRAPH USING CORRECT AGREEMENT) in your *Skills Practice Book.*

This next chart shows how verbs in their **past tense**—the message was true **earlier than now**—have NO CHANGES and THEREFORE NO SPECIAL AGREEMENT with a subject. See below for the verb *be*, the only exception.

SPELLING OF THE VERB *WANT* IN THE PAST TENSE THAT MATCHES CHANGES IN PERSON AND NUMBER OF SUBJECTS		
PERSON	**NUMBER**	
	Singular	**Plural**
FIRST	*I* **wantED**	*we* **wantED**
SECOND	*you* **wantED**	*you* **wantED**
THIRD	*he she it* **wantED**	*they* **wantED**

Agreement of the Verb *BE* with Its Subject

The verb *be* is unique because it must agree with its subject in **both** number **and** person **and** in **both** the present tense **and** the PAST TENSE. **The verb *be* alone has a different spelling for the FIRST PERSON SINGULAR in both its present and past tense.** Study these two charts.

SPELLINGS OF THE VERB *BE* IN THE PRESENT TENSE THAT MATCH CHANGES IN PERSON AND NUMBER OF SUBJECTS		
PERSON	**NUMBER**	
	Singular	Plural
FIRST	*I* **AM**	*we* **ARE**
SECOND	*you* **ARE**	*you* **ARE**
THIRD	*he* *she* **IS** *it*	*they* **ARE**

Notice that the verb *be* does **not** use the component spelling *be* itself to form any part of its present tense.

● Do <u>*PRACTICE F*</u> (USING THE VERB *BE* CORRECTLY IN THE PRESENT TENSE) in your *Skills Practice Book*.

SPELLINGS OF THE VERB *BE* IN THE PAST TENSE THAT MATCH CHANGES IN PERSON AND NUMBER OF SUBJECTS		
PERSON	**NUMBER**	
	Singular	Plural
FIRST	*I* **WAS**	*we* **WERE**
SECOND	*you* **WERE**	*you* **WERE**
THIRD	*he* *she* **WAS** *it*	*they* **WERE**

Notice that the verb *be* has the TWO spellings—*was* and *were*—for its past tense.

● Do **_PRACTICE G_** (USING THE VERB *BE* CORRECTLY IN THE PAST TENSE) in your *Skills Practice Book.*

Review

DEFINITIONS IN DARKER LETTERING MUST BE REMEMBERED.

Number: The way of writing a word to indicate whether it refers to one or more than one.

  Singular in Number: The way of writing a word to show that it refers to one or less than one.

  Plural in Number: The way of writing a word to show that it refers to more than one.

Person: The relationship to the sender of message of whoever or whatever is talked about.

  First Person: Sender himself/herself—the personal pronoun families *I, me, my, mine, myself* and *we, us, our, ours, ourselves.*

  Second Person: Audience—the personal pronoun family *you, your, yours, yourself, yourselves.*

  Third Person: Neither sender nor audience but someone or something else—ALL REMAINING PRONOUNS and ALL NOUNS.

Agreement: The way of writing a word to achieve a grammatically required "match" with a related word.

  Agreement in Number: The way of writing a word to achieve a "match" in number.

  Agreement in Person: The way of writing a word to achieve a "match" in person.

Chapter 4

More Information about Verbs

This chapter has three parts. First, it focuses on the unusual spellings that some verbs' components have. Then it stresses the role of verbs in sentences and dependent clauses. Lastly, it introduces two trustworthy strategies for finding verbs.

Spelling Patterns for Components of Main Verbs

All verbs have five component spellings—the BASIC, S/ES, ING, PAST TENSE, and AFTER-HAD SPELLINGS. However, they do not all form these spellings in the same way.

Here is a chart showing some of the differences.

Differences between the Spellings for the Verb *Halt* and the Verb *Wear*				
Basic	**S/es**	**Ing**	**Past Tense**	**After-Had**
halt	*halts*	*halting*	*HALT<u>ED</u>*	*HALT<u>ED</u>*
wear	*wears*	*wearing*	*WORE*	*WORN*

Verbs whose components CAN **have spellings like those for the verb *halt*** have the name REGULAR VERBS. All other verbs have the name IRREGULAR VERBS.

Regular Verbs

Grammarians use the name REGULAR VERB to mean A VERB WHOSE PAST TENSE AND AFTER-HAD COMPONENTS ALWAYS CARRY AN *ED* ENDING. More than 99% of the main verbs in English are REGULAR.

Regular Verb:
A verb whose past tense and after-had components end in *ed*.

This is a chart of the spellings for regular verbs.

EXAMPLES OF COMPONENTS FOR REGULAR VERBS				
Basic	**S/es**	**Ing**	**Past Tense**	**After-Had**
plant	*plants*	*planting*	*plant<u>ED</u>*	*plant<u>ED</u>*
pull	*pulls*	*pulling*	*pull<u>ED</u>*	*pull<u>ED</u>*
listen	*listens*	*listening*	*listen<u>ED</u>*	*listen<u>ED</u>*

Irregular Verbs

Grammarians use the name IRREGULAR VERB to mean VERBS WHOSE PAST TENSE OR AFTER-HAD COMPONENT CAN NOT CARRY A SPELLING WITH AN *ED* ENDING.

Some verbs are irregular because all **five** components carry different spellings.

> *break, breaks, breaking, broke, broken*

Others are irregular because **four** components carry different spellings.

> *lead, leads, leading, led, led*

Still others are irregular because **three** components carry different spellings.

> *cut, cuts, cutting, cut, cut*

Irregular Verb:

A verb whose past tense and/or after-had component does NOT end in *ed*.

English has far fewer irregular verbs than regular ones. However, the IRREGULAR VERBS ARE THE MOST COMMONLY USED VERBS IN OUR LANGUAGE. Therefore, **you must know the spellings for their components by heart**.

Here are charts showing the VARIETY of patterns of spellings for irregular verbs.

IRREGULAR VERBS WITH FIVE SPELLINGS				
Basic	**S/es**	**Ing**	**Past Tense**	**After-Had**
see	*sees*	*seeing*	*saw*	*seen*
freeze	*freezes*	*freezing*	*froze*	*frozen*
sing	*sings*	*singing*	*sang*	*sung*

● Do *PRACTICE A* (SUPPLYING COMPONENT SPELL-INGS FOR IRREGULAR VERBS WITH FIVE SPELLINGS) in your *Skills Practice Book.*

● Do *PRACTICE B* (MORE SUPPLYING OF COMPONENT SPELLINGS FOR IRREGULAR VERBS WITH FIVE SPELL-INGS) in your *Skills Practice Book.*

IRREGULAR VERBS WITH FOUR SPELLINGS				
Basic	**S/es**	**Ing**	**Past Tense**	**After-Had**
tell	*tells*	*telling*	*TOLD*	*TOLD*
bring	*brings*	*bringing*	*BROUGHT*	*BROUGHT*
say	*says*	*saying*	*SAID*	*SAID*

Notice why these components carry only four spell-ings—their past tense and after-had components carry identical spellings.

● Do *PRACTICE C* (SUPPLYING COMPONENT SPELL-INGS FOR IRREGULAR VERBS WITH FOUR SPELLINGS) in your *Skills Practice Book.*

- Do ***PRACTICE D*** (MORE SUPPLYING OF COMPONENT SPELLINGS FOR IRREGULAR VERBS WITH FOUR SPELLINGS) in your *Skills Practice Book*.

- Do ***PRACTICE E*** (STILL MORE SUPPLYING OF COMPONENT SPELLINGS FOR IRREGULAR VERBS WITH FOUR SPELLINGS) in your *Skills Practice Book*.

IRREGULAR VERBS WITH <u>FOUR</u> SPELLINGS— IN A DIFFERENT PATTERN				
Basic	S/es	Ing	Past Tense	After-Had
RUN	*runs*	*running*	*ran*	*RUN*
COME	*comes*	*coming*	*came*	*COME*
BECOME	*becomes*	*becoming*	*became*	*BECOME*

Notice that the past-tense and after-had components are NOT spelled the same for these verbs. However, they still have only four spellings because their after-had component has the same spelling as their basic component.

IRREGULAR VERBS WITH <u>THREE</u> SPELLINGS				
Basic	S/es	Ing	Past Tense	After-Had
HURT	*hurts*	*hurting*	*HURT*	*HURT*
RID	*rids*	*ridding*	*RID*	*RID*
COST	*costs*	*costing*	*COST*	*COST*

Note the sameness of spelling for the past tense, after-had, and basic components for all these verbs.

● Do *PRACTICE F* (SUPPLYING COMPONENT SPELL-
INGS FOR IRREGULAR VERBS WITH THREE SPELLINGS)
in your *Skills Practice Book.*

The Irregular Verb *Be*

There is only one verb in English that has more than
five components. It is the verb *be*, which has **eight**
components. It has so many components precisely
because it is our most commonly used verb and our most
important one.

Study this comparison of the components of the verb
be with those of the verb *break*. The verb *be* differs from
all other verbs in exactly the same way.

COMPARISON OF COMPONENTS FOR THE VERBS *BE* AND *BREAK*				
Basic	Present Tense	Ing	Past Tense	After-Had
break	*BREAK* *BREAKS*	*breaking*	*BROKE*	*broken*
be	*AM* *ARE* *IS*	*being*	*WAS* *WERE*	*been*

Notice that the verb *break*—like the usual verb in
English—has two present tense spellings, its BASIC
spelling and its S/ES spelling. The verb *be*, in contrast,
uses the three spellings *AM, ARE,* and *IS*—none of which
is its basic spelling. Here are examples.

I AM the goalie.
You ARE a forward.
She IS a halfback.

Notice, too, that the verb *break* has just one PAST

TENSE spelling. In contrast, the verb *be*—unlike any other verb in English—has two spellings. These are WAS and WERE. Here are examples.

He WAS the winner.
We WERE the winners.

Take note that the BASIC spelling for the verb *be* is the word *be* itself.

Also notice for the verb *be* that its ING spelling **being** is normal but that its AFTER-HAD spelling **been** is unique.

● Do *PRACTICE G* (IDENTIFYING COMPONENTS FOR THE VERB *BE*) in your *Skills Practice Book*.

The Irregular Verb *Have*

The verb *have* uses HAS (**not** ~~haves~~) for its **s/es component**. Here are its component spellings: *have, has, having, had,* and *had.*

Test of Knowledge of After-Had Components of Irregular Verbs

In the world of work, people judge others by the correctness of their use of English, including their use of the components of irregular verbs. To test how well you can spell after-had components, do the following practice.

● Do *PRACTICE H* (TEST OF KNOWLEDGE OF AFTER-HAD SPELLINGS FOR IRREGULAR VERBS) in your *Skills Practice Book*.

Importance of Verbs

The importance of verbs, in part, is that they are the core of both sentences and dependent clauses. Indeed, they are the core of English.

As Core of Sentences

In English, there can not even be a sentence (in the strictest sense) if no verb is present. This is why verbs in their primary role are the core ingredient of a sentence.

Here is a **review** of the types of wordings that make up a sentence (note the explanation for the command type that follows the review).

REVIEW OF SENTENCE TYPES	
TYPE	EXAMPLE
A QUESTION—when you use full wording.	*Is this a good answer?*
A STATEMENT—when you can turn the wording into a question.	*This is a good answer.*
A COMMAND—when you *omit* the subject.	*Write neatly.*

Explanation of the COMMAND type of sentence: When you write or say *Write neatly*, you **omit** the word *you* when you mean the sentence as a command. **The fact that you do NOT add the word *you* CAUSES the sentence *Write neatly* to be a command.**

IN ENGLISH, THE STRUCTURE OF THE SENTENCE—THE OMISSION OF THE WORD *YOU*—CAUSES THE WORDING TO BE A COMMAND. THIS IS A "CODE" THAT HAS BEEN BUILT INTO THE WAY ENGLISH IS USED.

Note these additional examples (the verb is in darker lettering).

Study with pen in hand.
*Please **move** to the right.*
[The word *please* is **not** a subject.]
***Do** not **tell** a lie.*

Sentence:

A fully worded question <u>or</u> wording that you can turn into a question <u>or</u> a command whose subject is omitted *you*.

● Do <u>*PRACTICE J*</u> (WRITING SENTENCES THAT EXPRESS A COMMAND) in your *Skills Practice Book*.

● Do <u>*PRACTICE K*</u> (MORE IDENTIFYING OF TYPES OF SENTENCES) in your *Skills Practice Book*.

As Core of Dependent Clauses

Verbs in their primary role are also one of the core ingredients of a dependent clause. (The other core ingredient is the subject. A subject, you remember, is the wording—usually before the verb—that the verb adds information about.)

The dependent clause **differs** from a sentence because it has wording **in addition to** its verb and subject—namely, an **introducer**. INTRODUCERS are everyday words like *if* or *though* whose effect is to make its accompanying verb and subject **dependent** on still more wording in order for the reader or listener to understand fully. (This is why this kind of clause is called a "dependent" clause.)

Here is a dependent clause.

if it rains

These three words leave the reader wondering what will happen. By adding more words, such as *the picnic will be postponed*, the writer can form a **sentence**.

If it rains, the picnic will be postponed.

For a fuller explanation of dependent clauses, see Chapter 13, 14, and 17.

Important Note: ALL THE DISCUSSION OF VERBS FOR THE REMAINDER OF THIS TEXT IS TRUE ONLY FOR VERBS IN THEIR PRIMARY ROLE AS CORE OF SENTENCES AND DEPENDENT CLAUSES—AND NOT IN THEIR SECONDARY ROLE.

In their secondary role, verbs serve as the core of smaller grammatical units known as "verbAL phrases." Verbal phrases are units of words that contain a verb and accompanying wording but whose verb has no accompanying subject inside the phrase.

As Carriers of Tense

You know that verbs are the carriers of tense. Now it is important to see how helping verbs and components of main verbs become the building blocks for a tense.

Present Tense versus Past Tense

To form the PRESENT TENSE (time now), you must choose a verb's BASIC COMPONENT or its S/ES COMPONENT. There are **two** present tense spellings. Here are examples.

I know the answer.
She knows the answer.

The verb *be* has the **three** spellings *am, are,* and *is.* Note these examples.

I am certain.
You are certain.
He is certain.

In contrast, to form the PAST TENSE (time earlier than now), you must choose the PAST TENSE COMPONENT.

(The verb *be* alone has the **two** spellings *was* and *were*.) Here is an example.

*He **knew** the answer yesterday.*

Grammarians use the name PRESENT TENSE to mean USE OF EITHER THE BASIC <u>OR</u> S/ES COMPONENT OF A VERB (except for the verb *be*) TO INDICATE THAT THE TIME OF THE HAPPENING IS NOW.

Present Tense:

Uses the BASIC or S/ES COMPONENT of the main verb to indicate that the time of the happening is NOW (uses *am, are,* or *is* for the verb *be*).

Grammarians use the name PAST TENSE to mean CHOICE OF THE PAST TENSE COMPONENT OF A VERB TO INDICATE THAT THE TIME OF THE HAPPENING WAS EARLIER THAN NOW.

Past Tense:

Uses the PAST TENSE COMPONENT of the main verb to indicate that the time of the happening was EARLIER THAN NOW (uses *was* or *were* for the verb *be*).

● Do *PRACTICE L* (WRITING SENTENCES USING THE BASIC SPELLING TO FORM THE PRESENT TENSE) in your *Skills Practice Book.*

● Do *PRACTICE M* (WRITING SENTENCES USING THE S/ES SPELLING TO FORM THE PRESENT TENSE) in your *Skills Practice Book.*

● Do **_PRACTICE N_** (WRITING SENTENCES USING THE PAST TENSE) in your *Skills Practice Book.*

Future Tense

To form the FUTURE TENSE (time later than now), you must choose the HELPER *WILL* and a verb's BASIC COMPONENT. Here is an example.

*We **will succeed** if we do our best.*

Grammarians use the name FUTURE TENSE to mean USE OF THE HELPER *WILL* AND A VERB'S BASIC COMPONENT TO INDICATE THAT THE TIME OF THE HAPPENING WILL BE LATER THAN NOW.

Future Tense:

Uses the helper *WILL* PLUS the BASIC COMPONENT of the main verb to indicate that the time of the happening will be LATER THAN NOW.

● Do **_PRACTICE P_** (WRITING SENTENCES USING THE FUTURE TENSE) in your *Skills Practice Book.*

As the Core of English

There are **rewards for students who master the verb.** Their insight into the verb helps them in all these ways:

• Those who can find verbs with total accuracy **can unravel the structure and meaning of even the most complex of sentences.**

• Those who can find verbs with total accuracy **can learn and master the key punctuation rules with relative ease.**

- Those who fully understand the role of verbs **will write and speak English with a sense of power and with special control over its structure.**

Misconceptions about Ways to Find Verbs

There is a common belief that you can define a verb as an "action" word or "state of being" word. This "definition" has glaring weaknesses. If you rely on it alone, you will **first** OVERLOOK MANY WORDS THAT ARE VERBS and **second** MISTAKE AS VERBS NUMBERLESS WORDS THAT ARE NOT VERBS.

The next three sections explain why this is so.

"State of Being" Words That Are <u>Not</u> Verbs

There are countless "state of being" words in English that are **not** verbs. First, there are nouns, such as *happiness, contentment,* and *prosperity.* In addition, there are adjectives, such as *happy* and *lifelike.*

Verbs That Are <u>Not</u> "Action Words"

Second, some verbs are not "action words." Note these examples—the **verbs** are in darker lettering.

*Fred **lacks** enough money.*
*A machine **rests** at night.*
*Frank **would have driven** if he **had been** able.*

"Action Words" That Do <u>Not</u> Function as Verbs

Third, countless "action words" perform jobs that are **not** the job of verbs. That is the case for the words in darker lettering in these sentences.

*My **swim** to the dock tired me.*
*The **limping** of the player was evident.*
*The **fast** train got delayed.*

Best Ways to Find Verbs

There are two unfailing strategies for finding verbs. You will learn these strategies in full in the next three chapters. The purpose of the two sections here is to reassure you that they exist.

Strategy When the Verb Has a Helper

There is a simple strategy that you can use if the verb starts with a helper. You first teach yourself to recognize the twenty starter helping verbs (see Chapter 5). As soon as you find one of these, such as the starter *could*, you then look for any accompanying verb words.

*This **could** have been prevented.*

Here the helper **could** marks the beginning of the verb phrase **could have been prevented.** See Chapter 6 for further explanation.

Strategy When the Verb Has No Helper

You use an entirely different strategy if the verb has no helper. Verbs that have no helper must be in their present or past tense. In English, there is a **two-word substitute** for these tenses—namely: you replace the main verb with a verb phrase that starts with the helper *do, does,* or *did.*

swims ➡ *does swim*

If the replacement fits, the word is a verb (provided that you have **first** found all verbs that do start with a helper). Otherwise, the word is not a verb. See Chapter 7 for further explanation.

Review

Sentence: A fully worded question or wording that you can turn into a question or a command whose subject is omitted *you*.

Dependent Clause: Wording that includes a verb, subject and "introducer" and that you can not turn into a question.

Tense: Way of writing a verb to indicate the time of happening of the message.

Present—Uses BASIC or S/ES COMPONENT of main verb to indicate that the time is now (uses *am, are,* or *is* for the verb *be*).

Past—Uses PAST TENSE COMPONENT of main verb to indicate that the time was earlier than now (uses *was* or *were* for the verb *be*).

Future—Uses helper WILL PLUS BASIC COMPONENT of main verb to indicate that the time will be later than now.

Components for Verb *Be* (the only verb with eight components):

Basic: *be*
Present Tense: *am, are, is*
S/ES: *is*
ING: *being*
Past Tense: *was, were*
After-Had: *been*

Regular Verbs: Past tense and after-had components end in ED.

Irregular Verbs: The past tense component and/or the after-had component does NOT end in *ed*.

Chapter 5

Helping Verbs

You remember that some verbs start with a helping verb while others do not. This chapter teaches you to recognize all the helping verbs (helpers) on sight. RECOGNIZING HELPERS ERRORLESSLY IS AN ESSENTIAL FIRST STEP FOR FINDING VERBS, ESPECIALLY VERB PHRASES. The importance of helpers is that they mark the presence of close to half the verb words in English.

As you learned in Chapter 1, there are two kinds of helping verbs (helpers). The STARTERS can start a verb phrase **or** stand alone and serve as a main verb.

The FOLLOWERS must follow a starter. In addition, they either hold the middle position in a verb phrase **or** stand as last word of the verb phrase and serve as a main verb.

Starters and followers are verbs and are the building blocks of verb phrases. These sections will help you find them.

Starter Helping Verbs

You remember that there are **twenty** starter helping verbs. Their importance is that they **are** verbs and that they **alone** can start a verb phrase.

YOU **MUST REMEMBER** THESE TWENTY WORDS—AND THEIR IMPORTANCE AS MARKERS OF THE PRESENCE OF A VERB.

Each of the next four sections shows you the four starter SETS and how easy they are to remember.

Starters in the *Do* Set

Three of the starters come from the present and past tense of the (main) verb *do*. Here is the set.

STARTERS FROM THE VERB *DO*

DO, DOES [from the present tense]

DID [from the past tense]

MEMORY AID
FOR *DO*-BASED STARTERS

DOES DID DO [it].

EXAMPLES OF *DO*, *DOES*, AND *DID* AS HELPING VERBS AND AS MAIN VERBS	
AS HELPING VERBS	AS MAIN VERBS
We DO work hard.	*We DO the job.*
He DOES work hard.	*He DOES the job.*
He DID work hard.	*He DID the job.*

● Do *PRACTICE A* (LABELING STARTERS FROM THE *DO* SET) in your *Skills Practice Book*.

Starters in the *Have* Set

Three more starters come from the present and past tense of the (main) verb *have*. Here is the set.

> ### STARTERS FROM THE VERB *HAVE*
>
> ***HAVE, HAS*** [from the present tense]
>
> ***HAD*** [from the past tense]

> ### MEMORY AID
> ### FOR *HAVE*-BASED STARTERS
>
> ***HAVE HAS HAD*** [it].

EXAMPLES OF *HAVE*, *HAS*, AND *HAD* AS HELPING VERBS AND AS MAIN VERBS	
AS HELPING VERBS	**AS MAIN VERBS**
We *HAVE* **won** the game.	We *HAVE* enough time.
He *HAS* **won** the game.	He *HAS* enough time.
He *HAD* **won** the game.	He *HAD* enough time.

● Do *PRACTICE B* (LABELING STARTERS FROM THE *HAVE* SET) in your *Skills Practice Book*.

● Do *PRACTICE C* (LABELING STARTERS FROM THE *DO* AND *HAVE* SETS) in your *Skills Practice Book*.

Starters in the *Be* Set

An additional five starters come from the present and past tense of the (main) verb *be*. Three are from the

63

present tense and two from the past. Note.

STARTERS FROM THE VERB *BE*

AM, ARE, IS [from the present tense]

WAS, WERE [from the past tense]

MEMORY AID
FOR *BE*-BASED STARTERS

AR'M'S WERE WA[ll]*S.* (Say: "Arms were walls.")

Explanation: *AR'* = *ARE*
'M = *AM*
'S = *IS*
WA[ll]*S* = *WAS*

EXAMPLES OF *AM*, *ARE*, *IS*, *WAS*, AND *WERE* AS STARTERS AND AS MAIN VERBS

As Starters	As Main Verbs
I AM *winning.*	I AM *present.*
You ARE *winning.*	You ARE *present.*
She IS *winning.*	She IS *present.*
He WAS *winning.*	He WAS *present.*
We WERE *winning.*	We WERE *present.*

● Do *PRACTICE D* (LABELING STARTERS FROM THE *BE* SET) in your *Skills Practice Book.*

● Do *PRACTICE E* (LABELING STARTERS FROM THE *DO, HAVE,* AND *BE* SETS) in your *Skills Practice Book.*

Starters in the *WILL* Set

The last nine starters do **not** come from any main verb. Nonetheless, they are easy to remember because you can arrange them in subsets. Here are the subsets.

STARTERS WITH NO MAIN VERB FUNCTION

WILL	*SHALL*	*CAN*	*MAY*
WOULD	*SHOULD*	*COULD*	*MIGHT*
			MUST

MEMORY AID FOR THE STARTERS WITH NO MAIN VERB FUNCTION

MAY COULD [and] *SHOULD CAN WOULD.*
SHALL WILL MUST[er] MIGHT?

Explanation: *May* is a woman's name. She is canning *would*, possibly for her pet termites.

EXAMPLES IN SENTENCES

You WILL succeed.

He WOULD succeed if he tried.

We CAN SUCCEED next time.

He COULD succeed if he tried.

You SHALL not tell anyone.

You SHOULD speak louder.

You MAY not win.

You MIGHT win.

You MUST win.

These memory aids can help you remember the four starter verb sets.

MEMORY AIDS
FOR THE STARTER GROUPS

WILL DOES HAVE AR'M'S.
or
WILL, DO BE·HAVE.

● Do *PRACTICE F* (LABELING STARTERS FROM THE WILL SET) in your *Skills Practice Book*.

● Do *PRACTICE G* (LABELING STARTERS FROM THE DO, HAVE, BE, AND WILL SETS) in your *Skills Practice Book*.

Truths about Starters to Note

The next three sections discuss three truths about starters that are important to know and that make them easier to find.

Truth A

A word with *n't* attached is always a starter.

You often add the word *not* to a sentence. You do this to deny or contradict a statement. For example, when you change *It is cold* to *It is **not** cold*, you deny or contradict the statement.

When you add *not* like this, you always add it RIGHT AFTER A STARTER. Almost always, the presence of the word *not* is an indicator of the presence of a starter (to its left).

In conversation and informal writing, you can **combine** *is* and *not* to form the CONTRACTION *isn't*. Note.

It ISN'T cold.

A CONTRACTION is THE COMBINING OF TWO WORDS BY THE OMISSION OF ONE OR MORE LETTERS FROM THE SECOND (USUALLY) AND REPLACING THEM (OR IT) WITH AN APOSTROPHE ('). Here are examples.

$$must + not \rightarrow \textbf{\textit{mustN'T}}$$
$$should + not \rightarrow \textbf{\textit{shouldN'T}}$$
$$can + not \text{ (or } cannot) \rightarrow \textbf{\textit{can'T}}$$

Note: The word that you add *n't* to—or just *'t* (as in *can't*)—is a STARTER. You label the starter—but **just** the starter—with a double underline. Be careful to **not** double underline the *n't* or *'t*. The reason is that *n't* and *'t* stand for a SECOND WORD, the word *not* (which is NOT a verb). Here is how you do the labeling.

He <u>can</u>'t say that we <u>didn</u>'t help.

Note Also: Usually the first word in a contraction has no change in spelling. Consequently, THE **SECOND** WORD LOSES ONE OR MORE LETTERS.

Contraction:

The combining of two words by the omission of one or more letters from the second (usually) and replacing them (or it) with an apostrophe (').

Note Again: The contraction *won't* stands for *will not*. Always rewrite this word as **two words** before doing labeling. Here is an example.

[<u>will</u> not]
*The rain **won't** ∧ last.*

> ## Labeling for Inserted Wording:
>
> Use a "CARET" (∧)—pronounced like *carrot*—to mark the place of insertion. Use SIDE BRACKETS ([ ]) on both sides of the wording to indicate that it is the wording of an EDITOR—NOT the author.

● Do *PRACTICE H* (LABELING STARTERS IN CONTRACTIONS WITH *NOT*) in your *Skills Practice Book*.

Truth B

Starters can form contractions with subjects.

In informal writing and conversation, you find starter verbs forming contractions with subjects, especially when these are personal pronouns. The eight starters that do this are *am, are, is, have, has, had, will,* and *would*. Here are examples.

I am	→	*I'M*
you are	→	*you'RE*
who is	→	*who'S*
we have	→	*we'VE*
she has	→	*she'S*
they had	→	*they'D*
it will	→	*it'LL*
he would	→	*he'D*

Here are example sentences.

> *I'D rather not talk about it.* [*I WOULD*]
> *We'D finished early that day.* [*We HAD*]

Notice that *'D* can mean **either** HAD **or** WOULD. In addition, *'S* can mean **either** IS **or** HAS. You can tell the meanings apart because starters must "match" the

component spellings of the verbs or other words that follow them. (See page 75 for a fuller explanation.)
Here are the correct "matches."

MAIN VERB COMPONENTS THAT CAN FOLLOW
'D AND 'S

He'D TAKEN his time.	[*HAD* + AFTER-HAD spelling]
He'D TAKE his time.	[*WOULD* + BASIC spelling]
He's TAKING his time.	[*IS* + ING spelling]
He's sick.	[*IS* + no other verb word]
He's TAKEN his time.	[*HAS* + AFTER-HAD spelling]

Note that you must always rewrite these contractions so that you separate the starter helper from its attached word. Here is an example.

[we have]
We'VE ∧ arrived early.

● Do *PRACTICE J* (REWRITING CONTRACTIONS OF STARTERS WITH SUBJECTS) in your *Skills Practice Book.*

● Do *PRACTICE K* (LABELING STARTERS THAT COME FROM CONTRACTIONS WITH SUBJECTS) in your *Skills Practice Book.*

● Do *PRACTICE L* (MORE LABELING OF STARTERS THAT COME FROM CONTRACTIONS WITH SUBJECTS) in your *Skills Practice Book.*

Truth C
Starters are often the first word in questions.

Background

In English, there is a simple way to change statements to questions. You reposition the starter helper to the front of the sentence. Here is an example.

A team's coach CAN *make a difference.*

[CAN]   [?]

  ∧ *A team's coach* ~~can~~ *make a difference.*

[**Note:** You can **not** say *can* in both places and have it be English. This is why you see a line through *can* (~~can~~) in its **inside**-the-sentence position.]

Sometimes the starter has N'T attached. When this is the case, you can reposition the starter **and** *n't* as if they were one word—or you can separate them and reposition just the starter. Here are examples.

Some of you DIDN'T *read the question carefully.* ➡

[DIDN'T]   [?]

  ∧ *Some of you* ~~didn't~~ *read the question carefully.*

OR

[DID]   [~~did~~ NOT]   [?]

  ∧ *Some of you* ~~didn't~~ ∧ *read the question carefully.*

Questions That Start with a Starter

Questions, therefore, can have STARTERS AS THEIR FIRST WORD. Here are examples.

ARE the number of leaves on trees countless?
CAN't you hear the rain coming?

When you see that a sentence is a question (it will end with a question mark), you must go to its FIRST WORD and label it as a starter. (In a later chapter, you will learn about questions whose first word is NOT a starter.) This kind of question has the name STARTER VERB QUESTION in this text.

> ## Starter Verb Question:
> **A question whose beginning word is a starter.**

- Do _**PRACTICE M**_ (LABELING STARTERS IN STARTER-VERB QUESTIONS) in your _Skills Practice Book._

- Do _**PRACTICE N**_ (LABELING STARTERS IN VARIED SENTENCES) in your _Skills Practice Book._

Follower Helping Verbs

There are only **four** follower helping verbs. They are important because they sometimes serve as main verbs and because they are the only verb words that can form a **bridge** between a starter helper and its main verb.

Note where these four words come from—three from the verb _be_ and one from the verb _have._

You MUST REMEMBER these four words—and THEIR IMPORTANCE as "followers" of a starter helping verb.

Followers in the _Be_ Set

Three of the followers come from the component spellings of the verb _be_. Note.

> ### FOLLOWERS FROM THE VERB _BE_
>
> _BE_ [BASIC spelling]
>
> _BEING_ [ING spelling]
>
> _BEEN_ [AFTER-HAD spelling]

Notice that all the component spellings of the verb *be* belong to either a follower set or a starter set. Study this chart.

COMPONENTS OF THE VERB *BE* ACCORDING TO HELPER VERB ROLE				
BASIC	PRESENT TENSE	ING	PAST TENSE	AFTER-HAD
BE	*am* *are* *is*	*BEING*	*was* *were*	*BEEN*
FOLLOWER	Starter	FOLLOWER	Starter	FOLLOWER

Note these example for *be, being,* and *been* in their two roles.

EXAMPLES OF *BE, BEING,* AND *BEEN* AS FOLLOWERS AND AS MAIN VERBS	
AS FOLLOWERS	AS MAIN VERBS
Jean will BE coming.	*Jean will BE here.*
Jean is BEING told.	*Jean is BEING a help.*
Jean has BEEN invited.	*Jean has BEEN a boon.*

Follower in the *Have* Set

The other (and last) follower is the word *have*—the SAME WORD that you already know can be a starter.

FOLLOWER FROM THE VERB *HAVE*
HAVE   [BASIC spelling]

Note these examples for *have* in its three roles.

EXAMPLES OF *HAVE* AS STARTER, FOLLOWER, AND MAIN VERB		
AS STARTER	**AS FOLLOWER**	**AS MAIN VERB**
They HAVE left.	*They will HAVE left.*	*They HAVE good news.*

MEMORY AID FOR THE FOUR FOLLOWERS

BE[es] HAVE BEEN BEING [busy].

● Do *PRACTICE P* (LABELING STARTERS AND FOLLOWERS) in your *Skills Practice Book.*

A Truth about Followers

Truth A

Expect followers and their starters to get separated from each other.

Often followers follow their accompanying starters immediately, as in the sentence *Eileen* **could** HAVE *called.* However, this does not have to be the case. Sometimes followers get separated from their accompanying starters. Study these examples.

This answer **must** NOT **be** *correct.*
Stars **can** SOMETIMES **be** *brighter than usual.*
Computers **have** NOT ALWAYS **been** *around.*

There is a "test" to determine whether a follower and starter belong to the same verb phrase. You see whether they **sound right together.** For example, the words *MAY HAVE* do sound right together, but the words ~~*may being*~~ do **not**.

● Do ***PRACTICE Q*** (FINDING FOLLOWERS WHEN SEPARATED FROM ACCOMPANYING STARTERS) in your *Skills Practice Book.*

● Do ***PRACTICE R*** (FINDING STARTERS AND FOLLOWERS) in your *Skills Practice Book.*

● Do ***PRACTICE S*** (MORE FINDING OF STARTERS AND FOLLOWERS) in your *Skills Practice Book.*

● Do ***PRACTICE T*** (STILL MORE FINDING OF STARTERS AND FOLLOWERS) in your *Skills Practice Book.*

There is one more truth about both starters and followers that is helpful to know as you proceed with the coming chapters.

A Truth about Starters and Followers

Truth A

**Starters and followers DICTATE THE SPELLING
for any verb word
that follows and accompanies it.**

In English, the helper CONTROLS the spelling you must choose for any verb that follows it. You **may** say *will ARRIVE* (*will* + BASIC SPELLING), but you may **not** say ~~will arrives~~ or ~~will arrived~~. Study the chart below that shows the "matches" that are allowed or required.

Spellings That Each Starter and Follower Requires or Allows for a Verb That Follows and Accompanies It		
Starter/ Follower	Spelling Required/ Allowed	Examples
do *does* *did*	BASIC only	*Ed does* SING *well.*
will *would* *shall* *should* *can* *could* *may* *might* *must*	BASIC only	*Ed will* SING *well.*
*being	AFTER-HAD only	*The song is being* SUNG.
am *are* *is* *was* *were* **be* **been*	ING or AFTER-HAD only	*I was* SINGING. *It was* SUNG. *The song has been* SUNG. *Ed may be* SINGING.
have *has* *had* **have*	AFTER-HAD only	*Ed has* SUNG *well.* *Ed could have* SUNG *well.*
*This is a follower.		

Notice that **no** starter or follower permits an S/ES or past tense spelling to follow and accompany it.

● Do *PRACTICE U* (Writing sentences using starters and followers) in your *Skills Practice Book*.

Review

Content in darker lettering must be remembered.

List of Starters:

From Verb *Do*: *Do, does, did.*
From Verb *Have*: *Have, has, had.*
From Verb *Be*: *Am, are, is, was, were.*
From no main verb: *Will, would, shall, should, can, could, may, might, must.*

List of Followers:

From Verb *Be*: *Be, being, been.*
From Verb *Have*: *Have.*

Starter Verb Question: A question whose beginning word is a starter.

Contraction: The combining of two words by the omission of one or more letters from the second (usually) and replacing them (or it) with an apostrophe (').

Labeling for Inserted Wording: Use a caret (ʌ) to mark the place of insertion and side brackets ([ ]) on both sides of the wording to indicate that it is the wording of an editor and NOT the author.

Chapter 6

Helping Verbs as Markers of Main Verbs

You now know the helping verbs on sight. You also know that they serve either as main verbs or as markers of where to look for a companion main verb.

The goals of this chapter, then, are to help you determine whether a helper has such a companion main verb and to determine just which word this main verb is.

Note that this is a much harder task than you might suspect. First, the helper by itself contains no clue as to whether it may be serving as a helping verb or not. In addition, even when a helper is serving as a helping verb, its companion main verb may **not** be the next word after it. See the list of truths about main verbs below.

Learn this chapter well. It is the KEY **to learning all the rest of this text.**

Truths about the Words That Make up Verb Phrases

This section states some helpful TRUTHS about the location of main verbs relative to other words in a sentence. In the example sentences, the whole verb is in darker lettering and its main verb has been capitalized.

Truth A

There is a main verb accompanying a starter or starter-plus-follower(s) most of the time.

Examples

*Jeff **has** FOUND his niche [slot] in life.*
*No one **could have** GUESSED the exact time
of the disabled satellite's reentry.*

Truth B

When there is a main verb after a helper, it is commonly the next word after it.

Examples

*Todd **is** RELACING his boots.*
*Little **has been** LEFT to chance.*

Truth C

The main verb gets separated from its starter or starter-plus-follower(s) sometimes.

Examples

*Even deep snow **will** EVENTUALLY MELT.*
*History **is being** TOO QUICKLY FORGOTTEN.*

Truth D

The main verb is sometimes the starter itself—that is, the starter does the job of main verb rather than that of helping verb.

Examples

Everyone IS out during the lunch hour.
Roses HAVE a delicate fragrance.

Truth E

The main verb is sometimes a follower— that is, a follower does the job of main verb rather than that of helping verb.

Examples

*Marge **will** BE the captain.*
*People in the suburbs **must** HAVE their own cars.*

There are three conclusions for you to draw now. First, you can expect to find a main verb after a starter or starter-plus-follower(s) MOST OF THE TIME.

Second, you must **NEVER** PRESUPPOSE that a main verb must come after one or more helpers because either a starter or a follower could ITSELF serve as main verb.

Third, starters and their followers are always verb words. You **must ALWAYS** DOUBLE UNDERLINE them.

Labeling for Verbs:
DOUBLE UNDERLINE all verb words— both helpers and main verbs.

Note this diagram of the order of verb words in a verb phrase (parentheses mean possible omission).

Start -er	+ (Other Word)	+ (Followers)	+ (Other Word)	+ (Main Verb)
___	___	___	___	___
		Examples		
HAS	(often)	*(BEEN BEING)*	(often)	*(DISCUSSED)*
WAS	(often)	*(BEING)*	(often)	*(TOLD)*
IS	(often)			*(ARRIVING)*

Introduction to the "Tests to Follow to Succeed"

In this text, the word TEST has a special meaning. A TEST is THE STEPS—AND ANY ACCOMPANYING GROUND RULES—THAT YOU CARRY OUT IN A FIXED ORDER TO HELP YOU IDENTIFY A PARTICULAR GRAMMATICAL ELEMENT. A side benefit of these tests is the **experiencing** of the structure of English that results.

ANY OMISSION OF A STEP, IGNORING OF A GROUND RULE, OR CARELESSNESS IN ORDER OF PROCEEDING CAN CAUSE FAILURE. Failure can also result from relying on less precise definitions or strategies than those taught in this text.

YOUR MASTERY OF THESE TESTS, WITH THEIR GROUND RULES AND STEPS, IS THE SECRET TO SUCCESS WITH THIS TEXT AND TO GAINING BETTER COMMAND OF ENGLISH. These are the reasons why these tests have the name **TESTS TO FOLLOW TO SUCCEED**.

The purpose of this chapter is to teach you the first of these tests.

The coming memory aid suggests a successful strategy for making the details of a test stick in your memory.

MEMORY AID
FOR MASTERING THE TESTS

- **Write out the steps and ground rules—in correct order.**
- **Use YOUR wording but keep the meaning.**
- **Explain how they work to someone else.**

This first (for now) test and the one that follows in

Chapter 7 are the foundation for all of grammar. Learn these tests to mastery.

TEST 1
The Helpers plus WHAT/ING Word Verb Test

This TEST, the Helpers plus WHAT/ING Word Verb Test, has no ground rules. Instead, it has three **sets** of steps—that is, three SUBTESTS. This section will teach these subtests one at a time. Here is an **overview** to help you see how they are interrelated.

OVERVIEW FOR

The Helpers plus WHAT/ING Word Verb Test

Part A	Part B	Part C
HELPERS SUBTEST	WHAT SUBTEST	ING SUBTEST
Label all starters and followers.	Find the right WHAT-answering word.	Check if the WHAT-answering word has an ING spelling.

A detailed explanation of each part of this test follows.

The first subtest, the Helpers Subtest, urges you to not miss a single starter or follower.

Part A
Helpers Subtest

The Helpers plus WHAT/ING Word Verb Test

Part A Helpers Subtest	Part B WHAT Subtest	Part C ING Subtest
1. **Label all starters.** 2. **Label all followers.**	Find the right WHAT-answering word.	Check if the WHAT-answering word has an ING spelling.

You know this subtest already. You learned it in Chapter 5. TAKE CARE TO NEVER MISS A SINGLE STARTER OR FOLLOWER—EVER.

Helper set

The term **HELPER SET** means simply **A STARTER PLUS ITS FOLLOWER(S)**. In the examples here, they are the words in capitalized and darker lettering.

Examples of Helper Sets

COULD HAVE come
COULD HAVE BEEN included
MIGHT then HAVE lost
SHOULD not ever HAVE BEEN
forgotten

Helper Set:
A starter plus its follower(s).

The WHAT Subtest (Part B) teaches you how to use a starter or helper set to pinpoint which word (if any) requires further testing to determine whether it is a main verb.

<table>
<tr><td colspan="3" align="center">Part B
WHAT Subtest</td></tr>
</table>

The Helpers plus WHAT/ING Word Verb Test

Part A Helpers Subtest	Part B WHAT Subtest	Part C ING Subtest
Label all starters and followers.	**Find the RIGHT WHAT-ANSWERING WORD:** 1. **Say the sentence through each starter or helper set AND ASK WHAT.** 2. **REQUIREMENTS (to be the right WHAT-answering word):** • **ONE word** • **MOST SENSE-COMPLETING WORD** • **NEARBY word.**	Check if the WHAT-answering word has an ING spelling.

The WHAT Subtest is more of a "test" than you might think. **First,** you must ask the question WHAT just right. **Second,** you must ask it repeatedly—that is, for each starter or helper set. **Third,** you must **carefully** weigh the correctness of the word you choose against ALL THREE of the requirements listed. ALL REQUIREMENTS must be met ALWAYS.

Asking *WHAT* Right the First Time

The goal in this subtest is to find the word that **might** be a verb—that is, to find the word that you must ALSO test with the ING Subtest. That is why you must, for now, place a **small circle** (°) under the WHAT-answering word **to mark it as a WORD FOR FURTHER TESTING.**

The test works this way: **First, you say to yourself all the words of the sentence through each starter or helper set—AND ASK WHAT.** You repeat the wording of the sentence so that you ask WHAT inside the sentence's own context.

Next, the WORD you are looking for must COMPLETE THE SENSE of the question WHAT. **It must be ONE word. It must be the MOST SENSE-COMPLETING word. It must also be a NEARBY word**—expect the WHAT-answering word to be nearby AS IF BY PREFERENCE.

Here are examples with commentary.

*Each person **will have** RECEIVED a turn.*
°

[You say *Each person **will have** WHAT?* The ONE, NEARBY, and MOST SENSE-COMPLETING word is ***received.*** You place a small circle under ***received***—to mark the word for further testing.]

*Carlos **has** a brand new SHIRT.*
°

[You say *Carlos has WHAT?* The answer is the ONE, MOST SENSE-COMPLETING WORD ***shirt.***]

*Pam **could** as easily CHANGE her plans.*
°

[You say *Pam could WHAT?* The answer is the MOST SENSE-COMPLETING word ***change.***]

Do not jump to conclusions. THE WORD YOU ARE TAKING SUCH CARE TO FIND MAY **NOT** BE A VERB AT ALL. That is why you will **not** use a double underline for them in the first practices here. Instead, you place the SMALL CIRCLE underneath the word (as demonstrated above.)

● Do **_PRACTICE A_** (LABELING *WHAT*-ANSWERING WORDS IN SHORTER SENTENCES) in your *Skills Practice Book.*

Asking *WHAT* Right Again

One sentence can have more than one verb or verb phrase in it. When this happens, you carry out the WHAT Subtest for **each** verb (phrase). You say to yourself the words of the sentence—or enough of them so you have sufficient context—and ask WHAT **for each starter helper (set).** Note the examples in this sentence.

*As the jogger **was** RUNNING, he **was** almost BLINDED*
*by the rays of the sun but **was being** CHEERED*
by the singing of the birds.

[You **first** say *As the jogger **was** WHAT?* You **next** say *As the jogger was running, he **was** WHAT?* **Third,** you say *...he was almost blinded by the rays of the sun but **was being** WHAT?* The WHAT-answering words are *running, blinded,* and *cheered.*]

● Do **_PRACTICE B_** (LABELING *WHAT*-ANSWERING WORDS IN LONGER SENTENCES) in your *Skills Practice Book.*

Asking *WHAT* in Sentences with *Not*

It is not natural to ask WHAT after a starter that has *not* after it. For example, for the sentence *Bill has **not** told me yet,* you could ask *Bill **has** WHAT?* The word that answers WHAT is clearly TOLD but the word **not** adds a degree of confusion because it adds the meaning that there was no "telling."

The solution is to combine the starter with the *not* in a CONTRACTION (when possible) and ask WHAT after the contraction. For example, you would rewrite the above sentence to read *Bill **hasn't** told me yet.* Now you would say *Bill **hasn't** WHAT?* This makes it much easier to tell that the WHAT-answering word is TOLD.

Here are examples of what you would do.

*The storm **has** not appeared yet.*

[hasn't]
*The storm **has** ~~not~~ ∧ APPEARED yet.*

*Some wildflowers **do** not bloom for long.*

[don't]
*Some wildflowers **do** ~~not~~ ∧ BLOOM for long.*

Note: The helper *will* and the word *not* form the contraction *WON'T*.

Note Also: The word *cannot* means (and can sometimes be written as) *can not*. The contraction for *cannot*, of course, is *CAN'T*.

● Do *PRACTICE C* (LABELING WHAT-ANSWERING WORDS IN SENTENCES WITH *NOT*) in your *Skills Practice Book*.

● Do *PRACTICE D* (MORE LABELING OF WHAT-ANSWERING WORDS IN SENTENCES WITH *NOT*) in your *Skills Practice Book*.

The ING Subtest (Part C below) is of critical importance. It helps you to determine whether a word you have isolated by the WHAT Subtest is or is not a verb. Learn this section well.

Part C
ING Subtest

The Helpers plus WHAT/ING Word Verb Test

Part A Helpers Subtest	Part B WHAT Subtest	Part C ING Subtest
Label all starters and followers.	Find the right WHAT-answering word: Say the sentence through each starter or helper set and ask WHAT. Requirements (to be the right WHAT-answering word): · One word · Most sense-completing word · Nearby word.	1. ADD ING to the WHAT-answering word AS IT STANDS and OUTSIDE THE SENTENCE—unless an exception. 2. EXCEPTIONS: • For ED WORDS, substitute an ing ending • For ING WORDS, drop the ing • For IRREGULAR VERBS, label them as verbs. 3. Test for SAMENESS OF DICTIONARY MEANING.

This ING Subtest is more like a double check as to whether the WHAT-answering word has the "makings" of a main verb—that is, whether it has an ING spelling that also has the same dictionary meaning. If it does, it must be a verb. If it does not, it cannot be a verb. This test is your **proof**.

To make this double checking easier, this subtest

divides the task into several steps.

The heart of the test, and the part you use most often, is to add *ing* to the WHAT-answering word. Step 1 in Part C tells you how to do this.

Part C: STEP 1—
Adding *ING* to the Word as It Stands
Add *ING* to the WHAT-answering word AS IT STANDS and OUTSIDE the sentence— unless an exception.

This first step works like this: **You take the word—JUST AS IT STANDS—OUTSIDE the sentence and ADD *ING* TO IT.** For the sentence *He **has** COME early*, you would say *COMING* APART **from the sentence.** This is an **acceptable spelling** in English (and has the same dictionary meaning). Therefore, you would **double underline** *come* because you have **proven** that it is a verb in this sentence. See this done for you.

He <u><u>has come</u></u> early.

However, for the sentence *He **has** DIMES in his pocket*, you would say ~~DIMESING~~, which is **unacceptable as English.** Consequently, you have **proven** that the word *DIMES* is **not** a verb.

Your label in the practices will be to place a check mark (✓) UNDER such a word to indicate that you have tested the word and proven to yourself that it was **not** a verb. See this labeling done for you.

He <u>HAS</u> dimes in his pocket.
✓

Notice that you did **not** drop the *s* before adding *ing*. You **never** drop an ending (other than *ED* and *ING*, the two exceptions about to be explained) as you carry out Step 1 for this test. Here are more examples.

Examples

They __will__ soon SUCCEED. [*Succeeding* **is** a word.]

Everyone __was__ LATE. [~~Lating~~ **is not** a word.]
        ✓

The wind __is__ STEADIER. [~~Steadiering~~ **is not** a word.]
       ✓

We __were__ the HELPERS. [~~Helpersing~~ **is not** a word.]
      ✓

● Do *PRACTICE E* (LABELING VERBS USING TEST 1
  THROUGH PART C, STEP 1—ADDING *ING*) **in your**
  Skills Practice Book.

● Do *PRACTICE F* (LABELING VERBS USING TEST 1
  THROUGH PART C, STEP 1—ADDING *ING*) **in your**
  Skills Practice Book.

● Do *PRACTICE G* (LABELING VERBS USING TEST 1
  THROUGH PART C, STEP 1—ADDING *ING*) **in your**
  Skills Practice Book.

● Do *PRACTICE H* (LABELING VERBS USING TEST 1
  THROUGH PART C, STEP 1—ADDING *ING*) **in your**
  Skills Practice Book.

The coming section explains the first exception to this
ING rule.

Part C: STEP 2—
The ED Exception
**For words that end in *ED*,
substitute an *ING* ending.**

The main verb in a verb phrase can stand in its BASIC
spelling—for example, *can* ***swim***. It can also stand in
its AFTER-HAD spelling—for example, *has* ***discovered*** or

*will be **arranged***. Main verbs (in verb phrases) that end in *ed* have this ending to match the requirements of the helper that immediately precedes them.

You know that an ED ending is attached to a BASIC spelling. Therefore, **to test whether an ED WORD at the end of a verb phrase is a verb, you DROP ED AND SUBSTITUTE ING.** If the word is a verb, the resultant word will be an acceptable English word. If the word is **not** a verb, the resultant word will be a **nonsense** word. Here are examples with accompanying explanations.

*A few **have WALKED** that far.*

[You can say *walking*—**outside** the sentence. Therefore, *walked* is a verb in this sentence.]

*This bench **is** RUGGED.*

[You can**not** say ~~rugging~~. Therefore, *rugged* is **not** a verb.]

● Do ***PRACTICE J*** (LABELING VERBS USING TEST 1 THROUGH PART C, STEP 2—*ED* EXCEPTION) **in your** *Skills Practice Book.*

● Do ***PRACTICE K*** (LABELING VERBS USING TEST 1 THROUGH PART C, STEP 2—*ED* EXCEPTION) **in your** *Skills Practice Book.*

This next section explains the *ing* ending exception.

Part C: STEP 2—
The ING Exception
For words that end in *ING*, drop *ing*.

The main verb in a verb phrase can also stand in its ING spelling—for example, *will be **arriving*** or *was **explaining***. Main verbs in a verb phrase often have this *ING* ending. It adds the meaning of "on-goingness."

To test whether an *ING* WORD at the end of a verb phrase is a verb, you simply DROP THE ING. The resultant word will be a verb if it is an acceptable word (and it has the same dictionary meaning—see Step 3 below). Here are examples with added explanation.

*Jack **is** FIXING his car.*

[You can drop the *ing* ending. English does have the word *fix* (and in the same dictionary meaning). Therefore, *fixing* is a verb.]

*Time **is** UNCEASING.*

[When you drop the *ing* ending from the word *unceasing*, you end up with a non-English word ~~uncease~~. Therefore, *unceasing* is **not** a verb.]

● Do *PRACTICE L* (LABELING VERBS USING TEST 1 THROUGH PART C, STEP 2—*ING* EXCEPTION) in your *Skills Practice Book.*

● Do *PRACTICE M* (LABELING VERBS USING TEST 1 THROUGH PART C, STEP 2—*ING* EXCEPTION) in your *Skills Practice Book.*

The next exception (and last one) involves irregular verbs. This is simply a matter of RECOGNIZING SUCH WORDS, as you will now see.

Part C: STEP 2—
Irregular Verb Exception
For words that are irregular verbs, just label them as verbs.

When the main verb stands in its AFTER-HAD spelling,

the main verb can be an irregular verb—for example, *is known* or *has sung*. In these cases, the verb does not end in ED (and you can **not** just add *ing* either). In such cases, YOU MUST RECOGNIZE THE WORD AS A SPELLING OF AN IRREGULAR VERB ON SIGHT.

Because such words are components of verbs, they do have an ING spelling. However, you have to **know** the BASIC spelling to arrive at it. Here are examples with explanation.

> *I have swum there.* [You can say **swimming**—out-
> side the sentence.]

[You have to **know** that *swum* comes from the verb *swim*, which has the ING spelling *swimming*.]

> *We are taught English.* [You can say **teach-
> ing**—outside the sentence.]

[You have to **know** that *taught* comes from the verb *teach*, which has the ING spelling *teaching*.]

● Do *PRACTICE N* (SUPPLYING THE BASIC SPELLING FOR VERBS IN THEIR AFTER-HAD SPELLING) in your *Skills Practice Book.*

● Do *PRACTICE P* (SUPPLYING THE BASIC SPELLING FOR VERBS IN THEIR AFTER-HAD SPELLING) in your *Skills Practice Book.*

● Do *PRACTICE Q* (SUPPLYING THE BASIC SPELLING FOR VERBS IN THEIR AFTER-HAD SPELLING) in your *Skills Practice Book.*

● Do *PRACTICE R* (SUPPLYING THE BASIC SPELLING FOR VERBS IN THEIR AFTER-HAD SPELLING) in your *Skills Practice Book.*

● Do *PRACTICE S* (LABELING VERBS USING TEST 1 THROUGH PART C, STEP 2—IRREGULAR VERB EXCEPTION) in your *Skills Practice Book.*

● Do **_PRACTICE T_** (LABELING VERBS USING TEST 1 THROUGH PART C, STEP 2—IRREGULAR VERB EXCEPTION) in your **_Skills Practice Book._**

● Do **_PRACTICE U_** (LABELING VERBS USING TEST 1 THROUGH PART C, STEP 2—IRREGULAR VERB EXCEPTION) in your **_Skills Practice Book._**

This last component of the ING Subtest requires your careful attention. When you apply this third step, you must take the time to do it right.

Part C: STEP 3— Testing for Sameness of Dictionary Meaning

The meaning of the word that you have added _ING_ to—or taken _ING_ from—must match the meaning of the original word. Compare the two meanings.

When you carry out the ING double check, you will find words to which you can add _ING_ **but this changes the word's meaning**. For example, for the sentence _The box is_ EMPTY, you can say _emptying_ but _emptying_ means "causing to spill out." In contrast, the word EMPTY—as used in the sentence—means "without any contents." When the meaning changes like this, the word tested is **not** a verb. You place a check mark under it as here.

The box **is** EMPTY.
✓

Note that this happens only about 10% of those times when you can add _ing_—and even more rarely for words that you take _ing_ from. In addition, as you come to understand our language better, you will be able to "sense" the difference instinctively.

Here are more examples with accompanying explanation.

*Paco **had** TROUBLE with his car yesterday.*
√

[*Troubling* means "disturbing," but in the sentence
TROUBLE means "difficulty."]

*Mary **is** WILLING to help.*
√

[*Will* means "to leave in a will," but in this sentence
WILLING means "disposed."]

● Do *PRACTICE V* (LABELING VERBS USING TEST 1
THROUGH PART C, STEP 3) in your *Skills Practice
Book.*

● Do *PRACTICE W* (LABELING VERBS USING TEST 1
THROUGH PART C, STEP 3) in your *Skills Practice
Book.*

Here is the whole Helpers plus WHAT/ING Word Verb
Test.

TEST 1: The Helpers plus WHAT/ING Word Verb Test

Part A	Part B	Part C
Helpers Subtest	**WHAT Subtest**	**ING Subtest**
1. Label starters.	1. Find the RIGHT WHAT-ANSWERING WORD.	1. ADD ING to the WHAT-answering word AS IT STANDS and <u>OUTSIDE</u> THE SENTENCE —unless an exception.
2. Label followers.	2. REQUIREMENTS (to be the right WHAT-answering word): • ONE word; • MOST SENSE-COMPLETING word; • NEARBY word.	2. EXCEPTIONS: • For ED WORDS, substitute an ING ending; • For ING WORDS, drop the ING ending; • For IRREGULAR VERBS, label as verbs.
		3. Test for SAMENESS OF DICTIONARY MEANING.

● Do *PRACTICE X* (LABELING VERBS USING TEST 1: STEPS 1, 2, AND 3) in your *Skills Practice Book.*

Endnotes

Verb Phrases as Units That Sound Right Together: As you might guess, all the words of a verb phrase—not just the starter and its followers—should sound as if they belong together. They should be "SAYABLE TOGETHER." Note these examples.

*Fred **may have been** only **kidding**.*
*Expensive items **can** sometimes **be** easily **broken**.*

The verbs ***may have been kidding*** and ***can be broken*** both sound as if they belong together. See the last note here for one application of this information.

Wording after Helpers That Answers WHEN or WHERE Rather than WHAT: Sometimes the wording that fills the territory after a helping verb will answer WHEN or WHERE rather than WHAT. Here are examples.

*The appointment will be **soon**. [**Soon** answers*
WHEN.]
*My book is **home**. [**Home** answers WHERE.]*

Such wording cannot serve as a WHAT-answering word. Instead, it serves as an ADVERB, the kind of word that answers questions like WHEN or WHERE when asked after a verb. See Chapter 16 for a fuller explanation.

Phrases and Noun Clauses That Serve as WHAT-answering Wording: You know that phrases and clauses are groups of words that—as a unit—can do the job of a noun (see Chapter 2). When such a group of words answers WHAT after helpers, it will never contain—**inside** it—a main verb that belongs to helpers that are **outside** (and **before**) it. Here are examples with explanation.

Tardiness is TO ARRIVE LATE FOR SOMETHING.
[The wording that answers WHAT after the verb *is* is
the **WHOLE PHRASE** TO ARRIVE LATE FOR SOMETHING.
Notice how you can **not** say the words ~~is arrive~~
together.]

The fact is THAT COLLEGE GRADUATES CAN EARN
IMPRESSIVE SALARIES.
[The wording that answers WHAT after the verb *is* is
the **WHOLE NOUN CLAUSE** THAT COLLEGE GRADUATES
CAN EARN IMPRESSIVE SALARIES. Notice that you find
a **second** verb phrase *can earn* **inside** the clause.]

You will learn more about both phrases and clauses as
you proceed through this text.

Review

Content in darker lettering
must be remembered.

Helper Set: A starter <u>plus</u> its follower(s).

Labeling for Verbs: Use a DOUBLE UNDERLINE for all
verb words—for both helpers and main verbs.

[continued]

Test 1: The Helpers plus WHAT/ING Word Verb Test:

Part A—Helpers Subtest:
1. Label starters.
2. Label followers.

Part B—WHAT Subtest:
1. Find the right WHAT-answering word.
2. Requirements (to be the right WHAT-answering word):
   - ONE word;
   - MOST SENSE-COMPLETING word;
   - NEARBY word.

Part C—ING Subtest:
1. Add ING to the WHAT-answering word AS IT STANDS and OUTSIDE THE SENTENCE—unless an exception.
2. Exceptions:
   - For ED WORDS, substitute an ING ending;
   - For ING WORDS, drop the ING ending;
   - For IRREGULAR VERBS, label as verbs.
3. Test for SAMENESS OF DICTIONARY MEANING.

Chapter 7

Remaining Main Verbs

You can now find starters and their companion verbs successfully. The goal of this chapter is to help you find all other main verbs with equal success.

The importance of this chapter cannot be overestimated because these main verbs make up close to TWO-THIRDS OF THE OCCURRENCES OF A VERB in written English.

Truths about Remaining Main Verbs

These "truths" are the foundation for the second key strategy for finding verbs, the "DO/DOES/DID TEST (TO FIND REMAINING MAIN VERBS)."

Truth A

Other than in commands, only main verbs in their present or past tense—that is, in their BASIC, S/ES, or PAST TENSE spelling—have no companion helping verb.

Examples

*That orange **tasted** good.*
*This orange **tastes** good.*
*Oranges **taste** good.*
*We **ate** the oranges.*

Other than in commands, these are the **only** ways you can use a verb like *taste* or *eat* without any helper. All other ways of writing main verbs (in their **primary** role) require the use of at least a starter helping verb.

Truth B

English has a substitute present and past tense—the *DO, DOES,* or *DID* + BASIC SPELLING substitution.

You can rewrite the four sentences you just saw by replacing the verb with its *do/does/did* + BASIC SPELL-ING substitutions. Notice in these examples that **the meanings are identical.**

*This orange **tasted** good.* ➡ *This orange **DID** **taste** good.* [Uses PAST TENSE spelling of helper *do*]

*This orange **tastes** good.* ➡ *This orange **DOES** **taste** good.* [Uses the S/ES spelling of helper *do*]

*Oranges **taste** good.* ➡ *Oranges **DO** **taste** good.* [Uses the BASIC spelling of helper *do*]

*We **ate** the oranges.* ➡ *We **DID** **eat** the oranges.* [Uses the PAST TENSE spelling of helper *do*]

Each of these new sentences is a perfect substitute for its earlier version. Each keeps the same tense and agreement. In addition, you add no new meaning—unless you say it with a special tone of voice.

Note that everybody who uses English is already familiar with these substitutions for two reasons. First, you need the substitution if you want to add *not* to such a sentence to reverse its meaning. Notice the example.

*That orange **tasted** good.* ➡ *That orange*
*DID NOT **taste** good.*

Second, you must make the substitutions before you can turn statements into starter-verb questions. Here is an example.

*That orange **tasted** good.* ➡ ***Did** that orange*
***taste** good?*

Truth C

You must use ONLY the
BASIC SPELLING of a main verb
AFTER *DO, DOES,* or *DID* AS HELPER.

Examples

*Joe **did** NEED a break.* [NOT ~~did needed~~]

*Joe **does** NEED a break.* [NOT ~~does needs~~]

*We **do** NEED a break.* [NOT ~~do needs~~ NOR ~~do needed~~]

*They **did** TAKE a break.* [NOT ~~did took~~]

Terms to Remember

You need to understand these terms and remember their meanings as you proceed through this chapter.

Do Substitution:

YOU WRITE OUT A WORD AND PLACE THE HELPER *DO* BEFORE IT.

Explanation: The purpose is to see if the **two** words can replace the original word and have the whole sentence be acceptable English.

Does Substitution:

YOU REWRITE A WORD THAT ENDS IN DE-
TACHABLE *S/ES*—YOU PLACE THE HELPER
DOES BEFORE IT, AND YOU DROP
THE WORD'S *S/ES* ENDING.

Explanation: The purpose is to see if the **two**
words can replace the original
word and have the whole sentence
be acceptable English.

Did Substitution:

YOU REWRITE A WORD THAT ENDS IN *ED*
OR IS A PAST TENSE SPELLING FOR
AN IRREGULAR VERB—YOU PLACE THE
HELPER *DID* BEFORE IT, AND YOU DROP
THE WORD'S *ED* ENDING OR CHANGE THE
IRREGULAR VERB BACK TO ITS
BASIC SPELLING.

Explanation: The purpose is to see if the **two**
words can replace the original
word and have the whole sentence
be acceptable English.

Truth D

You can use a *do/does/did* substitution to
PROVE that <u>a word still unlabeled as a verb</u>
(after the Helpers plus WHAT/ING Word Verb
Test) is a verb.

Example

[did cross]

A fox ∧ crossed the road.

The proof that *crossed* is a verb in this sentence is the fact that the *DID* SUBSTITUTION sounds correct in the context of the **whole sentence**—*A fox did cross the road.* The *DID* SUBSTITUTION **has** grammatical "fit."

Another Example

[did lack]

The borrowed rope that Ed used ∧ lacked the needed strength.

The proof that *lacked* is a verb in this sentence is the fact that the *DID* SUBSTITUTION makes the **whole sentence**—*The borrowed rope that Ed used did lack the needed strength*—an acceptable English sentence. The substitute spelling *did lack* has grammatical fit.

Truth E

You can use a *do/does/did* substitution to PROVE that <u>a word still unlabeled as a verb</u> (after the Helpers plus WHAT/ING Word Verb Test) is NOT a verb.

Example

[~~did cross~~]

The ∧ crossed wires caused a spark.
✓

The proof that *crossed* in this sentence is **not** a verb is the fact that the *DID* SUBSTITUTION does **not** sound right in the context of the whole sentence. Note.

~~the did cross wires caused a spark~~

The substitute spelling *did cross* does **not** have grammatical fit.

Truth F
Verbs can fill
any position in a sentence.

Examples

[Do speak]
∧ ***Speak*** *distinctly.*

[do know]   [do mean]
I ∧ ***know*** *the person you* ∧ ***mean.***

[did borrow] [does belong]
The book Paul ∧ ***borrowed*** ∧ ***belongs*** *to the library.*

In the sentence ***Speak*** *distinctly*, the verb fills the **first** position. In the sentence *I **know** the person you **mean***, the verbs fill the **second** and **last** positions. In the sentence *The book Paul **borrowed belongs** to the library*, the verbs fill middle positions and **positions right beside each other.**

Truth G
One sentence can contain
several verbs.

Example

[did carry]   [did fall]
The twig that the bird ∧ ***carried*** ∧ ***fell*** *to the ground*

[did surprise] [did frighten]
*when a sound **surprised** ∧ and ∧ **frightened** it.*

There are **four** verbs in this sentence. A sentence can have ANY NUMBER.

Ground Rules for the Tests to Follow to Succeed—a Special Note

Most of the Tests to Follow to Succeed have ground rules as well as steps. The GROUND RULES are **just as important as the steps.**

The GROUND RULES are THE ADDITIONAL ACTIONS OR PRECAUTIONS REQUIRED FOR THE SUCCESS OF THE STEPS.

You must LEARN and REMEMBER the ground rules **with the same urgency as the steps themselves.**

TEST 2
The Do/does/did Test (to Find Remaining Main Verbs)

This TEST—the DO/DOES/DID TEST—is the second of the two most important tests in this text. Learn it to mastery.

The next two sections explain its seven GROUND RULES and four STEPS.

Part A
Ground Rules

The Do/does/did Test
(to Find Remaining Main Verbs)

Part A	Part B
Ground Rules	Steps

	Part A — Ground Rules	Part B — Steps
1.	Apply the Helpers plus WHAT/ING Word Verb Test <u>BEFORE</u> THIS TEST ALWAYS.	Choose *do, does,* or *did* right.
2.	Test <u>ONLY</u> <u>NON</u>-DOUBLE UNDERLINED WORDS.	
3.	Test <u>ALL</u> <u>NON</u>-DOUBLE UNDERLINED WORDS.	
4.	Test with *DO/DOES/DID* + BASIC spelling.	
5.	Test with ENOUGH EARLIER **and** LATER WORDING.	
6.	Test with <u>WHOLE SENTENCE</u> AS THE ONLY TRUE PROOF.	
7.	Test with <u>ORIGINAL WORDING</u> for all other words.	

Your benefiting from these GROUND RULES is essential for your success. This section discusses the importance of each.

The DO/DOES/DID TEST causes failure IF YOU USE IT OUT OF TURN. It only works on words UNaccompanied by helping verbs. Therefore, it only works on those words that **remain** AFTER you have double underlined and (mentally) set aside all helpers and their companion main verbs. Note the example.

*He **has arrived** already.*

Explanation: If you use the *do/does/did* substitutions **before** applying the Helpers plus WHAT/ING Word Verb Test, neither *has* nor *arrived* would **appear** to be a verb. Note what would happen: ~~he does have arrived already~~ and ~~he has did arrive already~~.

You saw the importance of this in the above discussion about carrying out the two verb tests in the wrong order.

Once you have double underlined a word during the Helpers plus WHAT/ING-Word Verb Test, this word IS a verb word **for good**. You must **never** test it again.

Ground Rule 3
Test ALL NON-DOUBLE UNDERLINED WORDS.

As you saw in Truths 6 and 7, verbs have no predictable location in a sentence—THEY CAN APPEAR ANYWHERE, EVEN RIGHT BESIDE EACH OTHER. Therefore, you will **not** have found **every verb** UNLESS YOU HAVE TESTED EVERY SINGLE NON-UNDERLINED WORD—except the first word in the sentence (see below).

Special Note: Verbs in the FIRST POSITION in a sentence EXPRESS A COMMAND. The practices here do **not** include commands. Therefore, NEVER TEST A SENTENCE'S FIRST WORD. By the way, such testing could only cause the changing of a statement to a question—a NONpermitted change in the sense of a sentence (during this test). Note.

Deer eat the branches of young fruit trees. ➡

[do] Deer eat the branches of young fruit trees[?]

Ground Rule 4
Test with *do/does/did* plus BASIC spelling.

You learned in Chapter 5 and in Truth C above that *do, does,* and *did* **dictate** the spelling of the main verb that serves as their companion—this main verb must stand in its BASIC spelling. Note.

$$\underline{I} \quad \textbf{\textit{do}} \quad \text{CARE.}$$
$$\underline{He} \quad \textbf{\textit{does}} \quad \text{CARE.}$$
$$\underline{We} \quad \textbf{\textit{did}} \quad \text{CARE.}$$

The point is that when you test a word ending in *ed* or *s/es*, **you must remove these endings—but** THESE ENDINGS ONLY—AS YOU TEST. Note.

He cares. ➡ *He does CARE_.*

We careD. ➡ *We DID CARE_.*

Ground Rule 5
Test with ENOUGH EARLIER and LATER WORDING.

You must always do your testing IN CONTEXT. When a word is **not** a verb, the context of a NATURAL CLUSTER of **earlier wording** (never less than one word) and a NATURAL CLUSTER of **later wording** (never less than one word) can be enough. Note.

[~~did toast~~] [~~do sandwich~~]
A ⋀ *toasted* ⋀ *sandwich **has** special appeal.*

When you say ~~a did toast sandwich~~ or ~~a toasted do sandwich has~~, it is obvious that neither *toasted* nor *sandwich* is a verb.

Important Note: When a word obviously could be a verb (because it ends in *ed* or *s/es* or is a component of an irregular verb or is a word you can add *ing* to), YOU MUST USE THE CONTEXT OF THE WHOLE SENTENCE. Note this sentence.

[did object]
The people who ⋀ *objected* <u>were</u> *misinformed.*

If you test supplied *did object* with just **one** earlier and **one** later word—*who did object were*—you would be convinced that *objected* is not a verb. However, when you use the context of the whole sentence—*The people who did object were misinformed*—you find that the whole sentence **is** acceptable English.

This is the **proof** both that *objected* is a verb and that you must test words that might be verbs in the context of the <u>WHOLE SENTENCE</u>.

Ground Rule 6
Test with the <u>WHOLE SENTENCE</u>
AS THE ONLY TRUE PROOF.

You are **never sure** whether a word IS or IS NOT a verb UNTIL YOU SAY THE SUBSTITUTE SPELLING IN THE CONTEXT OF THE WHOLE SENTENCE. Note.

[did borrow]
He <u>used</u> some ∧ borrowed equipment.

If you test *borrowed* by saying only one word earlier and one later—*some did borrow equipment*—you can **think** that *borrowed* is a verb. However, in the context of the whole sentence ~~he used some did borrow equipment~~, the resultant wording is **un**acceptable as English. This is your **proof** that *borrowed* is **not** a verb in this sentence and that **only** the CONTEXT OF THE WHOLE SENTENCE GUARANTEES ACCURACY.

Ground Rule 7
Test with ORIGINAL WORDING
for all other words.

There are reasons why we do not use the *do / does / did* substitution in English unless we are adding *not* or creating a question. One reason is that the substitute spelling, though allowable, is wordy. The other reason is that THE USE OF MORE THAN ONE SUBSTITUTE SPELLING IN A SENTENCE SOUNDS AWKWARD. Note.

[did give] [did prove]
The answer John ∧ *gave* ∧ *proved wrong.*

Notice how awkward it would sound to use two substitute spellings at the same time.

~~the answer John did give did prove wrong~~

Therefore, you should use only one substitute spelling when you test *gave.*

The answer John **did give** PROVED *wrong.*

You should also use **only one** substitute spelling when you test *proved.*

The answer John GAVE **did prove** *wrong.*

Your care and accuracy in carrying out the steps that follow will directly influence your success with this test.

Part B
Steps

The Do/does/did Test
(to Find Remaining Main Verbs)

Part A	Part B
Ground Rules	**Steps**
1. Apply the "Helpers" Test BEFORE this test.	1. For *ED* WORDS, choose *DID*.
2. Test only non-underlined words.	2. For DETACHABLE *S/ES* WORDS, choose *DOES*.
3. Test all non-underlined words.	3. For IRREGULAR VERBS IN PAST TENSE, choose *DID*.
4. Test with *do/does/did* + basic spelling.	4. For ALL OTHER WORDS, choose *DO*.
5. Test with enough earlier and later wording.	
6. Test with whole sentence as the only true proof.	
7. Test with original wording for all other words.	

These four STEPS are so important that their correct use must become **natural** to you.

Another TRUTH about the *do/does/did* substitution is that *do, does,* and *did* are **not** interchangeable. When *did* is the correct choice, *DID* is the ONLY choice. Note.

*Joe need**ED** a break.* ➡ *Joe **DID** need a break.*

Explanation: Notice that the *ed* ending on *needed* is an INDICATOR OF PAST TENSE. However, *needed* **loses** its *ed* ending in the substitute spelling. Therefore, you **must** choose *DID* to preserve the past tense meaning. Here are more examples.

[did land]
The plane ∧ *landed safely.*

[did remain]
The sky ∧ *remained cloudless.*

Notice the use of the caret (∧) to indicate an insertion and the side brackets ([ ]) to indicate an editor's addition. You will be using these markings in the practices.

Ed Words That Cannot Be Verbs

Sometimes you can tell that an *ED* word is not a verb simply because you cannot say it with *DID*. Note the examples.

rugged ➡ *did rug* [This can **not** be a verb.]

unwanted ➡ *did unwant* [This can **not** be a verb.]

● Do *PRACTICE A* (ADDING THE *DID* SUBSTITUTION TO SINGLE WORDS) in your *Skills Practice Book.*

Spelling Tips

You know the chief SPELLING RULES that concern adding suffixes to root words. Here they are **in review**.

Spelling Rule for Changing *Y* to *I*:

When *Y* FOLLOWS A <u>CONSONANT</u>, change *Y* to *I*.

Examples

deNY + ed = deNIed
empTY + ed = empTIed

Spelling Rule for Dropping Final Silent *E*:

Drop final silent *E* before a suffix that begins with a vowel sound.

Examples

tracE + Ed = tracEd
debatE + Ed = debatEd

Spelling Rule for Doubling a Final Consonant:

Double a <u>single</u> FINAL consonant that comes AFTER a <u>single vowel</u> and BEFORE a <u>suffix that begins with a vowel sound</u>.

Examples

stoP + Ed = stoPPEd
triM + Ed = triMMEd

YOU MUST APPLY THESE RULES **IN REVERSE** WHEN YOU DROP *ED* FROM A WORD DURING THE ***DID*** **SUBSTITUTION.**

Spelling Tip A:
**When you add *DID* and drop
an *ed* after *I*, CHANGE *I* BACK TO *Y*.**

Examples
carrIed ➡ *did carrY*
replIed ➡ *did replY*

Spelling Tip B:
**When you add *DID* and drop an *ed*
where there was once a silent *E*,
RESTORE THE DROPPED SILENT *E*.**

Examples
placed ➡ *did placE*
quoted ➡ *did quotE*

Spelling Tip C:
**When you add *DID* and drop an *ed*
where a consonant has been doubled,
DROP THE ADDED CONSONANT.**

Examples
baTTed ➡ *did baT*
slIPPed ➡ *did slIP*

AS YOU CARRY OUT THE ABOVE TIPS, YOU ARE APPLYING
THE SPELLING RULES IN REVERSE.

● Do _PRACTICE B_ (APPLYING THREE SPELLING TIPS)
in your *Skills Practice Book*.

● Do *PRACTICE C* (ADDING THE *DID* SUBSTITUTION INSIDE SENTENCES WITH ONE *ED* WORD) in your *Skills Practice Book.*

● Do *PRACTICE D* (ADDING THE *DID* SUBSTITUTION INSIDE SENTENCES WITH EXTRA *ED* WORDS) in your *Skills Practice Book.*

● Do *PRACTICE E* (ADDING THE *DID* SUBSTITUTION AFTER CARRYING OUT THE HELPERS PLUS WHAT/ING WORD VERB TEST) in your *Skills Practice Book.*

Step 2
For DETACHABLE *S/ES* WORDS, choose *DOES.*

When a word ends in DETACHABLE S/ES, *DOES* is the only choice. Note the example.

Joe needs a break. ➡ *Joe DOES need a break.*

Explanation: The *s/es* ending on *needs* is an indicator of present tense and third person agreement. However, *needs* **loses** its *s/es* ending when you replace it with the substitute spelling. Therefore, you **must** choose *DOES* to preserve the present tense and *s/es* (third person singular) agreement. Here are more examples.

[does take]
Careful reading ∧ *takes longer.*

[does deserve]
A mistake ∧ **deserves** *analysis.*

Note that you will be inserting the *DOES* SUBSTITUTION in this way in the practices.

S/es Words That Are Not Detachable

Many words end in *s/es* because the *s/es* belongs to their root spelling. Examples are *glass, fuss, sometimes* [**not** *sometime*], and *his*. You test such words with DO. Note.

> *do glass   do fuss   do sometimes   do his*

[Note that *sometime* (with no *s*) is an English word too—an altogether different word. It has the meaning "former" or "one-time," as in *a SOMETIME boxer.*]

S/es Words That Cannot Be Verbs

Sometimes you can tell that an *s/es* word is not a verb simply because you cannot say it with the DOES or DO substitution. Three of the above words are of this sort—namely: *~~do glass, do sometimes,~~* and *~~do his~~*. Here are more examples.

ideas	➡	*~~does idea~~*
yes	➡	*~~do yes~~*
cars	➡	*~~does car~~*
moss	➡	*~~do moss~~*

● Do **_PRACTICE F_** (ADDING THE DO SUBSTITUTION TO SINGLE WORDS) in your *Skills Practice Book*.

Spelling Tips

There is another SPELLING RULE that concerns adding suffixes to root words. Here it is **in review**.

Spelling Rule for Changing *Y* to *IE*:

When *Y* FOLLOWS A <u>CONSONANT</u> and you are adding *S*, change *Y* to *IE*.

Examples

deNY + *S* = *deNIEs*
fanCY + *S* = *fanCIEs*

YOU MUST APPLY THIS RULE IN **REVERSE** WHEN YOU DROP *S/ES* FROM A WORD DURING A *DOES* SUBSTITUTION.

Spelling Tip D:

When you add *DOES* and drop an *S* after *IE*, CHANGE *IE* BACK TO *Y*.

Examples

carrIEs ➡ *does carrY*
replIEs ➡ *does replY*

Sometimes words end in *'s*. This is a special case.

Special Case—Words Ending in *'s*:

NOUNS can end in *'s* (say "APOSTROPHE *S*"). This *'s* is not detachable. You must test such a word with *DO*.

Examples

Fred's book ➡ ~~DO Fred's book~~
captain's table ➡ ~~DO captain's table~~

Do not confuse this *'s* with the *'s* that stands for a contraction of *is* or *has* with a pronoun and must be separated into its component words immediately. For example, you would rewrite *it's* as *it is* or *it has*.

Spelling Tip E:

Choose *DO* before a word that ends in *'s*. NEVER drop *'s*.

● Do <u>*PRACTICE G*</u> (APPLYING TWO SPELLING TIPS) in your *Skills Practice Book*.

● Do **_PRACTICE H_** (ADDING THE _DOES_ OR _DO_ SUBSTI-TUTION INSIDE SENTENCES FOR JUST _S/ES_ WORDS) in your **_Skills Practice Book._**

● Do **_PRACTICE J_** (ADDING THE _DOES, DID,_ OR _DO_ SUBSTITUTION INSIDE SENTENCES WITH BOTH JUST _S/ES_ AND _ED_ WORDS) in your **_Skills Practice Book._**

● Do **_PRACTICE K_** (ADDING THE _DOES, DID,_ OR _DO_ SUBSTITUTION AFTER CARRYING OUT THE HELPERS PLUS WHAT/ING WORD VERB TEST) in your **_Skills Practice Book._**

Step 3
For IRREGULAR VERBS IN THE
PAST TENSE, choose _DID_.

Unlike regular verbs, IRREGULAR VERBS do **not** have an _ed_ ending for their PAST TENSE SPELLING. Therefore, YOU MUST KNOW ALL THESE PAST TENSE SPELLINGS ON SIGHT.

When you find an irregular verb in its past tense spelling, _DID_ is your only choice. Here is an example.

Joe **broke** _his pen._ ➡ _Joe_ **DID** **break** _his pen._

Explanation: You must use _DID_ because _DID_ **alone** carries PAST TENSE MEANING. Here are more examples.

[did speak]
Everyone ∧ **_spoke_** _at once._

[did go]
The rehearsal ∧ **_went_** _well._

119

- Do _PRACTICE L_ (SUPPLYING THE BASIC SPELLING OR IRREGULAR VERBS IN THEIR PAST TENSE) in your _Skills Practice Book._

- Do _PRACTICE M_ (SUPPLYING THE BASIC SPELLING FOR IRREGULAR VERBS IN THEIR PAST TENSE) in your _Skills Practice Book._

- Do _PRACTICE N_ (SUPPLYING THE BASIC SPELLING FOR IRREGULAR VERBS IN THEIR PAST TENSE) in your _Skills Practice Book._

- Do _PRACTICE P_ (SUPPLYING THE BASIC SPELLING FOR IRREGULAR VERBS IN THEIR PAST TENSE) in your _Skills Practice Book._

- Do _PRACTICE Q_ (ADDING THE _DID_ SUBSTITUTION INSIDE SENTENCES FOR JUST IRREGULAR VERBS IN THEIR PAST TENSE) in your _Skills Practice Book._

- Do _PRACTICE R_ (ADDING THE _DOES, DID,_ OR _DO_ SUBSTITUTION INSIDE SENTENCES WITH _S/ES_ AND _ED_ WORDS AND IRREGULAR VERBS IN THEIR PAST TENSE) in your _Skills Practice Book._

- Do _PRACTICE S_ (ADDING THE _DOES, DID,_ OR _DO_ SUBSTITUTION AFTER CARRYING OUT THE HELPERS PLUS WHAT/ING WORD VERB TEST) in your _Skills Practice Book._

Step 4
For ALL OTHER WORDS, choose _DO._

When words do **not** end in _ed_ or detachable _s/es_ and are **not** irregular verbs in their past tense, _DO_ is your

only choice. Here is an example.

We *need* more money. ➡ We DO *need* more money.

Explanation: The lack of *ed* and *s/es* endings and of an irregular verb in its past tense **indicate** PRESENT TENSE **and** BASIC SPELLING. Therefore, you **must** choose *DO* because *DO* **alone** carries present tense in its basic spelling. Here are more examples.

arrival ➡ ~~do arrival~~
standing ➡ ~~do standing~~
talker ➡ ~~do talker~~
weak ➡ ~~do weak~~

Notice that you **never** change the spellings for these words. The **only** allowed changes—as you know—are to **drop** *s/es* **or** *ed* and to **change irregular verbs** in their past tense spelling to their basic spelling after adding *did*.

● Do *PRACTICE T* (ADDING THE *DO* SUBSTITUTION TO SINGLE WORDS) in your *Skills Practice Book.*

● Do *PRACTICE U* (ADDING THE *DO* SUBSTITUTION INSIDE SENTENCES JUST FOR WORDS OTHER THAN THOSE THAT END IN *S/ES* OR *ED* AND OTHER THAN IRREGULAR VERBS IN THEIR PAST TENSE) in your *Skills Practice Book.*

● Do *PRACTICE V* (ADDING THE *DOES, DID,* OR *DO* SUBSTITUTIONS FOR ALL WORDS) in your *Skills Practice Book.*

● Do *PRACTICE W* (ADDING THE *DOES, DID,* AND *DO* SUBSTITUTIONS AFTER CARRYING OUT THE HELPERS PLUS WHAT/ING WORD VERB TEST) in your *Skills Practice Book.*

Here is the whole Do/does/did Test (to Find Remaining Main Verbs).

The Do/does/did Test
(to Find Remaining Main Verbs)

Part A	Part B
Ground Rules	**Steps**

Part A — Ground Rules

1. Apply the Helpers plus WHAT/ING Word Verb Test BEFORE THIS TEST ALWAYS.

2. Test ONLY NON-DOUBLE UNDERLINED WORDS.

3. Test ALL NON-DOUBLE UNDERLINED WORDS.

4. Test with DO/DOES/DID + BASIC spelling.

5. Test with ENOUGH EARLIER and LATER WORDING.

6. Test with WHOLE SENTENCE AS THE ONLY TRUE PROOF.

7. Test with ORIGINAL WORDING for all other words.

Part B — Steps

1. For ED WORDS, choose DID.

2. For DETACHABLE S/ES WORDS, choose DOES.

3. For IRREGULAR VERBS IN PAST TENSE, choose DID.

4. For ALL OTHER WORDS, choose DO.

● Do *PRACTICE X* (Carrying out both verb tests) in your *Skills Practice Book.*

● Do *PRACTICE Y* (Carrying out both verb tests) in your *Skills Practice Book.*

Endnote

Occasional Need for an *Ing* Double Check as Well: There is one kind of sentence that requires extra care. In a sentence like *Children often play hopscotch*, you can say **both** *do often* **and** *do play* in the context of the whole sentence. However, **only** *play* is the verb. The reason is that the word *often* has no *ing* spelling.

This can happen only when the verb is in its DO substitute form and the prior word is an adverb.

Though this text tries to avoid such sentences, here is a rule you can follow: When two "verbs" in their "*do*" spelling stand beside each other, each is truly a verb **only** if EACH has an *ing* way in which you can write it.

Review

Content in darker lettering must be remembered.

Order for the Tests:
1. Helpers plus WHAT/ING Word Verb Test
2. Do/does/did Test

Do Substitution: You write out a word and place the helper *do* before it.

DOES SUBSTITUTION: You rewrite a word that ends in detachable *s/es*—you place the helper *does* before it, and you drop the word's *s/es* ending.

DID SUBSTITUTION: You rewrite a word that ends in *ed* or is a past tense spelling for an irregular verb—you place the helper *did* before it, and you drop the word's *ed* ending <u>or</u> change the irregular verb back to its basic spelling.

Spelling Tips:

When you add *DID* and drop an *ed* after *I*, CHANGE *I* BACK TO *Y*.

When you add *DID* and drop an *ed* where there was once a silent E, RESTORE THE DROPPED SILENT E.

When you add *DID* and drop an *ed* where a consonant has been doubled, DROP THE ADDED CONSONANT.

When you add *DOES* and drop an *s* after *IE*, CHANGE *IE* BACK TO *Y*.

Choose *DO* before a word that ends in *'s*. NEVER drop *'s*.

Test 2: The Do/does/did Test (to Find Remaining Main Verbs):

Part A—Ground Rules:
1. Apply the Helpers plus WHAT/ING Word Verb Test <u>BEFORE</u> THIS TEST ALWAYS.
2. Test <u>ONLY</u> NON-DOUBLE UNDERLINED WORDS.
3. Test <u>ALL</u> NON-DOUBLE UNDERLINED WORDS.
4. Test with *DO/DOES/DID* + BASIC spelling.
5. Test with EARLIER <u>and</u> LATER WORDING.
6. Test with <u>WHOLE SENTENCE</u> AS THE ONLY TRUE PROOF.
7. Test with ORIGINAL WORDING for all other words.

Part B—Steps:
1. For *ED* WORDS, choose *DID*.
2. For DETACHABLE *S/ES* WORDS, choose *DOES*.
3. For IRREGULAR VERBS IN PAST TENSE, choose *DID*.
4. For ALL OTHER WORDS, choose *DO*.

Chapter 8

Simpler Questions

Now you can find verbs without error. This ability will now be the chief tool to help you understand how sentences work.

The purposes of this chapter are to introduce you to the names for the chief parts of a sentence and to help you **experience**—by the strategy of repositioning verb words—how these parts work inside simpler questions.

Truths about
the Chief Parts of a Sentence

This background information will make the work of this and the following two chapters easier for you.

Truth A

Every verb has
a VISIBLE or INVISIBLE starter
that marks its beginning.

There are three ways in which a starter can mark the beginning of a verb.

First, the starter can **be** the verb. Note.

My book <u>was</u> in the kitchen.

Note here that the starter is *was* and that it is VISIBLE.
Second, the starter can start the verb phrase. Note.

My book <u>can be</u> in the kitchen.

Here the starter is *can*, and it too is VISIBLE.

Third, the starter can be INVISIBLE because it is
suppliable from a stand-alone main verb where it is
embedded. Here is an example.

[does stay]
My book _∧ <u>stays</u> in the kitchen.

In this sentence, the verb *stays* lacks a VISIBLE starter
UNTIL YOU REPLACE IT WITH *DOES STAY*. The ***does*** that
you SUPPLY was originally INVISIBLE.

Truth B

Every statement (versus "command") has a starter that you can reposition.

If a sentence is a statement, it will always have a
starter (visible or suppliable) that you can reposition to
turn the statement into a question. Here is an example.

*The wall clock <u>**has** lost</u> time.*

[has]   **[?]**
_∧ *The wall clock <s>has</s> <u>lost</u> time.*

Truth C

You can reposition the starter that begins and causes a question.

Just as you can reposition a starter (in a statement)
to cause a question, **similarly** you can reposition the
starter that begins a question to cause a statement.

126

Here is an example.

Can't advertising be misleading?

       [can]   [.]

➡ ~~*Can't*~~ *advertising* ∧ *be misleading?*

Truth D

Statements with two or more starters can have starters that you can NOT reposition.

It is easy to prove that statements with more than one starter can have starters that you can **not** reposition. Note.

*Air that **is** damp **can cause** discomfort.*

You can **not** say ~~*Is air that damp can cause discomfort*~~, but you **can** say *Can air that is damp cause discomfort?*

Truth E

The starter that you CAN reposition —in statements and questions—belongs to the chief verb in the sentence.

The CHIEF VERB in a sentence is THAT VERB WHOSE PRESENCE INDICATES THAT A GROUP OF WORDS (OR EVEN ONE WORD) MERITS THE NAME "SENTENCE."

When a sentence (other than a command) has only one verb (its chief one), its starter will always be movable and will therefore **be** the movable starter.

By extension, every starter that is movable must belong to a chief verb.

Preliminary Definitions

The chief verb in a sentence has the name CORE VERB in this text. The CORE VERB is THE VERB WHOSE STARTER YOU CAN REPOSITION.

By the way, the starter that you can reposition has the name MOVABLE STARTER. A MOVABLE STARTER is THE STARTER THAT HAS TWO POSITIONS IN A SENTENCE—AN ORIGINAL POSITION AND A POSITION YOU CAN SHIFT IT TO.

Labeling for the Core Verb

The CORE VERB needs no label. You will have identified it as soon as you identify its starter, which is the movable starter.

Labeling for Movable Starters

The **labeling** for a MOVABLE STARTER will be to place the LETTERS MS over it. It is preferable to label the starter in its place of origin in the sentence, **not** in the place that you reposition it to. Note.

[Can]   MS   [?]

  ∧ *A cloud ~~CAN~~ **shield** one's eyes from the sun.*

     MS   [does]

  ~~***DOES***~~ *acid rain* ∧ ***harm*** *plants?*

            MS

[Does]   [~~DOES~~ seem]   [?]

  ∧ *Rain without wind* ∧ ~~*seems*~~ *less threatening.*

Labeling for Movable Starters:

Place the lettering MS over the MOVABLE STARTER IN ITS ORIGINAL POSITION IN THE SENTENCE.

Truth F

ALL THE WORDS BETWEEN THE TWO POSITIONS OF A MOVABLE STARTER ARE USUALLY THE SUBJECT OF THE CHIEF VERB.

The wording between the two positions of the movable starter is precisely the wording that answers (or asks) WHO or WHAT before the core verb. Note how this works for the above sentences.

Sentence	WHAT—Asked before the Verb	Answer
A cloud can shield one's eyes from the sun.	***WHAT** can shield one's eyes from the sun?*	*A CLOUD*
Does acid rain harm plants?	***WHAT** does harm plants?*	*ACID RAIN*
Rain without wind seems less threatening.	***WHAT** seems less threatening?*	*RAIN WITHOUT WIND*

Main Subject (Preliminary Definition)

This subject has the name MAIN SUBJECT in this text. The MAIN SUBJECT is ALL THE WORDS BETWEEN THE TWO POSITIONS OF THE MOVABLE STARTER THAT DO THE JOB OF SUBJECT. The JOB OF SUBJECT, of course, is to fill the noun territory (usually before a verb) and to answer (or ask) WHO or WHAT before that verb.

Important Note about Asking WHAT: When you ask WHAT, you must know where to ask it and what you are looking for. Note this chart.

Test During Which You Ask *WHAT*	Where to Ask *WHAT*	Purpose for Asking WHAT
Helpers plus WHAT/ING Word Verb	AFTER A HELPING VERB	To find a POSSIBLE companion main verb
As you test for a subject	BEFORE A STARTER	To find the subject of the verb

In addition, you ask *WHAT* AFTER A MAIN VERB to help you find an object of verb and AFTER A PREPOSITION to help you find an object of preposition. See Chapters 2 and 14.

Labeling for Main Subjects

The **labeling** for the MAIN SUBJECT will be to use an OVERHEAD BRACKET over all the words and to place a CIRCLED *S* over the bracket. Note.

[Have] Ⓢ MS [?]
^ *Many hours* ~~have gone~~ by.

Labeling for Main Subjects:

Place an OVERHEAD BRACKET over the wording and a CIRCLED *S* over the overhead bracket.

Terms to Know

Movable Starter

This text uses the term MOVABLE STARTER to mean THE STARTER THAT YOU CAN SHIFT TO CAUSE OR "UNDO" A QUESTION. The MOVABLE STARTER has two positions—a GIVEN position and a SHIFTED-TO position.

Movable Starter:

The STARTER THAT YOU CAN SHIFT to turn a question into a statement or a statement into a question.

Core Verb

This text uses the term CORE VERB to mean A VERB WHOSE STARTER IS A MOVABLE STARTER. The CORE VERB is the most fundamental unit of a sentence. Its presence alone can permit you to punctuate wording as a sentence.

Core Verb:

A verb whose starter is a movable starter.

Main Subject

This text uses the term MAIN SUBJECT to mean ALL THE WORDS BETWEEN THE TWO POSITIONS OF A MOVABLE STARTER—WHEN THESE BELONG TOGETHER AS SUBJECT. This subject is always the SUBJECT OF THE CORE VERB.

> ## Main Subject:
> All the words between the two positions of a movable starter that belong together and do the job of subject.

Sentence Unit

This text uses the term SENTENCE UNIT to mean WORDING THAT HAS *AS ITS BASE* <u>A CORE VERB + MAIN SUBJECT</u> (OR <u>A CORE VERB THAT EXPRESSES A COMMAND</u>). In other words, it is WORDING THAT YOU CAN PUNCTUATE AS A SENTENCE. (The school grammar name for a sentence unit is MAIN CLAUSE.)

> ## Sentence Unit:
> Wording that has *as its base* <u>a core verb + main subject</u> (or <u>a core verb that expresses a command</u>).

> # NEW Test 1: The Main Subject Test—for Questions

This TEST shows you how to reposition the movable starter to locate main subjects in questions. You must carry out this test **first**. You carry out this test BEFORE the verb tests because in questions the movable starter and core verb have special locations.

This test has three GROUND RULES and five STEPS. The next two sections will explain these and provide practice.

Part A
Ground
Rules

The Main Subject Test
—for Questions

Part A	Part B
Ground Rules	Steps
1. DO THIS TEST BEFORE BOTH VERB TESTS.	Look for a question mark.
2. EXPECT GRAMMATICAL FIT.	Label the starter.
3. Expect to find another verb in the subject territory from time to time.	Reposition the starter.
	Label the main subject.
	Label the starter's companion verbs.

These ground rules are important for success with this test. Learn this section well.

Ground Rule 1
Do this BEFORE both verb tests.

If you apply the Helpers plus WHAT/ING Word Verb Test BEFORE THIS TEST, the WHAT Subtest will cause you to pick out the SUBJECT instead of the possible companion verb(s) that you are testing for—because in questions the SUBJECT has a position BEFORE any companion parts of a verb. Note this example.

Do sensible students check their own work?

If you ask WHAT after *do* in its beginning-of-the-QUESTION position, the answer is *students*—a word that is part of the subject. The proof is that when you ask WHO *do check*, the answer is *sensible students*.

Explanation: Notice what happens when you turn this sentence into a statement.

[DO]   [.]
Do sensible students ∧ check their own work?

Now—with the starter *do* in its INSIDE-THE SENTENCE position—you can successfully ask WHAT. The answer is the word *check*, which in this sentence is a verb. Here is the correct labeling for this sentence (so far).

[DO]   [.]
Do sensible students ∧ check their own work.

In conclusion, you can apply the Helpers plus WHAT/ING Test successfully ONLY when a starter is in its INSIDE-THE-SENTENCE position—that is, only AFTER you have carried out the Main Subject Test—for Questions. YOU MUST USE THIS NEW ORDER FOR THE TESTS.

Ground Rule 2
Expect GRAMMATICAL fit.

This test asks you to TAMPER with someone else's sentences. You will be changing another writer's question into a statement that he/she did not write nor intend to write. Therefore, you cannot expect that the statement will always make good sense.

Notice what happens when you change this question to a statement.

[aren't]   [.]

~~Aren't~~ birds ∧ considered animals?

The statement *Birds aren't considered animals* is untrue. The writer did not expect the question to be turned into this statement.

There are two points to remember. First, what **counts** is grammatical fit. Clearly, the word *aren't* has no other place to move to (to turn this question into a statement) other than before *considered*. Unquestionably, that is where it fits.

The second point is that there is nothing sacred about *n't* or *not*. As an EDITOR, you can add or subtract *not* or *n't* (but ONLY *not* or *n't*) from a sentence at any time if it improves the sense of the sentence. Feel free to turn the above question into the statement *Birds **are** considered animals.*

Here is another example.

Is all drinking water free of minerals?

You can—and should—rewrite this as *All drinking water **is not**/**isn't** free of minerals.*

Here is one more example.

Can't children also help with the dishes?

You would rewrite this as *Children **can** also help with*

the dishes.

Ground Rule 3

Expect to find another verb in the subject territory from time to time.

When you "UNDO" A QUESTION, you shift the movable starter to an inside-the-sentence position. You can **not** assume that there are no verbs between these two positions of the movable starter. There can be. You must look for them when you carry out the Helpers plus WHAT/ING Word Verb Test and Do/does/did Test.

Here are two examples.

[does use]   [should]   [.]
~~Should~~ SOMEONE WHO ∧ USES A SAW ∧ wear goggles?

~~Can~~ A GIRL WHO IS GETTING GOOD GRADES

[can]   [.]
∧ overwork?

Part B
Steps

The Main Subject Test—for Questions

Part A	Part B
Ground Rules	**Steps**
Do this test BEFORE both verb tests.	1. Look for a question mark.
Expect GRAMMATI-CAL fit.	2. If a question, label as MS the starter that begins it.
Expect to find another verb in the subject territory from time to time.	3. Reposition the starter to where it fits inside the sentence.
	4. Label the in-between words as the main subject.
	5. Locate and label companion verbs (if any) that FOLLOW the starter in its INSIDE position.

You must learn to use these steps in the right order and without omission. They are the means to success with this test.

Step 1
Look for a question mark.

This is the easiest step but the one most easily overlooked. The end punctuation is the surest guide to the type of word order to expect. You might circle the end punctuation to force yourself to see whether it is a period or question mark before you proceed further.

● Do **PRACTICE A** (TAKING NOTE OF END PUNCTUA-
TION) in your **Skills Practice Book.**

Step 2

If a question, label as MS
the starter that begins it.

If the sentence is a question, a starter will begin the
question (for now). Double underline it and write MS
over it at once. (Note that in a later chapter you will
learn of two other kinds of questions that can occur.)
Here is an example.

MS
<u>Do</u> *few birds stay in the same location all summer?*

● Do **PRACTICE B** (LABELING THE MOVABLE STARTER
IN STARTER-VERB QUESTIONS) in your **Skills Practice Book.**

Step 3

Reposition the starter to where
it fits inside the sentence.

As you shift the movable starter to the right, you will
find a place where it fits. Place it there and enclose it in
side brackets. Also use a caret (∧) to mark the place of
insertion. See the example below. You should leave the
original *do* unchanged. The line through it is to remind
you that you must cover it as you do the shifting.

MS   [do]
<s>Do</s> *few birds* ∧ *stay in the same location all summer?*

Note that there will be ONLY ONE PLACE where a starter
WILL FIT as it "undoes" the question.

138

● Do *PRACTICE C* (REPOSITIONING THE MOVABLE STARTER IN STARTER-VERB QUESTIONS) in your *Skills Practice Book.*

Step 4
Label the in-between words as the main subject.

YOU LABEL ALL THE WORDS BETWEEN THE TWO POSITIONS OF THE MOVABLE STARTER—its position at the start of the question and its inside-the-sentence position—AS A MAIN SUBJECT. You place both an OVERHEAD BRACKET over all the words and a CIRCLED S over the bracket. Here is the same example again.

MS   S   [do]   [.]
<u>Do</u> ⌐few birds⌐ stay in the same location all summer?

● Do *PRACTICE D* (LABELING MAIN SUBJECTS IN STARTER-VERB QUESTIONS) in your *Skills Practice Book.*

● Do *PRACTICE E* (CARRYING OUT STEPS 1-4) in your *Skills Practice Book.*

Step 5
Locate and label companion verbs (if any) that FOLLOW the starter in its INSIDE position.

It is risky to save this step until later. It is too easy to forget that this shifted starter can stand at the start of a verb phrase. Note the example again.

MS   S   [do]   [.]
<u>Do</u> ⌐<u>few birds</u>⌐_∧ <u>stay</u> in the same location all summer?

When you ask *Few birds do* WHAT, the answer is the verb *stay*.

● Do **_PRACTICE F_** (LABELING COMPANION VERBS TO THE MOVABLE STARTER IN STARTER-VERB QUESTIONS) in your *Skills Practice Book.*

Here is the test as a whole.

TEST 1: The Main Subject Test —for Questions

Part A Ground Rules	Part B Steps
1. Do THIS TEST <u>BE-FORE</u> BOTH VERB TESTS.	1. Look for a question mark.
	2. If a question, label as MS the starter that begins it.
2. EXPECT GRAMMATI-CAL FIT.	3. Reposition the starter to where it fits inside the sentence.
3. Expect to find another verb in the subject territory from time to time.	4. Label the in-between words as the main subject.
	5. Locate and label the companion verbs (if any) that FOLLOW the starter in its INSIDE position.

- Do *PRACTICE G* (CARRYING OUT THE MAIN SUBJECT TEST—FOR QUESTIONS) in your *Skills Practice Book.*

- Do *PRACTICE H* (CARRYING OUT TESTS 2 AND 3) in your *Skills Practice Book.*

- Do *PRACTICE J* (CARRYING OUT TESTS 1, 2, AND 3) in your *Skills Practice Book.*

- Do *PRACTICE K* (CARRYING OUT ALL TESTS) in your *Skills Practice Book.*

Endnotes

Counterpart Subjects: Sometimes it sounds unnatural when you shift a movable starter to the place of grammatical fit inside a sentence. Here is an example.

Doesn't anybody agree?

It is clear that *doesn't* can shift and FITS before *agree*. For this to SOUND RIGHT, too, you would have to change *anybody* to its counterpart wording *somebody*. Note.

Somebody doesn't agree.

This less common type of sentence will not be used in the practice sentences here.

Job of NONmovable Starters: Except in command sentences, every starter that is **not** a movable one is the MARKER OF A DEPENDENT CLAUSE. It will always have an accompanying NONmain subject and a visible or suppliable introducer. Note.

We were enjoying the movie THOUGH WE HAD ALREADY SEEN IT.

The NONmovable starter *had* marks the presence of the verb phrase *had seen* **and** of the dependent clause

141

THOUGH WE HAD ALREADY SEEN IT. The subject of the clause is the second *we*, and the introducer of the clause is *though*.

Review

CONTENT IN DARKER LETTERING MUST BE REMEMBERED.

Movable Starter: A starter that you can shift to turn a question into a statement or a statement into a question.

Core Verb: The verb whose starter is the movable one.

Main Subject: All the words between the two positions of a movable starter that belong together and do the job of subject.

Sentence Unit: The wording that has AS ITS BASE either the core verb plus main subject or a core verb that expresses a command.

Labeling for the Core Verb: (ITS STARTER IS ALWAYS THE MOVABLE STARTER.)

Labeling for Movable Starters: Place the lettering MS over the MOVABLE STARTER IN ITS ORIGINAL POSITION IN THE SENTENCE.

Labeling for Main Subjects: Place an OVERHEAD BRACKET over the wording and a CIRCLED S over the overhead bracket.

Editor: The person who makes changes in someone else's piece of writing.

Order for the Tests:
1. **Main Subject Test—for Questions**
2. **Helpers plus WHAT/ING Word Verb Test**
3. **Do/does/did Test**

TEST 1: The Main Subject Test—for Questions:

Part A—Ground Rules:

1. Do this test BEFORE both verb tests.
2. Expect GRAMMATICAL fit.
3. Expect to find another verb in the subject territory from time to time.

Part B—Steps:

1. Look for a question mark.
2. If a question, label as MS the starter that begins it.
3. Reposition the starter to where it fits inside the sentence.
4. Label the in-between words as the main subject.
5. Locate and label the companion verbs (if any) that FOLLOW the starter in its INSIDE position.

Chapter 9

The Helper That Shifts— in Statements

You now know how easy it is to find the helper that shifts in questions. It is often the first word of the sentence, and it will shift to inside the sentence. (As you recall, the words between its two locations—its original location and its shifted-to location—are always the main subject.)

In statements, you use a reverse strategy. You first find all helpers and then test to see which one you can shift FROM **inside the sentence** TO the **front of the sentence** to turn the statement into an acceptable question.

The helper that can shift—in **both** types of sentences—has the name MOVABLE STARTER.

Truths about the Ways to Find Main Subjects

Truth A

The strategy of repositioning the movable starter to find main subjects has many advantages.

The strategy for finding main subjects in statements that this text teaches—the repositioning of the movable starter to find the words that stand between its two positions—has three advantages.

First, it is accurate.

Second, it is "natural" for those who are at home with English.

Third, it WORKS no matter how long the subject is and no matter how many verbs a sentence has.

This is **not** true for other ways of finding subjects.

Truth B

The main subject is NOT "what is talked about."

There are two problems with the definition of a main subject as "what is talked about." First, there are sentences in which people can **disagree** over "what is talked about." Here is an example.

My sister saw smoke outside her window that looked as if it was coming from a fire.

Some would say that *smoke* is what is talked about here while others would say it is *my sister*.

Second—and more importantly—it is the WHOLE SENTENCE that any sentence "talks about." In the above example, what is ACTUALLY being talked about is MY SISTER'S SEEING SMOKE OUTSIDE HER WINDOW THAT LOOKED AS IF IT WAS COMING FROM A FIRE.

Truth C

A WHO or WHAT test for a main subject presupposes that you have already found the core verb.

When a sentence unit has more than one verb, the main subject is the one that answers *WHO* or *WHAT* before the CORE verb. Here is an example.

The bike I am now riding lacks the brakes I need for steep hills.

Since this sentence has THREE verbs, you must KNOW which verb is the one to ask *WHO* or *WHAT* before. You must have an accurate strategy for knowing BEFORE-HAND which verb is the core verb.

You now know that the STRATEGY THAT WORKS is to find the core verb's movable starter. Here is the sentence with all its starters made visible.

The bike I am now riding

[does lack]   **[do need]**
∧ *lacks* the brakes I ∧ *need* for steep hills.

You can now see that it is the supplied *does* alone that turns this statement into an acceptable question—and that the verb *lacks (does lack)* is the core verb. Note.

Does *the bike I am riding* **lack** *the brakes I need for steep hills?*

Of course, this strategy also pinpoints the words between *[does]* and *does—THE BIKE I AM NOW RIDING*—as the MAIN SUBJECT.

THIS IS AN EASY AND SAFE WAY TO FIND THE MAIN SUBJECT FOR ALL SENTENCES—both simpler and more complicated ones.

Truth D

Strategies that find just the chief word in the subject (versus the whole subject) are less accurate.

When two or more words do the job of main subject, these words do the job AS A UNIT—that is, they answer WHO or WHAT **as a unit**. Here is an example.

[Does]   Ⓢ

  ʌ*The midsummer variety of birds*

MS
[~~does~~ differ]   [?]

  ʌ~~*differs*~~ *from the spring variety.*

The CHIEF WORD in this subject is *variety*. Clearly, this one word is an inadequate substitute for the WHOLE SUBJECT *the midsummer variety of birds*—especially from a reader's vantage point.

Truths about the Chief Parts of Sentences

There are a few truths about movable starters and main subjects that will help you with **this** chapter **and the next**.

Truth A

Most statements—even those with many verbs—have only one starter that is movable.

Statements, as a rule, have only ONE movable starter. This is because the extra starters in a sentence often serve as the core of dependent clauses (groups of words that have a verb and subject but that you can **not** turn into a question). In short, dependent clauses have starters that are **not** movable. Here is an example.

[did bring]
The thunderstorm that ∧ *brought much-needed*

[did cause]
coolness ∧ *caused unneeded flooding.*

The first starter (the supplied *did* that came from *brought*) is NOT "movable." You can **not** say ~~Did the thunderstorm that bring much-needed coolness caused unneeded flooding~~. In this sentence, the verb *brought* is the core of the DEPENDENT CLAUSE *that brought much-needed coolness.*

In contrast, the remaining starter in this sentence (the supplied *did* that came from *caused*) **is** movable. Note.

DID the thunderstorm that brought much-needed coolness CAUSE unneeded flooding?

You may remember that the starter that is movable belongs to the core verb, the verb that makes the whole group of words a true sentence.

Truth B

The proof that a starter is the movable one is that its repositioning turns the entire sentence unit into a grammatically acceptable question.

You noticed in the above example that the repositioning of the *did* from *did bring* caused UNacceptable English. In contrast, you COULD reposition the *did* from *did cause* and create an acceptable question.

Truth C

It is easier to turn your own statements into questions than someone else's.

You can create your own questions easily because you know what you want to ask.

When you try to change someone else's statements into questions, you may find that their statements are overlong, complex, or both.

For these reasons, the steps given here have extra importance. Their purpose is to help you work with anybody's statements.

Truth D

The work of this chapter gets easier with practice.

Since this chapter spells out the steps that you have been using since you first learned English, you will find the practices getting easier and easier as you proceed.

Truth E

An essential rule for successfully changing someone else's statements into correct questions is to use every word—but only once—and to make no substitutions other than the *do/does/did* substitutions.

You can always achieve grammatical fit as you reposition a starter if you follow these two rules **strictly**. YOU USE THE WORDS OF THE SENTENCE ONLY ONCE, **and** YOU MAKE NO SUBSTITUTIONS OTHER THAN THE UNAVOIDABLY NECESSARY *DO/DOES/DID* SUBSTITUTIONS.

You will learn how to do this successfully as you proceed through this chapter.

Test 4:
The Movable Starter Test

This TEST is the FIRST STAGE of the strategy for finding main subjects in statements. BECAUSE IT IS SO CHALLENGING TO LEARN TO DO RIGHT, THIS CHAPTER WILL TREAT THIS TEST ALONE.

It is the foundation for the next chapter, where it will be the first—and most important—strategy for finding main subjects errorlessly.

Note the ORDER FOR THE TESTS here. The tests now include the Movable Starter Test.

Order in Which to Carry out the Tests

1. Main Subject Test—for Questions
2. Helpers plus WHAT/ING Word Verb Test
3. Do/does/did Test
4. MOVABLE STARTER TEST

Note that the Movable Starter Test has two parts. These consist of two STEPS and eight GROUND RULES. Look for detailed explanations in the sections that follow this OVERVIEW.

Overview for Test 4:
The Movable Starter Test

Part A	Part B
Steps	**Ground Rules**
Test each starter to find the ONE that you can shift to the front to form an acceptable question.	Keep covered any inside-the-sentence duplicate wording. Ask the question as if you expect it to work.

Test 4: The Movable Starter Test

Part A Steps	Part B Ground Rules
1. **When there is only one starter, shift it to the front and label it "MS."**	Keep covered any inside-the-sentence duplicate wording.
2. **When there are two or more starters, test each to find and label as "ms" the ONE that you can shift to the front to form an acceptable question.**	Ask the question as if you expect it to work.

Step 1
When there is only one starter, shift it to the front and label it "MS."

When there is only one verb, you can ALWAYS shift its starter to the front to form an acceptable question. Note.

[Had]   **MS**   **[?]**

∧ *The tomatoes in the bag* *h̶a̶d̶ fallen* *through.*

For this sentence, you can ask *Had the tomatoes in the bag fallen through?* Therefore, *had* is the movable starter. Incidentally, all the words between the two positions of *had* (the position it came from and the position it shifted to)—*THE TOMATOES IN THE BAG*—make up the main subject.

● Do *PRACTICE A* (CARRYING OUT TESTS 2-4) in your *Skills Practice Book.*

Important Note: As you know from Chapter 8, the two positions of a movable starter always mark the outside boundaries of the main subject. You will not be labeling these while you do the practices for the Movable Starter Test SO THAT YOU CAN MASTER ONE IMPORTANT SKILL AT A TIME.

Note Again: You need to pay close attention to the ground rules to come because finding the movable starter is much more challenging when the sentences are someone else's **and** when there are two or more verbs.

Step 2

When there are two or more starters, test each to find and label as "MS" the ONE that you can shift to the front to form an acceptable question.

In a sentence with many starters, the one that "fits" could be the first ...or last ...or one in between. You must test the FIRST AND EACH NEXT ONE until you find—and are sure that you have found—the ONE that fits. Note.

The place where Dad <u>had put</u> the old toy that we <u>were looking</u> for <u>was</u> the garbage can.

For this sentence, neither of the first two starters is movable. Observe why this is so.

Had the place where Dad put the old toy that we were looking for was the garage can?

Were the place where Dad had put the old toy that we looking for was the garage can?

Only the last starter in the sentence is movable. Note.

Was the place where Dad had put the old toy that we were looking for ... the garage can?

WHENEVER A SENTENCE HAS MORE THAN ONE VERB, YOU MUST REMEMBER TO APPLY THIS STEP.

The ground rules that follow are the vitally important guidelines for your success with these steps.

Part B
Ground Rules

Test 4: The Movable Starter Test

Part A Steps	Part B Ground Rules
When there is only one starter, shift it to the front and label it "MS." When there are two or more starters, test each to find and label as "MS" the ONE that you can shift to the front to form an acceptable question.	1. Leave *n't* attached. 2. Change STARTER/ *not* to START-ER/*n't* (if possible). 3. WRITE OUT all *do/does/did* substitutions. 4. Write out the substitute spellings for the words *do, does, did, have, has,* and *had* WHENEVER THESE ARE MAIN VERBS. 5. <u>Keep covered</u> ALL <u>INSIDE</u> DUPLICATES of words. 6. For all words NOT now being tested, USE ONLY the <u>ORIGINAL SPELLING</u>—NOT its *do/does/did* substitute spelling. 7. Use a question-asking tone of voice. 8. As you ask the question, PAUSE briefly at the position of the INSIDE—AND NOW COVERED STARTER.

As you learn the reasons for these ground rules (see below), you will have accompanying practice work.

When you test a starter that has *n't* attached, reposition the <u>starter + *n't*</u> AS ONE WORD—do **not** separate them. This will always sound "natural" because it is the way you ask questions in conversation. Note.

*The train **hasn't** left yet.* ➡

[hasn't]   MS   **[?]**
∧ *The train ~~hasn't~~ left yet.*

● Do <u>*PRACTICE B*</u> (FINDING AND LABELING MOVABLE STARTERS WITH *N'T* ATTACHED) in your *Skills Practice Book.*

When a starter has *not* after it, combine the two words into a contraction before testing, whenever possible. Note.

*The delay **was not** longer than expected.* ➡

MS
[wasn't]
The delay ∧ <u>*was*</u> *not longer than expected.* ➡

MS
[wasn't]   **[~~wasn't~~]**   **[?]**
∧*The delay* ∧ <u>~~was not~~</u> *longer than expected.*

● Do **_PRACTICE C_** (FINDING AND LABELING MOVABLE STARTERS FOLLOWED BY *NOT*) in your *Skills Practice Book.*

● Do **_PRACTICE D_** (MORE FINDING AND LABELING OF MOVABLE STARTERS FOLLOWED BY *NOT*) in your *Skills Practice Book.*

● Do **_PRACTICE E_** (FINDING AND LABELING OF MOVABLE STARTERS) in your *Skills Practice Book.*

Ground Rule 3

You must WRITE OUT all *DO/DOES/DID* SUBSTITUTIONS.

If you do not write out the *do/does/did* substitutions, you could be omitting the starter that is the only one that you can reposition. Here is an example.

*The bat that Pete **thinks** he **broke needs** some tape.*

[**Does**]   [does think] [did break] [~~does~~ **need**]
   ∧*The bat that Pete* ∧*thinks he* ∧*broke* ∧~~*needs*~~

[?]
some tape.

As you say this question, be sure that you pause at the place of the repositioned helper *does—**Does** the bat that Pete thinks he broke ... **need** some tape?* See Ground Rule 8 below.

Notice that if you were to fail to write out the *does need* substitution for *needs*, you would miss the only starter that works.

Ground Rule 4

Write out the SUBSTITUTE SPELLINGS for the words *DO, DOES, DID, HAVE, HAS,* and *HAD* whenever these are MAIN verbs.

When the HELPERS IN THE *DO* AND *HAVE* SETS HAVE NO MAIN VERB COMPLETING THEIR SENSE, YOU MUST CHANGE THEM TO THEIR *DO/DOES/DID* SUBSTITUTE SPELLING. If you neglect to do this, you will be unable to turn statements that contain them into acceptable questions. Note.

Andrew <u>does</u> his work rapidly.

You can **not** say ~~Does Andrew his work rapidly~~. However, if you change the word *does* to its *does* substitute spelling *does do*, you **can** say *Does Andrew do his work rapidly?*
Note again.

Maria <u>had</u> band in the sixth period today.

You can **not** say ~~Had Maria band in the sixth period today?~~ In contrast, you **can** use the *did* substitute spelling for the verb *had*—namely: *did have*—and say *Did Maria have band in the sixth period today?*

Notice the difference in these sets of contrasting uses of *do, does,* and *did.*

Sentences Contrasting the Uses of *Do, Does,* and *Did* as Helping Verbs and as Main Verbs

As Helping Verb	As Main Verb
Tom <u>does work</u> hard.	Tom <u>does</u>/[*does do*] well.
I <u>do play</u> the piano.	I <u>do</u>/[*do do*] my best.
They <u>did leave</u> early.	They <u>did</u>/[*did do*] a lot.

● Do *PRACTICE F* (WRITING OUT THE *DO/DOES/DID* SUBSTITUTIONS FOR *DO, DOES,* AND *DID*) in your *Skills Practice Book.*

● Do *PRACTICE G* (CARRYING OUT THE *DO/DOES/DID* SUBSTITUTIONS FOR *DO, DOES,* AND *DID* WHEN MAIN VERBS) in your *Skills Practice Book.*

Notice the difference in these sets of contrasting uses of *have, has,* and *had.*

Sentences Contrasting the Use of *Have, Has,* and *Had* as Helping Verbs and as Main Verbs

As Helping Verb	As Main Verb
Tom <u>has left</u>.	Tom <u>has</u>/[*does have*] plans.
I <u>have won</u>.	I <u>have</u>/[*do have*] some.
They <u>had forgotten</u>.	They <u>had</u>/[*did have*] fewer players.

● Do *PRACTICE H* (WRITING OUT THE *DO/DOES/DID* SUBSTITUTIONS FOR *HAVE, HAS,* AND *HAD*) in your *Skills Practice Book.*

● Do *PRACTICE J* (CARRYING OUT THE *DO/DOES/DID* SUBSTITUTIONS FOR *HAVE, HAS,* AND *HAD* WHEN MAIN VERBS) in your *Skills Practice Book.*

● Do *PRACTICE K* (CARRYING OUT THE *DO/DOES/DID* SUBSTITUTIONS FOR *DO, DOES, DID, HAVE, HAS,* AND *HAD* WHEN MAIN VERBS) in your *Skills Practice Book.*

TAKE CAREFUL NOTE of the **expanded—and extremely important—wording** for Ground Rule 5 (below). Both the rule and all its subparts will have separate treatment and, as appropriate, accompanying practice.

Ground Rule 5

<u>Keep covered</u> ALL *INSIDE* DUPLICATES of words:

a. The <u>INSIDE STARTER</u>—with or without *n't.*

b. ALSO the <u>ORIGINAL STARTER + *NOT*</u> that you contracted.

c. ALSO the <u>ORIGINAL MAIN VERB</u>—for the substitute spelling that you are now testing.

Ground Rule 5

<u>Keep covered</u> ALL *INSIDE* DUPLICATES OF WORDS.

HEED THIS REQUIREMENT. You must PHYSICALLY COVER—with pen, pencil, or your finger—any INSIDE word that is present TWICE. **If you ever include this**

SECOND inside word as you ask the question, YOU WILL MISLEAD YOURSELF.

YOU MUST ALWAYS HIDE THE EXTRA INSIDE WORD.

Ground Rule 5a

Keep covered the INSIDE STARTER—
with or without *n't*.

You can **not** say the same starter twice in one sentence and have the sentence be acceptable English. Note.

> *The house is large.*

You simply cannot say ~~Is that house is large?~~

- Do *PRACTICE L* (CARRYING OUT TESTS 2-4 AND COVERING INSIDE STARTERS) in your *Skills Practice Book.*

- Do *PRACTICE M* (MORE CARRYING OUT OF TESTS 2-4 AND COVERING OF INSIDE STARTERS) in your *Skills Practice Book.*

Ground Rule 5b

Keep covered the
ORIGINAL STARTER + *NOT*
that you contracted.

You cannot use the contraction of a starter + *n't* FOR TESTING **and** LEAVE THE ORIGINAL TWO WORDS (the starter + *not*) UNCOVERED at the same time. Note.

> [haven't]
> *The buses ∧ have not left yet.*

160

You cannot say ~~Haven't the buses have not left yet?~~
Instead, you would say **Haven't** the buses **left** yet?

- Do _PRACTICE N_ (CARRYING OUT TESTS 2-4 WHILE COVERING INSIDE STARTERS AND ORIGINAL <u>STARTERS + _NOT_</u>) in your *Skills Practice Book*.

- Do _PRACTICE P_ (MORE CARRYING OUT OF TESTS 2-4 WHILE COVERING INSIDE STARTERS AND ORIGINAL STARTERS + _NOT_) in your *Skills Practice Book*.

Ground Rule 5c

<u>Keep covered</u> the
<u>ORIGINAL MAIN VERB</u>—for the substitute spelling that you are now testing.

You cannot—AT THE SAME TIME—use a SUPPLIED starter (from a *do/does/did* substitution) **and** THE ORIGINAL MAIN VERB THAT YOU SUPPLIED IT FROM. Remember that the original main verb CONTAINS the starter INVISIBLY. Note.

[did give]
  He ∧ <u>gave</u> an incomplete answer.
You can **not** say ~~Did he give gave an incomplete answer?~~

- Do _PRACTICE Q_ (CARRYING OUT TESTS 2-4 WHILE COVERING INSIDE STARTERS AND ORIGINAL MAIN VERBS FOR A SUBSTITUTE SPELLING NOW BEING TESTED) in your *Skills Practice Book*.

- Do _PRACTICE R_ (MORE CARRYING OUT OF TESTS 2-4 WHILE COVERING INSIDE STARTERS AND ORIGINAL MAIN VERBS FOR A SUBSTITUTE SPELLING NOW BEING TESTED) in your *Skills Practice Book*.

Ground Rule 6

For all words NOT now being tested, USE ONLY the ORIGINAL SPELLING—NOT its *do/does/did* substitute spelling.

Sentences will rarely sound better when you use substitute spellings **unnecessarily**. Therefore, always say sentences with only their original wording except when you cannot because a substitute spelling (or *n't* contraction) is needed for testing. Here is an example.

[did come]
The package that ˄came yesterday had been damaged.

You test *had* in this sentence by asking **Had** the package that CAME yesterday **been damaged?**

You can cover these left-over substitute spellings too if you find it helpful. See this simulated.

[had]   **[did come]**   **[?]**
˄*The package that ˄came yesterday had been damaged.*

● Do *PRACTICE S* (CARRYING OUT TESTS 2-4 WHILE USING ONLY ORIGINAL WORDING FOR VERBS NOT NOW BEING TESTED) in your *Skills Practice Book*.

Ground Rule 7

Use a QUESTION-ASKING TONE of voice.

When you reposition a starter to the left, you are creating a question. Therefore, use your voice so the sentence SOUNDS like a question. Note that the first word—now the repositioned starter—and the last word get a noticeably RISING pitch or intonation. Note the illustration.

$\overset{\frown}{}$ MS $\overset{\frown}{}$

[will] The apples ~~will~~ be plentiful this year.[?]

Ground Rule 8

As you ask the question, PAUSE briefly at the position of the INSIDE—AND NOW COVERED—STARTER.

When asking a question, you should pause briefly—AS IF FOR A BREATH—at the very spot where the starter (that you are testing) was **originally**. ALWAYS PAUSE as you test—**as a person who expects this question to make complete sense.**

Here is a sentence for illustration.

[is]   [does stay]   MS   **[?]**
ᴀA bird that ᴀstays north in the winter ~~is~~ the chickadee.

[is]   [does stay]   **[?]**
ᴀA bird that ᴀstays north in the winter ... the chickadee.

YOU MUST ALWAYS PAUSE AT THE PLACE OF THE COVERED MOVABLE STARTER SO THAT YOUR QUESTIONS WILL SOUND NATURAL.

● Do **_PRACTICE T_** (USING A QUESTION-ASKING TONE OF VOICE AND PAUSING RIGHT WHEN ASKING SOMEONE ELSE'S QUESTION) in your *Skills Practice Book.*

Here is the complete Movable Starter Test.

Part B
Steps

Test 4: The Movable Starter Test

Part A	Part B
Steps	**Ground Rules**

Part A — Steps

1. When there is only one starter, shift it to the front and label it "MS."

2. When there are two or more starters, test each to find and label as "MS" the ONE that you can shift to the front to form an acceptable question.

Part B — Ground Rules

1. Leave *n't* attached.

2. Change STARTER + *not* to STARTER/*n't* (if possible).

3. WRITE OUT all *do/does/did* substitutions.

4. Write out the substitute spellings for the words *do, does, did, have, has,* and *had*— WHENEVER THESE ARE MAIN VERBS.

5. Keep covered ALL *INSIDE* DUPLICATES of words:

   a. The INSIDE STARTER—with or without *n't*.

   b. ALSO the ORIGINAL STARTER + *NOT* that you contracted.

   c. ALSO the ORIGINAL MAIN VERB—for the substitute spelling that you are now testing.

6. For all words NOT now being tested, USE ONLY the ORIGINAL SPELLING—NOT its *do/does/did* substitute spelling.

7. Use a question-asking tone of voice.

8. As you ask the question, PAUSE briefly at the position of the INSIDE—AND NOW COVERED—STARTER.

● Do *PRACTICE U* (CARRYING OUT TESTS 1-4 IN THEIR ENTIRETY) in your *Skills Practice Book.*

● Do *PRACTICE V* (CARRYING OUT TESTS 1-4 IN THEIR ENTIRETY) in your *Skills Practice Book.*

Accuracy in identifying the movable starter is the means to success at finding main subjects errorlessly— the work of the next chapter.

Review

CONTENT IN DARKER LETTERING MUST BE REMEMBERED.

Order for the Tests:
1. Main Subject Test—for Questions
2. Helpers plus WHAT/ING Word Verb Test
3. Do/does/did Test
4. Movable Starter Test

[continued]

TEST 4: The Movable Starter Test:

Part A—Steps:

1. When there is only one starter, shift it to the front and label it "MS."
2. When there are two or more starters, test each to find and label as "MS" the ONE that you can shift to the front to form an acceptable question.

Part B—Ground Rules:

1. Leave *n't* attached.
2. Change STARTER + *not* to STARTER/*n't* (if possible).
3. WRITE OUT all *do/does/did* substitutions.
4. Write out the substitute spellings for the words *do, does, did, have, has,* and *had*— WHENEVER THESE ARE MAIN VERBS.
5. Keep covered ALL INSIDE DUPLICATES of words:
   a. The INSIDE STARTER—with or without *n't*.
   b. ALSO the ORIGINAL STARTER + *NOT* that you contracted.
   c. ALSO the ORIGINAL MAIN VERB—for the substitute spelling that you are now testing.
6. For all words NOT under test, USE ONLY the ORIGINAL SPELLING—NOT its do/does/did substitute spelling.
7. Use a question-asking tone of voice.
8. As you ask the question, PAUSE briefly at the position of the INSIDE—AND NOW COVERED—STARTER.

Chapter 10

Finding Main Subjects in Statements

This chapter completes the information you need to find main subjects without error.

Test 5:
The Main Subject Test— for Statements

This test will always follow right after the Movable Starter Test. It is the FINAL STAGE of the strategy for finding main subjects.

Note the ORDER FOR THE TESTS. The list now includes the Main Subject Test—FOR STATEMENTS.

Order in Which to Carry out the Tests

1. Main Subject Test—for Questions
2. Helpers plus WHAT/ING Word Verb Test
3. Do/does/did Test
4. Movable Starter Test
5. MAIN SUBJECT TEST—FOR STATEMENTS

The test to find main subjects for statements consists of the two STEPS that you see here.

Test 5: The Main Subject Test— for Statements

STEPS

1. Label as main subject the words between the two positions of the movable starter that sound as if they belong together and serve as subject.

2. When the word *there* fills the subject territory, label as subject THOSE WORDS AFTER THE VERB THAT CAN REPLACE THE WORD *THERE*, and label *there* as the subject's space filler.

The heart of the Main Subject Test—for Statements is this first step, which you already know from the Main Subject Test—for Questions.

Note: From now on, the example sentences will show no strike-through line (to indicate which words you must keep covered). The reason for this is that you should no longer need such a reminder.

Step 1

Label as main subject the words between the two positions of the movable starter that sound as if they belong together and serve as subject.

You have already learned how to find the two positions for the movable starter. Commonly, these words do sound as if they belong together and do serve as subject. Note.

$$\overset{\text{[Does]}}{\wedge} \overset{\text{⑤}}{\lceil} \textit{The first frost of the fall}\rceil \overset{\text{MS}}{\underset{\wedge}{\underline{\text{[does kill]}}}} \textit{flowers that}$$

$$\overset{\text{[haven't]}}{\underset{\wedge}{\underline{\textit{have}}}} \textit{not} \overset{\text{[?]}}{\underline{\textit{been covered.}}}$$

● Do **_PRACTICE A_** (CARRYING OUT TESTS 1-5) in your *Skills Practice Book.*

● Do **_PRACTICE B_** (CARRYING OUT TESTS 1-5) in your *Skills Practice Book.*

● Do **_PRACTICE C_** (CARRYING OUT TESTS 1-5) in your *Skills Practice Book.*

WORDING THAT DOES NOT BELONG WITH THE SUBJECT

SOMETIMES YOU FIND THAT THE WORDS BETWEEN THE TWO POSITIONS OF THE MOVABLE STARTER DO **NOT** SOUND RIGHT TOGETHER. Note.

$$\overset{\text{[Did]}}{\wedge} \overset{?}{\overbrace{\textit{We seldom}}} \overset{\text{MS}}{\underset{\wedge}{\underline{\text{[did discuss]}}}} \textit{the matter.}$$

The words ~~we seldom~~ do **not** sound right together
BECAUSE THEY DO NOT BELONG TOGETHER. The word *we*
alone is serving as subject **because** when you ask *WHO
discussed the matter*, the answer is clearly the word *we*.
Note the correct way to label this sentence.

MS
[Did] Ⓢ   [did discuss]   [?]
  ∧ ⌐We⌐ *seldom* ∧*discussed* the matter.

Notice how the remaining word (here *seldom*) belongs
more with the verb—you **can** say *seldom discussed*. For
this reason, it is the kind of word called an ADVERB. See
Chapter 16 for a full discussion of adverbs.

YOU MUST ALWAYS TEST WHETHER THE WORDS IN
THE SUBJECT TERRITORY SOUND AS IF THEY BELONG
TOGETHER. The SUBJECT TERRITORY FOR THE MAIN
SUBJECT, of course, IS THE SPACE BETWEEN THE TWO
POSITIONS OF THE MOVABLE STARTER.

● Do *PRACTICE D* (CARRYING OUT TESTS 1-5 AND
MAKING SURE THAT THE WORDS IN THE SUBJECT
TERRITORY SOUND AS IF THEY BELONG TOGETHER) in
your *Skills Practice Book.*

● Do *PRACTICE E* (CARRYING OUT TESTS 1-5 AND
MAKING SURE THAT THE WORDS IN THE SUBJECT
TERRITORY SOUND AS IF THEY BELONG TOGETHER) in
your *Skills Practice Book.*

Step 2

When the word *there* fills the subject
territory, label as subject THOSE WORDS
AFTER THE VERB THAT CAN REPLACE THE
WORD *THERE*, and label *there*
as the subject's space filler.

The English language has a special kind of sentence. It is one in which the word *there* fills the subject territory but does not serve as subject. Note.

[Is] $\underbrace{\quad?\quad}$ **MS**   **[?]**
  ∧ *There* <u>is</u>   a   new   plan.

There are three things to take note of here. First, the word *there*—as used in this sentence—has no meaning of its own.

Second, the subject is the wording *a new plan*. One proof is that if the wording were TWO *new plans*, the verb would have to change to *are* to "agree" with it. Note.

There **ARE** TWO *new plans.*

Another proof is that you can change the sentence so that *a new plan* fills the subject territory. Note.

A NEW PLAN is [= EXISTS].

Third, you use *there* in this way primarily with the verb *be* as main verb. However, the verb *be* takes on FOUR new meanings in this type of sentence. It can mean *exists* (as you just saw), *takes place*, *is at hand*, or *is present*. Here are more examples.

There is nothing to fear. ➡
NOTHING TO FEAR is [=IS AT HAND].

There was an explosion. ➡
AN EXPLOSION was [=TOOK PLACE].

There are answers here. ➡
ANSWERS are [=ARE PRESENT] here.

Term to Know: Space-filler *There*

SPACE-FILLER *THERE* is the name for THE WORD *THERE* WHEN IT OCCUPIES THE SUBJECT TERRITORY AS A SPACE FILLER.

Labeling for Space-filler *There*

The LABEL for space-filler *there* is an OVERHEAD
BRACKET WITH A CIRCLED S ON TOP OF IT AND WITH A
STRIKE-THROUGH ARROW THAT POINTS TO THE RIGHT
WRITTEN THROUGH THE S. The purpose of the arrow is to
indicate that you must look TO THE RIGHT for the real
subject. Note.

$$[\text{Is}] \quad \overset{\rightarrow}{\ominus} \quad \text{MS} \qquad \text{\textcircled{S}} \qquad [?]$$

$$\overset{\wedge}{\lceil} \textit{There} \rceil \ \underline{\underline{is}} \ \lceil a \ \ new \ \ plan\rceil$$

Note that the real subject *a new plan* has the plain
CIRCLED S label, as it should.

Important Note: In the practices, you will be looking
AFTER THE VERB for the words that can replace *there* in
the subject territory. When you do this, you will need to
know (and use) the different meanings for the verb *be*
that were mentioned earlier. See them again in this
chart.

```
┌─────────────────────────────────────────┐
│  MEANINGS THAT THE VERB BE CAN            │
│  HAVE AFTER SPACE-FILLER THERE            │
│     exist         be at hand              │
│     take place    be present              │
└─────────────────────────────────────────┘
```

● Do **_PRACTICE F_** (DETERMINING THE MEANING OF THE VERB *BE* IN SPACE-FILLER *THERE* SENTENCES) in your *Skills Practice Book.*

● Do **_PRACTICE G_** (CARRYING OUT TESTS 1-5 AND LABELING SPACE-FILLER *THERE* CORRECTLY) in your *Skills Practice Book.*

● Do **_PRACTICE H_** (MORE CARRYING OUT OF TESTS 1-5 AND LABELING OF SPACE-FILLER *THERE* CORRECTLY) in your *Skills Practice Book.*

WORDING THAT DOES NOT BELONG WITH A SUBJECT IN SPACE-FILLER *THERE* SENTENCES

In some sentences with space-filler *there*, there are words after the verb that you can **not** bring to the subject territory. Note.

There was a tornado here last year.

You would change this sentence to *A tornado was [=took place]* **here last year.** You could **not** change it to ~~*A tornado here last year was [=took place]*~~. The wording *here last year* belongs WITH THE VERB, **not** with the subject.

Notice the correct labeling for this sentence.

[Was] ⟲⃗   MS ‾‾‾‾‾ Ⓢ ‾‾‾‾‾   [?]
   ^ ⌈There⌉ <u>was</u> ⌈a tornado⌉ here last year.

173

● Do **_PRACTICE J_** (IDENTIFYING THE TRUE SUBJECT
IN SPACE-FILLER _THERE_ SENTENCES) in your _Skills
Practice Book._

Note the whole Main Subject Test—for Statements
once again.

Test 5: The Main Subject Test— for Statements

STEPS

1. Label as main subject the words between
   the two positions of the movable starter
   that sound as if they belong together and
   serve as subject.

2. When the word _there_ fills the subject territory, label as subject THOSE WORDS AFTER
   THE VERB THAT CAN REPLACE THE WORD
   THERE, and label _there_ as the subject's
   space filler.

● Do **_PRACTICE K_** (CARRYING OUT TESTS 1-5 IN
THEIR ENTIRETY) in your _Skills Practice Book._

● Do **_PRACTICE L_** (CARRYING OUT TESTS 1-5 IN
THEIR ENTIRETY) in your _Skills Practice Book._

Writing Tips
for Using Space-filler _There_

There are advantages to your using sentences that
begin with space-filler _there_ in your own writing.
  The first advantage is that this kind of sentence
enables you to write with greater VARIETY. You use

sentences that start with space-filler *there* among sentences that start in other ways. This makes your writing more INTERESTING to read and, therefore, more INVITING.

A second advantage is that it lends itself to expressing some truth that you can then "prove." In other words, this kind of sentence is ideal for use as a TOPIC SENTENCE—that is, as the first or leading (lead-in) sentence in a paragraph. For example, you might start your paragraph *There are several reasons why a person should exercise.* The following sentences would then list and/or discuss the reasons.

The third advantage is that space-filler *there* is handy for introducing items in a list in a more interesting way. For example, you could say: *"First, there are those.... Second, there are others.... Finally, there are still others...."*

● Do *PRACTICE M* (WRITING SENTENCES USING SPACE-FILLER *THERE*) in your *Skills Practice Book.*

Endnotes

Questions with Space-filler *There*: You can find space-filler *there* used in questions too. Note.

Is there a white birch on your property?

Aren't there good reasons why lumberjacks wear hard hats?

These are easy to label after you reposition the movable starter. This is because the question then becomes a statement exactly like the ones that you have just been working with. Note the labeling for these two sentences.

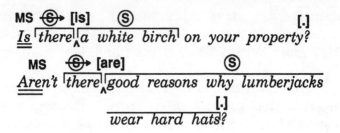

MS ⊖ [is] Ⓢ   [.]
Is ⌐there⌐*a white birch*⌐ *on your property?*

MS ⊖ [are]   Ⓢ
Aren't ⌐there⌐*good reasons why lumberjacks*
                              [.]
              wear hard hats?

You will not find questions like this in the practices in this text.

Reversal of Word Order: There are certain sentences in English (other than those with *there* as space filler) when a main subject can **follow** a subject. Note.

MS
[does come]   Ⓢ
Here ∧*comes* ⌐*your brother.*⌐

It is characteristic of sentences like this that they are easy to read and interpret despite the change in word order. (Of course, you can **not** turn them into questions by moving a starter to the left.)

These types of sentences are restricted in their use. Some are restricted to certain tenses and certain types of verbs. Others are found only when the style is rather formal or literary. Still others have a rhetorical tone, such that they would be appropriate only in speeches or in more formal types of persuasive writing.

This kind of sentence has been excluded from the practice work accompanying this text.

Review

Space-filler *There*: The word *there* when it fills
the space of the subject territory in place of
the real subject.

Labeling for Space-filler *There*: Use an OVERHEAD
BRACKET, and place a CIRCLED *s* that has a RIGHT-
POINTING ARROW THROUGH IT on top of the brack-
et.

Order for the Tests:
1. Main Subject Test—for Questions
2. Helpers plus WHAT/ING Word Verb Test
3. Do/does/did Test
4. Movable Starter Test
5. Main Subject Test—for Statements

TEST 5: The Main Subject Test—for Statements
1. Label as main subject the words between
the two positions of the movable starter
that sound as if they belong together and
serve as subject.
2. When the word *there* fills the subject territory, label as subject THOSE WORDS
AFTER THE VERB THAT CAN REPLACE THE
WORD *THERE*, and label *there* as the
subject's space filler.

Chapter 11

Front Wording

You know how sentences usually begin—as a question, statement, or command.

There is **another way** that sentences can begin. This is because there is a position IN FRONT OF a question, statement, or command that a SPECIAL KIND OF WORDING can occupy.

The goal of this chapter is to inform you about this special kind of wording and to help you use it in your own writing.

Truths about Wording in the Front Position

Here are some truths about English that you should know and that will help you understand this special wording better.

Truth A

Sentences have a FRONT position BEFORE the start of any question, statement, or command.

Examples

BY THE END OF SUMMER, we anticipate school.
AFTER SUMMER, weren't you eager for a change?
IF YOU HAVE A QUESTION, raise your hand.

Truth B

There is a type of front wording that can shift from the start of a sentence unit to the end of a sentence unit.

Examples

WHEN THE HALFTIME ARRIVED, the commercials resumed. ➡
The commercials resumed WHEN THE HALFTIME ARRIVED.

IF YOU LIKE TO READ IN BED, you must have proper lighting. ➡
You must have proper lighting IF YOU LIKE TO READ IN BED.

Note about Sentence Units: For now, all sentences will have only one sentence unit.

Truth C

Commonly, such front wording has a COMMA after it that serves as a MARKER FOR THE END OF THE FRONT WORDING.

Examples

WHEN THE SUN BREAKS THROUGH THE CLOUDS, the brightness causes cheeriness. ➡

The brightness causes cheeriness WHEN THE SUN BREAKS THROUGH THE CLOUDS.

IF WE SPEAK INDISTINCTLY, we can be misunderstood. ➡

We can be misunderstood IF WE SPEAK INDISTINCTLY.

Note: Ordinarily you USE A COMMA when this kind of wording comes BEFORE the question, statement, or command. **However,** you ordinarily OMIT THE COMMA when such wording comes AT THE END of the sentence (because this is the location where the reader expects to find it).

Truth D

When such front wording has no comma, it sometimes shifts to the end of the sentence AUTOMATICALLY—AS YOU TEST FOR THE MOVABLE STARTER.

Examples

Occasionally the showers are downpours. ➡

Are the showers downpours OCCASIONALLY?

Perhaps you should exercise more. ➡

Should you exercise more PERHAPS?

Truth E

Even when such wording has no comma and does not shift automatically for you, you can still sense its presence BECAUSE YOU SENSE THAT YOU <u>COULD</u> PLACE A COMMA THERE.

Examples

Due to occasional daydreaming a student can miss important information.

Almost by chance Mike had offered an invaluable suggestion.

Explanation: For both these sentences, your voice's pitch has a falling sound and you pause slightly RIGHT AFTER THE FRONT WORDING—both after *DUE TO OCCASIONAL DAYDREAMING* and after *ALMOST BY CHANCE*. For both sentences, the wording to the left of where you pause and where the voice trails can shift to the end of the sentence. Note.

A student can miss important information
DUE TO OCCASIONAL DAYDREAMING.

*Mike had offered an invaluable suggestion **ALMOST BY CHANCE.***

Truth F

When wording before a comma is NOT this type of wording, you will (usually) be <u>UN</u>able to shift it to the end of the sentence unit.

Examples

Tiny, darting humming birds hover for seconds at a time.
[You can **not** say ~~darting humming birds hover for seconds at a time tiny~~.]

The Andersons, who are our neighbors, like to go camping.
[You can **not** say either ~~who are our neighbors like to go camping the Andersons~~ or ~~like to go camping the Andersons who are our neighbors~~.]

Term to Know: Front Adverbial

This front wording that can shift to the end of a sentence unit has its own name in this text.

Because it always does the job of an ADVERB, it has the word **ADVERBIAL** as part of its name. Briefly an ADVERB (a single word) or ADVERBIAL (a group of words) is WORDING THAT YOU CAN SAY TOGETHER WITH THE VERB OR WITH THE VERB AND ITS ACCOMPANYING WORDS. See Chapter 16 for a fuller discussion.

Because this special wording occupies the front position in a sentence—that is, it comes IN FRONT OF any question, statement, or command—it has the word **FRONT** as part of its name too. Its full name, then, is **FRONT ADVERBIAL**.

This text uses the term FRONT ADVERBIAL to mean WORDING AT THE FRONT OF A SENTENCE UNIT THAT YOU CAN SHIFT TO THE END OF THE SENTENCE UNIT WHERE IT HAS GRAMMATICAL FIT.

Front Adverbial:

Wording at the front of a sentence unit that you can shift to the end of the sentence unit with grammatical fit.

Labeling for a Front Adverbial

Because of the special nature of a front adverbial, it has its own label. You place a LEFT-pointing arrowhead BEFORE it and a RIGHT-pointing arrowhead WHERE IT ENDS. You then place the lettering *FAV* over the first (**left**-pointing) arrowhead. Note.

FAV

⟨*Due to the rain,*⟩ *the snow has disappeared.*

Labeling for Front Adverbials:

Place a left-pointing arrowhead before its first word, a right-pointing arrowhead after its last word, and the lettering *FAV* over the first arrowhead.

NEW (AGAIN!) Test 1: The Comma Test (to Find Front Adverbials)

This test must come BEFORE all the other tests because failure to recognize front adverbials can undermine your success with several of the later tests.

Take note of this **new** ORDER OF THE TESTS.

1. COMMA TEST
2. Main Subject Test—for Questions
3. Helpers + WHAT/ING Word Verb Test
4. Do/does/did Test
5. Movable Starter Test
6. Main Subject Test—for Statements

Here is an OVERVIEW of the Comma Test (to Find Front Adverbials). In the detailed explanations that follow, there will be FIVE ground rules and TWO steps.

Overview for Newest Test 1:

The Comma Test (to Find Front Adverbials)

Part A Ground Rules	Part B Steps
Do this test BEFORE all others. Do this test RIGHT. Cover the front adverbial when you do your testing.	Look for a comma. Label as FAV all the wording before the comma that you can shift TO THE END WITH GRAMMATICAL FIT.

Test 1: The Comma Test (to Find Front Adverbials)

Part A
Ground Rules

Part A Ground Rules	Part B Steps
1. Carry out this test BEFORE ALL OTHERS.	Look for a comma.
2. Test by shifting the wording from LEFT to RIGHT ONLY.	Label as FAV all the wording before the comma that you can shift to the end of the sentence unit with grammatical fit.
3. Always shift to the END of the sentence unit.	
4. Keep the front wording COVERED while you test it.	
5. Keep the front adverbial UNcovered when carrying out the two verb tests.	

Ground Rule 1

Carry out this test BEFORE ALL OTHERS.

Remember that the front adverbial occupies the front or first section of a sentence. Therefore, you must identify it first. Then you can cover it so that for a starter-verb question the (now) **"front" wording will be a STARTER** and during the Movable Starter Test the **starter can move to the "front" of the sentence** (as it now appears).

This **must** now be TEST ONE.

Ground Rule 2

Test by shifting <u>from</u> LEFT <u>to</u> RIGHT ONLY.

When testing front wording, you must take the wording FROM THE FRONT and shift it TO THE RIGHT. The reason is that you are testing to see whether A FRONT ADVERBIAL stands BEFORE the sentence's **core verb and main subject**—that is, before the question, statement, or command has begun—but **not** whether "end wording" stands after them.

Ground Rule 3

Always shift to the END of the sentence unit.

There are several kinds of grammatical elements that can shift from the start to **before the END** and **not** be a front adverbial. Here is one example.

Carlos, my friend, loaned it to me.

[You **may** say *My friend Carlos loaned it to me.* However, you may **not** say ~~Carlos loaned it to me my friend.~~ The words *my friend* are **not** a front adverbial.]

Ground Rule 4

Keep the front wording COVERED while you test it.

As is the case with any testing inside a sentence, you may **not** use the same wording **twice** in the same sentence and have it be acceptable English.

For example, you may **not** say ~~Occasionally it rains occasionally~~.

Therefore, you should PHYSICALLY COVER—use a pen or pencil or your finger—the front part of the sentence as you do your testing. Note.

~~Occasionally~~ *it rains* OCCASIONALLY

Note again.

When you smile, you cheer others up. ➡

~~When you smile~~, *you cheer others up* WHEN YOU SMILE

● Do **PRACTICE A** (IDENTIFYING FRONT ADVERBIALS) in your **Skills Practice Book**.

Ground Rule 5

Keep the front adverbial UNcovered when carrying out the two verb tests.

Front adverbial wording can be of ANY length and **can contain** ONE OR MORE VERBS. Therefore, you must UNcover it as you carry out BOTH VERB TESTS. Here is an example.

*IF A STUDENT **IS EXPLAINING** WHY HIS/HER WORK **IS** LATE, won't a teacher usually listen?* ➡

*won't a teacher usually listen IF A STUDENT **IS** **EXPLAINING** WHY HIS/HER WORK **IS** LATE*

● Do **PRACTICE B** (LABELING VERBS INSIDE FRONT ADVERBIALS) in your **Skills Practice Book**.

Part B
Steps

Test 1: The Comma Test (to Find Front Adverbials)

Part A Ground Rules	Part B Steps
1. Carry out this test BEFORE ALL OTHERS.	1. Look for a comma.
2. Test by shifting the wording <u>from</u> LEFT <u>to</u> RIGHT ONLY.	2. Label as FAV all the wording before the comma that you can shift to the end of the sentence unit with grammatical fit.
3. Always shift to the END of the sentence unit.	
4. Keep the front wording COVERED while you test it.	
5. Keep the front adverbial UNcovered when carrying out the two verb tests.	

Note that this is also the WHOLE TEST. You have already learned these two steps.

Step 1
Look for a comma.

You know that a comma often marks the end of front adverbial wording. You must NOTICE COMMAS. If you disregard a comma, you could be overlooking this truly important grammatical feature.

● Do *PRACTICE C* (TAKING NOTE OF COMMAS) in your *Skills Practice Book.*

Step 2
Label as FAV
all the wording before the comma
that you can shift to the end of the
sentence unit with grammatical fit.

You now **test** ALL THE WORDS BEFORE THE COMMA. You say them—AS A UNIT—at the end of the sentence unit. **As you test them at the end of the sentence unit,** YOU COVER THEM IN THEIR FRONT POSITION. The words must SOUND AS IF THEY BELONG WITH GRAMMATICAL FIT. Note.

> *BECAUSE THE SNOW TURNED TO RAIN, the drifts disappeared.* ➡

~~Because the snow turned to rain,~~ *the drifts disappeared* *BECAUSE THE SNOW TURNED TO RAIN*

Notice that you **can** shift the wording with grammatical fit. Therefore, you would add the necessary labeling—the LEFT-POINTING ARROWHEAD, the RIGHT-POINTING ARROWHEAD, and the LETTERING *FAV* (over the FIRST arrowhead). Note.

FAV
⟨*Because the snow turned to rain,*⟩*the drifts*

disappeared.

● Do *PRACTICE D* (LABELING FRONT ADVERBIAL WORDING CORRECTLY) in your *Skills Practice Book.*

You know from Truth F (above) that wording before a comma will **not** always shift with grammatical fit. You must now be on the lookout for such wording. Note these examples.

Our plumber, a neighbor's son, does first-rate work. ➤

~~a neighbor's son does first rate work our plumber~~

[You may **not** shift the wording *our plumber* to the end of the sentence unit. These two words are not functioning as a front adverbial in this sentence.]

Our plumber, a neighbor's son, does first-rate work. ➤

~~does first rate work our plumber, a neighbor's son~~

[You may **not** shift the wording before the second comma *our plumber, a neighbor's son* to the end of the sentence unit either. Therefore, this sentence has **no** front adverbial.]

● Do *PRACTICE E* (DETERMINING WHETHER FRONT WORDING IS OR IS NOT A FRONT ADVERBIAL) in your *Skills Practice Book.*

Changes Required for Other Tests

The three subsections here are extremely important. The first two explain how important it is to cover the front adverbial as you carry out the Main Subject—for Questions Test and the Movable Starter Test.

The third subsection explains how you can find front adverbials when the author does **not** use a comma.

Change Required for the Main Subject Test—for Questions

The Main Subject Test—for Questions requires you first to take note of any question mark and **then** to find the starter that "begins the question." TAKE NOTE THAT THE FRONT ADVERBIAL COMES **BEFORE** THE QUESTION.

Therefore, you **must** KEEP THE FRONT ADVERBIAL COVERED while you carry out this test so that the starter you are looking for WILL ACTUALLY BE LOCATED WHERE THE QUESTION BEGINS.

Here is an example.

If the ground is soft, can a car get stuck? ➡

FAV

⟨*If the ground is soft,*⟩*can a car get stuck?* ➡

FAV

⟨
                     MS Ⓢ [can]
⟩ *can* ⌐*a car*⌐*get stuck?* ➡

FAV
                      MS Ⓢ [can]
⟨*If the ground is soft,*⟩*can* ⌐*a car*⌐*get stuck?*

Explanation: First, you test for the front adverbial. Then you COVER THE FRONT ADVERBIAL.

Third, you look for the starter that begins this question at the start of the REMAINING WORDS of the sentence.

Fourth, you label *can* as the movable starter and shift it to its inside position before *get*. In addition, you label the words between its two positions—*a car*—as main subject.

Finally, you carry out the WHAT and ING Subtests for the starter *can*—in its **inside** position—to find the companion main verb *get*.

After these steps, you label remaining verbs.

Now note the wording for this new STEP and how it fits into the whole Main Subject Test—for Questions.

NEW Step 1
KEEP COVERED any front adverbial.

TEST 2: REVISED Main Subject Test —for Questions

Part A Ground Rules	Part B Steps
1. DO THIS TEST BE- FORE BOTH VERB TESTS.	1. KEEP COVERED ANY FRONT ADVERBIAL.
2. EXPECT GRAMMATI- CAL FIT.	2. Look for a question mark.
	3. If a question, find the starter that begins it (if any) and label it MS.
3. Expect to find an- other verb in the sub- ject terri- tory from time to time.	4. Reposition the starter to where it fits inside the sentence.
	5. Label the in-between words as the main sub- ject.
	6. Locate and label the com- panion verbs (if any) that FOLLOW the starter in its INSIDE position.

● Do *PRACTICE F* (CARRYING OUT THE COMMA TEST, MAIN SUBJECT TEST—FOR QUESTIONS, AND THE TWO VERB TESTS) in your *Skills Practice Book*.

Change Required for the Movable Starter Test

The Movable Starter Test requires you to test starter verbs by shifting each to the "front." This means to the

FRONT of the wording AFTER the front adverbial. Therefore, you **must** KEEP THE FRONT ADVERBIAL COVERED while you carry out this test so that you can shift the starter and have the result be acceptable English. Here is an example.

If you are forgetful, you need reminders. ➡

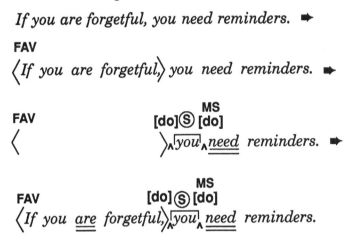

Explanation: You test the first starter **after** the COVERED FRONT ADVERBIAL—namely, supplied *do*. You cause the acceptable question *Do you need reminders?* Therefore, supplied *do* is the movable starter and the word *you* is the main subject. You then carry out the remaining tests.

Note: You NEVER USE THIS TEST ON A STARTER INSIDE A FRONT ADVERBIAL. The reason is that front adverbials fit AFTER THE CORE VERB and MAIN SUBJECT. Consequently, FRONT ADVERBIALS NEVER CONTAIN A MAIN SUBJECT.

Note the wording for this NEW STEP, and note that it becomes the FIRST STEP for the Movable Starter Test.

NEW Step 1

KEEP COVERED ANY FRONT ADVERBIAL.

Test 5: REVISED
Movable Starter Test

Part A
Steps

1. KEEP COVERED ANY FRONT ADVERBI- AL.

2. When there is only one starter, shift it to the front and label it "MS."

3. When there are two or more starters, test each to find and label as "MS" the ONE that you can shift to the front to form an accept- able ques- tion.

Part B
Ground Rules

1. Leave *n't* attached.

2. Change STARTER/ *not* to start- er/*n't* (if possible).

3. WRITE OUT all *do/does/did* substitutions.

4. Write out the substitute spell- ings for the words *do, does, did, have, has,* and *had*— WHENEVER THESE ARE MAIN VERBS.

5. Keep covered ALL *INSIDE* DU- PLICATES of words:

   a. The INSIDE STARTER—with or without *n't*.

   b. ALSO the ORIGINAL STARTER + *NOT* that you contracted.

   c. ALSO the ORIGINAL MAIN VERB—for the substitute spelling that you are now testing.

6. For all words NOT now being tested, USE ONLY the ORIGINAL SPELLING—NOT its *do/does/did* substitute spelling.

7. Use a question-asking tone of voice.

8. As you ask the question, PAUSE briefly at the position of the INSIDE—AND NOW COV- ERED—STARTER.

● Do *PRACTICE G* (Carrying out all tests) in your *Skills Practice Book.*

● Do *PRACTICE H* (Carrying out all tests) in your *Skills Practice Book.*

Precaution regarding the Main Subject Test—for Statements When Front Adverbials Have No Commas after Them

As you learned in Truths D and E above, front adverbials occasionally have **no comma** after them.

When this happens, you might find yourself shifting the front adverbial automatically as you test for the movable starter. Alternatively, you might sense its presence due to your voice's falling sound and your pausing as you proceed through the sentence.

Even if you do not recognize a front adverbial by one of these strategies, you can come to recognize it if you are careful during the main subject test.

You remember that the words that make up the main subject—that is, the words between the two positions of the movable starter—must **both** SOUND AS IF THEY BELONG TOGETHER **and** SERVE AS SUBJECT.

You remember also that wording can come between the two positions of a movable starter—**and to the** RIGHT **of the subject**—that does **not** belong to the subject. See the example again.

$$\underset{\wedge \ We \quad seldom \ \wedge \underline{discussed} \quad the \quad matter.}{\text{[Did]} \underbrace{\qquad\qquad}_{} \overset{\text{MS}}{\text{[did discuss]}} \qquad \text{[?]}}$$

In this sentence, the word *seldom* neither sounds right with the main subject *we* nor answers WHO or WHAT when asked before the verb *discussed*. It is the kind of ADVERB that can come right before a verb and is sayable with it.

When you find wording between the two positions of a movable starter—but to the LEFT of the subject—that do **not** belong to the subject, you have found a front adverbial. Note.

[has]　　　　　　　　　　　　　　　　MS

ᴧ*Fortunately the sweltering heat has subsided.*

Though you can say *Has fortunately the sweltering heat subsided* (if you use your voice right), you can **not** say the words ~~fortunately the sweltering heat~~ together. The words that answer WHO or WHAT before the verb *subsided* for this sentence are *the sweltering heat*. The remaining word—because it occupies the front position of the sentence AND BECAUSE IT SHIFTS TO THE END OF THE SENTENCE—is a FRONT ADVERBIAL. Note.

*The sweltering heat has subsided **FORTUNATELY**.*

Note the correct labeling for this sentence.

FAV　　　　　　[has]　　　S　　　　MS
⟨*Fortunately*⟩ᴧ*the sweltering heat¹ has subsided.*

Here is another example.

?

[should] 　　　　　　　　　　　　MS
ᴧ*In a minute the phone should ring again.*

For this sentence, you cannot say the words ~~in a minute the phone~~ together. In addition, the words that answer WHAT when asked before *should ring* are *the phone*. Finally, you can shift the wording *in a minute* to the end of the sentence unit. Note.

the phone should ring again in a minute

The correct labeling for this sentence, then, is as follows.

FAV   **[should]** Ⓢ   MS

⟨*In a minute⟩ the phone* should ring *again.*

- Do *PRACTICE J* (TELLING FRONT ADVERBIALS FROM MAIN SUBJECTS IN SENTENCES WITHOUT A COMMA) in your *Skills Practice Book.*

- Do *PRACTICE K* (IDENTIFYING FRONT ADVERBIALS IN STATEMENTS WITH AND WITHOUT COMMAS) in your *Skills Practice Book.*

- Do *PRACTICE L* (CARRYING OUT ALL THE TESTS) in your *Skills Practice Book.*

Changes You Must Make as an Editor

You know that authors have rules to follow when they change their own sentences. Editors, too, must follow these rules. When you change someone else's sentences BY SHIFTING FRONT WORDING TO THE END OF A SENTENCE UNIT, you are acting as an EDITOR. Therefore, when you do this, you too must follow the rules.

One rule for writers and editors is to USE THE NAME (THE NOUN) for a person, idea, or thing **the first time** but to USE A PRONOUN INSTEAD **the second time.** If you **rearrange a sentence** so that a **pronoun comes first,** YOU MUST SUBSTITUTE THE NOUN FOR THE PRONOUN so that the noun will again be first, as the rule requires. You would **not** use the noun twice (ordinarily). Consequently, you would USE A **PRONOUN**—INSTEAD OF THE NOUN—IN ITS **SECOND** POSITION.

A Single Switch When Shifting

Here is an example of a SINGLE SWITCH you must make as you shift front wording to test it.

When WINTERS are too mild, THEY cause loss of jobs.

Notice the use of the name WINTERS **first** but of the pronoun THEY to replace it **afterwards**.

When you edit the sentence by shifting the words *when winters are too mild* to the end of the sentence unit, you must replace the PRONOUN *they* (now earlier) with the NOUN *winter* and the NOUN *winter* (now later) with the PRONOUN *they*. In other words, the NOUN must always come **first** and the PRONOUN **second**. Note.

*WINTERS [**not** they] cause loss of jobs when THEY [**not** winters] are too mild.*

Explanation: Note the effect if you do **not** make the switch—*they cause loss of jobs when winters are too mild.* First, the front adverbial has obvious fit at the end of the sentence unit. However, THE SENTENCE PUZZLES THE READER because he/she does not know what the word *they* refers to until too late in the sentence.

● Do *PRACTICE M* (REWORDING SENTENCES WITH A SINGLE SWITCH WHEN TESTING FOR FRONT ADVERBIALS) in your *Skills Practice Book*.

● Do *PRACTICE N* (CARRYING OUT LABELING USING ALL TESTS) in your *Skills Practice Book*.

● Do *PRACTICE P* (CARRYING OUT ALL THE TESTS) in your *Skills Practice Book*.

A Pair of Switches When Shifting

Sometimes you must make a PAIR OF SWITCHES as you test front wording. Here is an example.

When MY COUSIN took THE DRIVER'S TEST, HE failed IT.

MY COUSIN failed THE DRIVER'S TEST
when HE took IT.

Notice the **pair of switches** required here. You had to substitute the words *my cousin* for *he* at the start of the new sentence (and *he* for *my cousin* afterward) and the words *the driver's test* for *it* after the verb *failed* (and *it* for *the driver's test* afterward).

Note that the words *when my cousin took the driver's test* are clearly a front adverbial both because they have grammatical fit at the end of the sentence and because you can make the above changes.

● Do **_PRACTICE Q_** (REWORDING SENTENCES WITH PAIRS OF SWITCHES WHEN TESTING FOR FRONT ADVERBIAL WORDING) in your *Skills Practice Book.*

● Do **_PRACTICE R_** (CARRYING OUT LABELING USING ALL TESTS) in your *Skills Practice Book.*

● Do **_PRACTICE S_** (CARRYING OUT ALL THE TESTS) in your *Skills Practice Book.*

More Complicated Switching When Shifting

Sometimes you must do more than make a pair of switches. You must also add other wording or make more extensive changes. Note.

If ANTS suddenly appear everywhere in A HOUSE, THEY have been forming a nest NEARBY.

ANTS have been forming a nest NEAR A HOUSE if THEY suddenly appear everywhere in IT.

Notice how the word NEARBY had to be replaced by the **three** words NEAR A HOUSE.

Despite the extra wording change (which you sense is possible even if you do not actually think through to the exact wording), it is clear that the words *if ants sudden-*

ly appear everywhere in a house make up a front adverbial. The reasons are that they fit grammatically at the end of the sentence **and** that all the necessary changes are reasonable and possible.

●Do _PRACTICE T_ (REWORDING SENTENCES REQUIRING MORE COMPLICATED SWITCHING WHEN TESTING FOR FRONT ADVERBIALS) in your *Skills Practice Book.*

Identifying Front Adverbials inside Paragraphs

When you test front wording INSIDE PARAGRAPHS, you will **often** find that you seem to be committing a fault as a writer/editor by shifting it. The wording can seem OUT OF PLACE or even MISPLACED in an end-of-sentence-unit location.

The reason for this is that front adverbials serve to connect a new sentence with wording in an earlier one. Therefore, good writing requires that the front (connecting) wording be as close to the earlier wording as possible. Note.

There are many rules that good drivers follow. FIRST, they anticipate problems. FOR EXAMPLE, when another car slows down without warning, they expect some unpredictable action to take place.

A good writer would **not** place *first* at the end of its sentence because at the end of the sentence the word *first* no longer necessarily means that this is the first "rule." Nor would a good writer place *for example* at the end of its sentence because the reader has to be **fore**warned that this is an "example" and **not** a rule. Nonetheless, both of these expressions **are** front adverbials BECAUSE THEY FIT AT THE END OF THEIR RESPECTIVE SENTENCES GRAMMATICALLY.

Though such shifting may seem awkward or even

misplaced, you should still label the wording as front adverbial as long as there is a grammatical fit.

● Do *PRACTICE U* (CARRYING OUT LABELING USING ALL TESTS) in your *Skills Practice Book.*

Final Truth about Front Adverbials

Truth A

Though sentences often DO have front adverbials, they also often do NOT.

Do NOT expect every sentence to have a front adverbial. Writers do use them, but they often do **not** use them as well. The practices to come will have an assortment of sentences both WITH and WITHOUT front adverbials.

● Do *PRACTICE V* (CARRYING OUT ALL THE TESTS) in your *Skills Practice Book.*

● Do *PRACTICE W* (CARRYING OUT ALL THE TESTS) in your *Skills Practice Book.*

Writing Tips for Using Front Adverbials

Just as there are advantages to your using sentences that begin with spacer-filler *there,* so there are advantages to your using sentences that begin with a front adverbial.

One type of front adverbial is a specific set of words and phrases that help you keep clear for your reader where this new sentence fits in relative to what you just wrote. This "set" includes words like *first, in addition, moreover, however, for example,* and so forth.

When you use these front adverbials, you are providing a service for your readers. You are acting as their "tour guide." Your writing has extra CLEARNESS and CONNECTEDNESS (more technically called COHERENCE).

The front adverbials in this set also have the name TRANSITIONAL ADVERBIALS.

Transitional Adverbial:

One of a listable set of adverbials that serves to connect a new sentence unit with earlier wording.

Lists of Common Transitional Adverbials according to Type of Message Conveyed

Indicating "Here is one more"	Indicating "Here is another/the last in a list"	Indicating "Here is something in contrast"
also	*another*	*however*
too	*second / third / ...*	*nonetheless*
similarly	*next*	*nevertheless*
in addition	*again*	*on the other*
moreover	*last(ly)*	*hand*
furthermore	*final(ly)*	*on the contrary*
Indicating "Here is a consequence"	**Indicating "Here is an example"**	**Indicating "Here is a conclusion"**
consequently	*for example*	*in summary*
therefore	*for instance*	*in conclusion*
thus	*namely*	*in short*
as a result	*by way of illus-*	*to conclude*
then	*tration*	*in brief*

Another type of front adverbial also begins the new sentence by relating its content to what you said earlier. However, this type does not rely on a list of words or expressions. Instead, it "echoes" the very wording that went before it. Note this example.

*The baby **woke** up early as usual. AFTER HE HAD ALSO **WOKEN** UP HIS MOTHER AND FATHER, he sucked on his bottle contentedly.*

Notice the repetition ("echoing") of the verb *woke*. Notice, too, the use of the transitional adverbial *also* in accompaniment with the echoing. Also notice how the starting word *after* establishes the time connection between the two statements.

Such an "echoing" type of front adverbial also enables you to guide the tour of the reader through your writing in a clear and helpful way.

A third advantage of front adverbials is that they enable you to write with greater VARIETY. You can intermix sentences that start with front adverbials with those that do not to make your writing much more interesting to read.

Punctuation Rule
for WRITING FRONT ADVERBIALS:
Always use a COMMA to separate front adverbials from the rest of the sentence.

EXAMPLES

Provided that you have read the directions carefully, you may proceed to take the test.

Actually, haven't deer become overabundant lately?

To check his spelling, he consulted a dictionary.

Explanation: Writers use a comma after a front adverbial because it helps the main part of the sentence stand out better. (They do **not** omit the comma unless the sentence is EASY TO READ WITHOUT IT **and** the front adverbial is FOUR WORDS—OR LESS—LONG.)

● Do _PRACTICE X_ (WRITING SENTENCES WITH FRONT ADVERBIALS) in your _Skills Practice Book._

Endnote

Two Commas as Markers of Front Adverbials: Sometimes you find TWO commas and TWO front adverbials beside each other. Note.

Yesterday, despite the snow, we still had school.

Note that you can say **both** _Despite the snow, we had school yesterday_ **and** _We had school yesterday despite the snow._

In such cases, it would be best to treat the two front adverbials as if they were just one. Note the labeling.

                              MS
    FAV   [did]Ⓢ   [did have]
⟨_Yesterday, despite the snow_⟩ˏ⎡_we_⎤ _still_ˏ_had_ _school._

This text will avoid such sentences in its accompanying practice material.

Review

CONTENT IN DARKER LETTERING
MUST BE REMEMBERED.

Front Adverbial: Wording at the front of a sentence unit that you can shift to the end of the sentence unit with grammatical fit.

Transitional Adverbial: One of a listable set of front adverbials that serves to connect a new sentence unit with earlier wording.

Labeling for Front Adverbials: Place a left-pointing arrowhead before its first word, a right-pointing arrowhead after its last word, and the lettering *FAV* over the first arrowhead.

Punctuation Rule for WRITING FRONT ADVERBIALS: Always use a COMMA to separate front adverbials from the rest of the sentence.

Order of the Tests:
1. COMMA TEST
2. Main Subject Test—for Questions
3. Helpers + WHAT/ING Word Verb Test
4. Do/does/did Test
5. Movable Starter Test
6. Main Subject Test—for Statements

Test 1: The Comma Test (for Front Adverbials):
Part A—Ground Rules:
1. Carry out this test BEFORE ALL OTHERS.
2. Test by shifting the wording <u>from</u> LEFT <u>to</u> RIGHT ONLY.
3. Always shift to the END of the sentence unit.
4. Keep the front wording COVERED while you test it.
5. Keep the front adverbial <u>UN</u>covered when carrying out the two verb tests.

Part B—Steps:
1. Look for a comma.
2. Label as FAV all the wording before the comma that you can shift to the end of the sentence unit with grammatical fit.

CHANGE FOR Test 2: Main Subject Test—for Questions; Part B—Steps:
1. <u>KEEP COVERED</u> ANY FRONT ADVERBIAL.

CHANGE FOR Test 5: Movable Starter Test; Part A—Steps:
1. <u>KEEP COVERED</u> ANY FRONT ADVERBIAL.

Chapter 12

Introduction
to Conjunctions and
Punctuation

This chapter has three goals. The first is to introduce you to conjunctions, which are another kind of grammatical word.

The second goal is to alert you to the importance of correct punctuation.

The third goal is to help you use conjunctions and punctuation in ways that will improve the effectiveness of your writing.

The Punctuation Marks
of Greatest Importance

The punctuation marks of greatest importance for the purpose of this chapter are the period (.), the question mark (?), the semi-colon (;), and the comma (,).

Period

The most important use of the PERIOD is to MARK THE END OF A SENTENCE.

Note that in addition to placing a period at the end of a sentence, you **must also** make the FIRST LETTER of every sentence a CAPITAL LETTER.

Question Mark

The QUESTION MARK is another way to MARK THE END OF A SENTENCE. In addition, the question mark informs readers that they must use a QUESTION-ASKING TONE OF VOICE as they read the sentence.

Note that because questions are sentences, you must make the first letter of every question a capital letter too.

Comma

The job of a comma is to be A SEPARATOR **INSIDE** A SENTENCE. It indicates a **MINOR** PAUSE or interruption in a string of words.

When commas separate items IN A SERIES (a group of three or more ALIKE grammatical elements), they also carry the meaning of either *and* or *or*. In fact, the comma DOES THE JOB OF one or the other of these coordinating conjunctions—acting as **separator** and **joiner** at the same time. Note.

Tom, Bill, Joe, and Jim are coming.
[This means *Tom **and** Bill **and** Joe **and** Jim are coming.*]

Tom, Bill, Joe, or Jim is coming.
[This means *Tom **or** Bill **or** Joe **or** Jim is coming.*]

Be aware that because commas come **inside** a sentence, they have **no influence** on the capitalization of any word that follows them.

Note that a GRAMMATICAL ELEMENT is any word or

group of words that does a single grammatical job.

Grammatical Element:

Any word or group of words that does a single grammatical job.

Series:

A string of three or more ALIKE grammatical elements.

Semi-colons

The job of a SEMI-COLON, like the job of the comma, is to be a SEPARATOR **INSIDE A SENTENCE**. However, semi-colons indicate a **MAJOR** PAUSE or interruption in a string of words.

You use semi-colons to SEPARATE **SENTENCE UNITS** (elements of a HIGHER ORDER) rather than to separate less important grammatical elements (elements of a LOWER ORDER).

Semi-colons That Separate Items in a Series: You use semi-colons to separate elements in MAJOR SERIES. A MAJOR SERIES is a series **either** of SENTENCE UNITS **or** of LESSER GRAMMATICAL ELEMENTS THAT HAVE INTERNAL PUNCTUATION OR ARE EXTRA LONG.

Just like commas, semi-colons carry the meaning of the word *and* or *or* when they separate items in a series.

Examples

School was not called off; the buses arrived late because of the slippery conditions; AND all the classes were shortened.
[The semi-colons carry the meaning of *AND* in this sentence.]

There are three strategies for writing a report: students can write them out using longhand; they can use a typewriter and add corrections on the good copy; OR they can use a computer but not print it out until they have already corrected any mistakes.
[The semi-colons carry the meaning of OR
in this sentence.]

Semi-colons That Serve as Joiners of Sentence Units: Semi-colons—without any conjunction—can connect two sentence units. When they do this, they carry the meaning of *and, but,* or *for.*

Examples

He works the whole day; he relaxes the whole evening.
[The semi-colon carries the meaning AND.]

He lost his watch Friday; he found it Sunday.
[The semi-colon carries the meaning BUT.]

He could not open his locker; he had lost the key.
[The semi-colon carries the meaning FOR.]

Key Punctuation Marks and Their Chief Roles		
Name	**Mark**	**Purpose**
PERIOD	.	To mark END OF SENTENCE.
QUESTION MARK	?	To mark END OF SENTENCE.
COMMA	,	To mark MINOR PAUSES.
SEMI-COLON	;	To mark MAJOR PAUSES.

Terms to Know

Note that there are TWO kinds of conjunctions to learn about.

Conjunctions

The words like *and* and *but* belong to a group of words called CONJUNCTIONS. A CONJUNCTION IS A WORD OR WORDING USED TO JOIN TWO GRAMMATICAL ELEMENTS.

The two kinds of conjunctions have the names COORDINATING CONJUNCTION and SUBORDINATING CONJUNCTION.

Coordinating Conjunction

One kind of conjunction joins EQUALLY IMPORTANT or "COORDINATE" ELEMENTS. This kind has the name COORDINATING CONJUNCTION. Note this example.

Tom AND Bill are coming.
[The coordinating conjunction *and* joins the two subjects *Tom* and *Bill*.]

Coordinating Conjunction:

A word (wording) that joins grammatical elements of equal importance.

There are THREE coordinating conjunctions that are so

common that you **must know them** ON SIGHT. These are *AND, OR,* and *BUT.*

List of Most Common Coordinating Conjunctions:

AND   *OR*   *BUT*

Subordinating Conjunction

The other kind of conjunction joins elements when one of them is OF A LOWER ORDER than the other or "SUBORDINATE." This kind has the name SUBORDINATING CONJUNCTION. Note this example.

Tom left BECAUSE he was sick.

[The subordinating conjunction *BECAUSE* belongs to the dependent clause *because he was sick* (which is of a lower order) and joins it to the core verb and main subject *Tom left*.]

Note that a HIGHER ORDER UNIT is **either** a SENTENCE UNIT **or** a CORE VERB PLUS MAIN SUBJECT.

Higher Order Unit:

A SENTENCE UNIT <u>or</u> a CORE VERB PLUS MAIN SUBJECT.

Lower Order Unit:

Any grammatical element that does NOT contain a core verb and main subject.

> ## Subordinating Conjunction:
> **A word (wording) that joins a dependent clause to the rest of its sentence unit.**

There are more than a dozen subordinating conjunctions because these are the INTRODUCERS OF DEPENDENT CLAUSES. Take careful note of this list of the subordinating clauses that you must KNOW ON SIGHT from now on.

Subordinating Conjunctions That You Must Know on Sight:

BECAUSE	*BEFORE*
SINCE	*AFTER*
THOUGH/ALTHOUGH	*WHILE*
IF	*UNTIL*

Predicate

A PREDICATE is those words in a sentence or dependent clause that include the verb and all the words (other than its subject) that belong with it—such as an object of verb or adverb. Note.

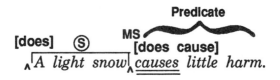

$\overbrace{\quad}^{\text{Predicate}}$

[does] ⓢ MS [does cause]

ᴬA light snow ᴬcauses little harm.

Predicate

[does] ⓢ MS [does cause]

ᴬA freezing rain always ᴬcauses hazardous driving.

Predicate:
A core verb together with all the words that belong with it other than its main subject.

The Job of Coordinating Conjunctions

The JOB OF COORDINATING CONJUNCTIONS is to JOIN ALIKE GRAMMATICAL ELEMENTS of almost any kind. Note.

ANN and LIZ are coming. [two SUBJECTS joined—both NOUNS]

THE LARGE BOX and THE SMALL ONE must come. [two SUBJECTS joined—both NOUN CLUSTERS]

Tom COULD and SHOULD mow the lawn. [two STARTERS joined]

Tom has COME and LEFT. [two MAIN VERBS joined]

Joanne SPOKE and WAS HEARD. [two (WHOLE) VERBS joined]

*Joanne SPOKE HER MIND OPENLY and WAS RESPECT-
FULLY LISTENED TO.* [two PREDICATES joined]

JOANNE SPOKE HER MIND, and SHE WAS HEARD. [two
SENTENCE UNITS joined]

Joanne spoke to KELLY and ME. [two OBJECTS
OF PREPOSITIONS JOINED]

Joanne ran FOR FUN and FOR EXERCISE.
[two PREPOSITIONAL PHRASES joined]

Telling
What a Coordinating Conjunction Joins

You might presuppose that you can tell what a
coordinating conjunction joins by first looking before it
and then looking after it. Here is the proof that this is
not so.

> *Sue went to the LIBRARY and BANK.*
> *Sue went TO THE LIBRARY and TO THE BANK.*
> *Sue WENT TO THE LIBRARY and STAYED THERE.*
> *SUE WENT TO THE LIBRARY, and SHE STAYED.*

Notice that all **four** sentences START ALIKE—they all
start with exactly the SAME five words *Sue went to the
library.* Therefore, the **only way you can really know**
what the conjunction *and* is joining is to **first** look
AFTER it and **then** look BEFORE IT TO FIND A MATCH.

Take careful notice of the difference between the third
and fourth sentences. In the third sentence, the first
word after the coordinating conjunction *and* is the VERB
stayed. **Therefore, *and*** is joining PREDICATES and NO
COMMA COMES BEFORE *AND.*

In contrast, in the fourth sentence the first word
after the coordinating conjunction *and* is the SENTENCE
UNIT *she stayed* (you can cause the question *Did she
stay?*). **Therefore, *and*** is joining SENTENCE UNITS and
BOTH A **COMMA** AND *AND* MUST COME BEFORE THE
SECOND SENTENCE UNIT.

214

Punctuation Rule for JOINING TWO PREDICATES:

When using a coordinating conjunction to join two PREDICATES (verbs plus words that belong just with them), PLACE NO COMMA BEFORE THE SECOND PREDICATE.

Examples

The baby could not stand up BUT could not stay still either.

Many questions were raised AND were answered.

The teacher sits at his desk OR stands by the lectern.

● Do *PRACTICE A* (PUNCTUATING JOINED PREDICATES) in your *Skills Practice Book.*

● Do *PRACTICE B* (WRITING ONE'S OWN SENTENCES WITH PROPERLY JOINED PREDICATES) in your *Skills Practice Book.*

Punctuation Rule for JOINING TWO SENTENCE UNITS:

When using a coordinating conjunction to join two SENTENCE UNITS, FIRST place a COMMA and THEN add the CONJUNCTION before starting the second one.

Examples

You can send a letter the usual way, **OR** *you can send it by "Priority Mail."*

Your answers should be short, **AND** *they must be to the point.*

The hill was perfect for sledding, **BUT** *it was too near a main road.*

● Do *PRACTICE C* (PUNCTUATING JOINED SENTENCE UNITS) in your *Skills Practice Book.*

● Do *PRACTICE D* (WRITING ONE'S OWN SENTENCES WITH PROPERLY JOINED SENTENCE UNITS) in your *Skills Practice Book.*

Using Conjunctions to Join Elements in a Minor Series

Coordinating conjunctions can also join a SERIES of alike grammatical elements.

A MINOR SERIES is a series of elements **both** of a lower order **and** without either internal punctuation or extra length.

For a minor series, it is customary to use COMMAS **instead of a conjunction** until you reach the last element. However, it makes sense to use a **comma plus conjunction between the last two elements too** because often you must use both to assist the reader. Note.

ELLEN, DONNA, and MARIA are coming.

We WENT, STAYED A WHILE, and LEFT.

Notice how the first comma takes the place of *and* in both sentences. Notice, too, the use of a comma PLUS *AND* to join the last two elements. Though this COMMA is sometimes optional, it is SOMETIMES REQUIRED so that it is **wiser to ALWAYS use it.**

Minor Series:

A series of elements both of a lower order and without either internal punctuation or extra length.

Punctuation Rule for Separating Elements in a Minor Series:

When using commas to punctuate elements in a minor series, place them BETWEEN EACH OF THE ELEMENTS <u>and</u> add the coordinating conjunction AFTER the last comma.

● Do *PRACTICE E* (PUNCTUATING SENTENCES THAT CONTAIN A SERIES) in your *Skills Practice Book.*

● Do *PRACTICE F* (WRITING SENTENCES OF YOUR OWN THAT CONTAIN A SERIES) in your *Skills Practice Book.*

Special Sentence Combining Strategies

You learned (above) that you can COMBINE TWO SENTENCE UNITS by placing **first** a COMMA and **then** a COORDINATING CONJUNCTION between them (you must also change the capital letter to a lower-case one). Here are THREE ADDITIONAL WAYS IN WHICH YOU CAN COMBINE SENTENCE UNITS.

Combining by Use of Just a Semi-colon

First, a semi-colon without a coordinating conjunction can serve to separate two sentence units. When it does this, it carries the meaning of a coordinating conjunction. Therefore, a SEMI-COLON without a coordinating conjunction—and without a capital letter at the start of the second unit—can correctly separate two sentence units. Note.

Example

The snow has melted.
Winter has stayed.
➡ *The snow has melted; winter has stayed.*
[Here the semi-colon means *HOWEVER* or *BUT*.]

● Do <u>*PRACTICE G*</u> (USING A SEMI-COLON TO JOIN TWO SENTENCE UNITS) in your *Skills Practice Book*.

Combining by Use of a Semi-colon and a Transitional Adverbial

An alternative way to use a semi-colon to combine sentences is to use **both** a SEMI-COLON **and** a TRANSITIONAL ADVERBIAL. You remember (from Chapter 11) that these are words like *therefore* and *however* that connect a new sentence unit with earlier wording. Be sure to add a comma after such wording.

An advantage of this strategy over using a coordinating conjunction is that you can state the exact relationship of the second sentence unit to the first.

Example

Dad types it.
Mom proofreads it.
➡ *Dad types it; however, Mom proofreads it.*

● Do *PRACTICE H* (USING A SEMI-COLON AND TRAN-
SITIONAL ADVERBIAL TO JOIN SENTENCE UNITS) in
your *Skills Practice Book.*

Combining by Use of a Dependent Clause instead of a Second Sentence Unit

Sometimes the smoothest strategy of all for combining
two sentence units is to change one of them to a dependent clause that has a subordinating conjunction as its
introducer.

This strategy, too, has the added advantage that it
enables the writer to express the precise connection
between sentence units. It also has the advantage that
the writer can place the dependent clause in a front
adverbial position for variety and for the bridging of
ideas.

Example

The snow kept falling. It did not amount to much. ➡

*THOUGH THE SNOW KEPT FALLING, it did not amount
to much.*

OR

*The snow did not amount to much THOUGH IT KEPT
FALLING.*

● Do *PRACTICE J* (JOINING TWO SENTENCE UNITS BY
CHANGING ONE TO A DEPENDENT CLAUSE) in your
Skills Practice Book.

Remedying Punctuation Faults

The reason why writers use punctuation is to help the
reader follow their meaning.   In conversation, the

VOICE tells the listener how he/she should group and interpret words. **In writing, the PUNCTUATION MARK (and accompanying capital letter, when appropriate) alone can tell the reader how to group words and interpret them.**

WHEN A WRITER MISLEADS A READER AS TO WHERE SENTENCE UNITS BEGIN OR END, HE/SHE MISLEADS THE READER IN A MOST SERIOUS WAY.

There are THREE types of FAULTS related to punctuating sentence units that students can commit—the FRAGMENT FAULT, the COMMA SPLICE FAULT, and the RUN-ON SENTENCE FAULT. Each of these faults has its own section here.

Fragment Fault

The first fault that you could commit is to place a period after a NON-sentence unit—that is, after wording that is not a fully worded question, nor a command, nor wording that you can turn into a question. When you do this, you write FRAGMENTS of a sentence unit.

Fragment:
The punctuation fault of placing a PERIOD AFTER WORDING THAT YOU CAN NOT TURN INTO A QUESTION (and that does not express a command).

Remedying the Fragment

The way to REMEDY A FRAGMENT is to ADD ENOUGH WORDS **BEFORE** OR **AFTER** IT to make it an acceptable sentence—that is, to make it a fully worded question or command, or to make it wording that you can turn into a question.

Example

~~Though he was not happy at the time.~~ ➡

HE SAID NOTHING though he was not happy at the time.
[You can ask *Did he say nothing though he was unhappy at the time?*]

OR

Though he was not happy at the time, HE DID NOT MENTION THIS TO ANYONE.
[You can ask *Didn't he mention this to anyone though he was not happy at the time?*]

Note: Students can mistakenly use a period to separate words that grammatically belong INSIDE THE SAME SENTENCE. When you find that you have written a fragment, see whether this has happened to you. See whether you can combine your fragment with either the "sentence" right before it or the one right after it.

● Do *PRACTICE K* (CHANGING FRAGMENTS TO SENTENCES) in your *Skills Practice Book*.

Comma Splice Fault

The second fault that you could commit is to use a COMMA WITH NO COORDINATING CONJUNCTION to separate sentence units. This fault has the name COMMA SPLICE FAULT (a "splice" is a "connection").

> ## Comma Splice:
> **The punctuation fault of using a**
> COMMA ALONE TO JOIN TWO SENTENCE
> UNITS.

Remedying Comma Splices

The way to REMEDY A COMMA SPLICE is to **either** ADD A COORDINATING CONJUNCTION AFTER THE COMMA **or** USE A SEMI-COLON in its place.

Note that all of the strategies for combining sentences that you saw demonstrated earlier in this chapter are effective remedies for a comma splice.

● Do _PRACTICE L_ (REMEDYING COMMA SPLICES) in your *Skills Practice Book.*

Run-on Sentence Fault

The third fault that you could commit is to combine sentence units WITHOUT AN ACCEPTABLE SEPARATOR—that is, with NO period, NOR semi-colon, NOR comma plus coordinating conjunction to separate them. This fault has the name RUN-ON SENTENCE.

Run-on Sentence:
The punctuation fault of FAILING TO SEPARATE SENTENCE UNITS CORRECTLY.

Remedying Run-on Sentences

There are two ways to REMEDY RUN-ON SENTENCES.

First, you must train yourself to be conscious of every sentence unit you use as you write. You do this by taking note of all verbs. You must then mentally test each verb to see whether you can shift its starter to cause a question. Of course, you have a new sentence unit for every starter that you can shift.

Second, you must take care either to punctuate each sentence unit as a separate sentence **or** to combine sentence units with correct punctuation and/or with correct punctuation plus conjunction.

● Do _PRACTICE M_ (COMBINING PAIRS OF SENTENCE UNITS CORRECTLY) in your _Skills Practice Book._

Endnote

Punctuating Sentence Units in a Series: When you write sentence units in a series—that is, when you write three or more as a kind of listing—you should usually USE SEMI-COLONS in preference to commas. Note.

Example

When you shovel a lot of snow, you should use a shovel with a nonstick surface; you should shovel before anyone walks over the path; **and** you should wear gloves so you do not get frostbite.

Review

CONTENT IN DARKER LETTERING MUST BE REMEMBERED.

Coordinating Conjunction: A word (wording) that joins grammatical elements of equal importance.

Most Common Coordinating Conjunctions Listed: AND, OR, BUT.

Subordinating Conjunction: A word (wording) that joins a dependent clause to the rest of its sentence unit.

Subordinating Conjunctions Know on Sight: BECAUSE, SINCE, THOUGH/ALTHOUGH, IF, BEFORE, AFTER, WHILE, UNTIL.

Grammatical Element: Any word or group of words that does a single grammatical job.

Higher Order Unit: A SENTENCE UNIT or a CORE VERB PLUS MAIN SUBJECT.

Lower Order Unit: Any grammatical element that does NOT contain a core verb and main subject.

Series: A string of three or more ALIKE grammatical elements.

Major Series: A series either of SENTENCE UNITS or of LESSER GRAMMATICAL ELEMENTS THAT HAVE INTERNAL PUNCTUATION OR ARE EXTRA LONG.

Minor Series: A series of elements both of a lower order and without either internal punctuation or extra length.

Predicate: A core verb together with all the words that belong with it other than its main subject.

Punctuation Rule for JOINING TWO PREDICATES: When using a coordinating conjunction to join two PREDICATES (verbs plus words that belong just with them), PLACE NO COMMA BEFORE THE SECOND PREDICATE.

Punctuation Rule for JOINING TWO SENTENCE UNITS: When using a coordinating conjunction to join two SENTENCE UNITS, FIRST place a comma and THEN add the conjunction before starting the second one.

Punctuation Rule for SEPARATING ELEMENTS IN A MINOR SERIES: When using commas to punctuate elements in a series, place them BETWEEN EACH OF THE ELEMENTS and add the coordinating conjunction AFTER the last comma.

Fragment: The punctuation fault of placing a PERIOD AFTER WORDING THAT YOU CAN NOT TURN INTO A QUESTION (and that does not express a command).

Comma Splice: The punctuation fault of using a COMMA ALONE TO JOIN TWO SENTENCE UNITS.

Run-on Sentence: The punctuation fault of FAILING TO SEPARATE SENTENCE UNITS CORRECTLY.

Chapter 13

Questions That Start with a Question Word

So far you have learned only how questions caused by starter verbs work. There is another kind of question that is caused instead by a QUESTION WORD.

The goal of this chapter is to teach you how this second kind of question works.

Truths about Question Words and Question Word Questions

The various truths unfolded here should help you with the later work of this chapter.

Truth A

There are NINE "question words" that can cause the start of a question—namely, *who, whom, whose, which, when, where, why, what,* and *how.*

Examples

WHO came?
WHOM have you called?
WHOSE hat is this?
WHICH day is best?
WHEN is the play?
WHERE have you placed it?
WHY has this happened?
WHAT do we do next?
HOW did you manage that?

Here is a list of these words arranged in a way to help you remember them.

Questions Words Listed Alphabetically					
NON-wh.. Word	Wh.. Words (Alphabetically)				
HOW	*WHAT*	*WHEN* *WHERE*	*WHICH*	*WHO* *WHOM* *WHOSE*	*WHY*

TRUTH B

Questions caused by question words differ from starter-verb questions in important ways.

Example of a Starter-Verb Question

Is your watch gaining time?
[This **must be** a starter-verb question because it
STARTS WITH A STARTER **and** CONTAINS NO QUESTION-
ASKING QUESTION WORD.]

Example of a Question Caused by a Question Word

WHAT will happen?

[This question does **not** start with a starter verb and **DOES** CONTAIN A QUESTION-ASKING QUESTION WORD.]

Term to Remember: Question-Word Question

Questions that are caused by question-asking question words have their own name in this text. They have the name QUESTION-WORD QUESTIONS.

Question-Word Question:

A question caused by a question-asking question word near its start.

Important Note: THE END PUNCTUATION FOR EVERY QUESTION MUST BE THE **QUESTION MARK**.

This chart summarizes the above information.

Comparison of Starter Verb Questions and Question Word Questions

| SIMILARITY | DIFFERENCES | |
	Starter Verb Question	Question Word Question
BOTH MUST END WITH A QUESTION MARK.	MUST START WITH A START-ER. DOES NOT CON-TAIN A QUES-TION-ASKING QUESTION WORD.	NEVER STARTS WITH A STARTER. DOES CONTAIN A QUESTION-ASKING QUESTION WORD.

Truth C

The FIRST WORD of a question-word question is sometimes NOT a question word.

Occasionally, the question word itself will be INSIDE a beginning GROUP of words and therefore will **not** be the first word of the group. Note.

*FOR **HOW MANY MINUTES** have you been practicing?*

As you can see, the GROUP is the prepositional phrase *FOR HOW MANY MINUTES.* Notice how the preposition *for* and **not** the question word *how* is the beginning word of the group.

Truth D

Sometimes "question words" do NOT cause a question.

Examples

*A bike **WHOSE** tires are soft should not be ridden.*
*She speaks **WHEN** she is called on.*
***HOW** we should proceed is unclear.*

Notice that each of these sentences ends in a PERIOD. The clue, therefore, that a question word is **not** asking a question is the **PERIOD** AT THE END OF THE SENTENCE.

Note that in sentences like these the question words are usually serving as INTRODUCERS OF DEPENDENT CLAUSES. The dependent clauses are *WHOSE tires are soft, WHEN she is called on,* and *HOW we should proceed.*

Whenever a question word **is** asking a question, the end punctuation must be a **QUESTION MARK and** the QUESTION WORD MUST BE PART OF THE BEGINNING WORDING OF THE QUESTION.

Truth E

**When a SUBJECT comes BEFORE A STARTER,
you have "STATEMENT ORDER";
when a STARTER comes BEFORE A SUBJECT,
you have "QUESTION ORDER."**

Examples

Statement Order: $\overset{\text{Ⓢ}}{\ulcorner Sally \urcorner}\ \overset{\text{MS}}{\underline{has\ left}}$ already.

Question Order: $\overset{\text{MS}}{\underline{Has}}\ \overset{\text{Ⓢ}}{\ulcorner Sally \urcorner}\ \underline{left}$ already?

Explanation: It is easy to see the difference between STATEMENT ORDER and QUESTION ORDER from these two sentences. The wording *Sally has already left* is a statement **because** the SUBJECT *Sally* comes **BEFORE THE MOVABLE STARTER** *HAS*. Contrariwise, the wording *Has Sally left already* is a question **because** the MOVABLE STARTER *has* comes **BEFORE** the SUBJECT *Sally*. Note the following graphic illustration of this.

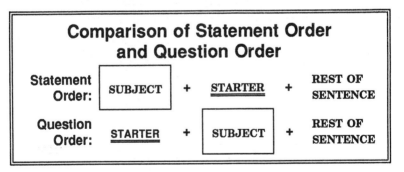

Comparison of Statement Order and Question Order

Statement Order:	SUBJECT	+	<u>STARTER</u>	+	REST OF SENTENCE
Question Order:	<u>STARTER</u>	+	SUBJECT	+	REST OF SENTENCE

Terms to Remember

Statement Order:
A SUBJECT comes BEFORE ITS STARTER.

Truth F

Some question-word questions have statement order.

Example

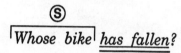

⎡Whose bike⎤ *has fallen?*

Explanation: This sentence has statement order because its SUBJECT *whose bike* comes BEFORE its STARTER *has*.

Important Note: There is a way to prove that *whose bike* is the main subject and that *has* is a movable starter. The PROOF is the fact that **all the words of a question always have the SAME GRAMMATICAL JOB as all the CORRESPONDING WORDS in the answer.**
Here is how this works.

Whose bike has fallen? ➡

Ed's bike has fallen. ➡

[has] Ⓢ MS
∧⎡*Ed's bike*⎤ *has fallen.* ➡

Ⓢ MS
⎡*Whose bike*⎤ *has fallen?*

NOTICE THAT YOU TRANSFER THE LABELS IN THE ANSWER TO THE CORRESPONDING WORDS IN THE QUESTION. (When you begin labeling every word, the question word itself will get the label of the word that serves as its answer.)

Note: For this to work, you must answer the question fully. First, you must REPEAT each word of the question. Second, you must PROVIDE A ONE-WORD ANSWER for the question word itself. Note how you should answer the question *How often does Ed run?*

Ed does run VERY *often.*

[Notice that this answer repeats each word possible and does provide the one-word answer *very* to the question word *how*.]

Truth G

Some question-word questions have question order.

Example

$$\overset{\text{(S)}}{}$$
Whose bike $\underline{\underline{has}}$ *⌐Carl⌐ borrowed?*

Explanation: This sentence has question order because the STARTER *has* comes BEFORE the SUBJECT *Carl.*

Another Important Note: You can prove that *Carl* is the subject by answering the question and noting the corresponding grammatical job. Note.

Whose bike has Carl borrowed? ➡

[has] Ⓢ **MS**
˄ *Carl* ⌐*has borrowed* *Joe's bike.* ➡

MS Ⓢ
⟨*Whose bike*⟩ *has* ⌐*Carl* *borrowed?*

As in Truth F, you transfer the labels of the answer to the corresponding words of the question.

The purpose for the **left- and right-pointing arrowheads** is TO INDICATE THAT THESE WORDS SHIFT AS YOU ANSWER THE QUESTION. However, they are **not**—nor could they be—front adverbials. In fact, the words *Joe's bike* have the job of object of verb in the answer, and therefore the words *whose bike* have the job of object of verb in the question.

Truth H

In question-word questions, the question word itself and/or the group of words that contains it have the name QUESTION-WORD WORDING.

Examples

WHO is coming?
WHOSE CUP is this?
AT WHICH LIGHT should I turn?
HOW SOON can you come?

In the examples, the question-word wording is in capitalized lettering.

Notice, first of all, that a VERB WORD marks the end of the question-word wording. This verb's starter is **always** the MOVABLE STARTER.

Second, notice that each of the question words does

TWO jobs at once. On the one hand, it causes the question. On the other, it has a job to do as part of its sentence. In the first sentence, *WHO* is serving as main subject. In the second sentence, *WHOSE* belongs with *cup* (in the same way that *Bill's* could belong with *cup*). In the third sentence, *WHICH* is part of the prepositional phrase *at which light*. In the fourth sentence, *HOW* belongs with *soon* (just as *very* could belong with *soon*).

Term to Remember: Question-Word Wording

> ## Question-Word Wording:
> **The wording at the beginning
> of a question-word question
> that includes the
> question word and ends
> at the movable starter.**

Truth J

You may NEVER shift a movable starter to the LEFT in question-word questions.

The reason for this is that these sentences **already are questions**. The English language does not permit you to make a group of words that is already a question into a question again. Note.

Who has left? ➡ ~~has who left~~

Truth K

When the starter after question-word wording CAN SHIFT TO THE RIGHT, you have QUESTION ORDER after the question-word wording. Therefore, you find the main subject TO THE RIGHT OF THE STARTER (between the starter's two positions).

Examples

MS Ⓢ [will]

For how long will⌐it⌐rain?

MS Ⓢ [does]

How often does⌐the river⌐overflow its banks?

Explanation: Only question order permits a starter to shift to the right—that is, to shift to the other side of its subject. In these questions, **expect the SUBJECT to stand immediately to the right of the starter that shifts.**

Helpful Note: It is allowable in English to start questions like this WITH THE FIRST WORD OF THE SUBJECT—THAT IS, WITH THE FIRST WORD AFTER THE MOVABLE STARTER—instead of starting them with question-word wording. **As soon as you do this, you find that the question-word wording immediately shifts to somewhere after the verb.** Note.

For how long will IT rain? ➡
It will rain for how long?

How often does THE river overflow its banks? ➡
THE RIVER does overflow its banks how often?

Here is the full labeling for these sentences.

$$\langle\textit{For how long}\rangle \overset{\text{MS}}{\textit{will}} \overset{\text{\textcircled{S}}}{\ulcorner\textit{it}\urcorner} \overset{\text{[will]}}{\underset{\wedge}{\textit{rain?}}}$$

$$\langle\textit{How often}\rangle \overset{\text{MS}}{\textit{does}} \overset{\text{\textcircled{S}}}{\ulcorner\textit{the river}\urcorner} \overset{\text{[does]}}{\underset{\wedge}{\textit{overflow}}} \textit{ its banks?}$$

Note that the main subject will be the words between the two positions of the movable starter. Note also that any companion verbs to the starter will follow it ONLY IN ITS AFTER-THE-SUBJECT LOCATION.

Truth L

When the starter after question-word wording can NOT shift to the RIGHT, it is part of the PREDICATE. Therefore, the question-word wording must BE the MAIN SUBJECT.

Examples

$$\overset{\text{\textcircled{S}}}{\ulcorner\textit{Which tree}\urcorner} \overset{\text{MS}}{\textit{has}} \textit{ lost its branch?}$$

$$\overset{\text{\textcircled{S}}}{\ulcorner\textit{Whose quarter}\urcorner} \overset{\text{MS}}{\underset{\wedge}{\textit{fell}}} \textit{ through the grate?}$$

Explanation: Only statement order will **not** permit a starter to move to the right. Consequently, the subject **must** be TO ITS LEFT—in other words, the SUBJECT MUST BE THE QUESTION-WORD WORDING ITSELF.

Labeling for Question-Word Wording

When question-word wording **is** the main subject, you label it as the main subject in the usual way (see Truth L).

When the movable starter shifts to the right, the

question-word wording will always shift too. It will shift to somewhere after the already shifted movable starter and its companion verb words. **Because it always shifts**, you will use a PAIR OF ARROWHEADS to mark the beginning and end of the question-word wording.

Labeling for Question-Word Wording That Can NOT Shift:

Place an OVERHEAD BRACKET over it with a CIRCLED S on top of the bracket.

Labeling for Question-Word Wording That CAN Shift:

Place an arrowhead on both sides of it. (Use NO other labeling for now.)

Test 2:
The Main Subject Test—for Questions (Expanded)

The time to note the existence of a question-word question and label it is during Test 2.

From now on, Test 2 will have some ADDED STEPS (but **no** new ground rules).

You will see the test (as expanded) first. Detailed explanation of the steps will then follow.

Test 2: The Main Subject Test—for Questions (Expanded)

STEPS (EXPANDED)

I. Note whether there is a <u>question mark</u>;

II. <u>Cover</u> any front adverbial if "yes";

III. If YES, SEE IF IT IS A <u>STARTER</u> QUESTION:
- A. If YES:
    1. Label the starter "MS";
    2. Reposition the starter INSIDE;
    3. Label the main subject;
    4. Label (inside) companion verb;
- B. If NO:
    1. Find first starter—label it "MS";
    2. Test if MS is shiftable TO <u>RIGHT</u>:
        - a. If YES:
            ① Reposition MS to right;
            ② Label main subject;
            ③ Label companion verb;
            ④ Label question-word wording (arrowheads);
        - b. If NO: Label question-word wording as "main subject."

IV. If A <u>PERIOD</u>: Proceed to Test 3.

Step I
Note whether there is a <u>question mark</u>.

You now know how important this is.

For a sentence that ends in a period, you go immediately to the tests that follow this—EVEN IF THE SEN-

TENCE STARTS WITH A QUESTION WORD. Note.

```
[hasn't]          Ⓢ                    MS
                                     [hasn't]
 ⌐How early we should leave⌐ has not been decided.
 ^                         ^
```

You apply the rest of this test ONLY when the end punctuation mark is a QUESTION MARK.

Step II
Cover any front adverbial if "yes."

It is especially important for **questions** that you cover the front adverbial. The reason is that you must find the FIRST WORD OF THE QUESTION TO SEE WHETHER IT IS OR IS NOT A STARTER—**the simplest way to tell the two types of questions apart.**

Step III, A

III. **If** YES, SEE IF IT IS A STARTER QUESTION:

    A. **If** YES:

        1. **Label the starter "MS";**
        2. **Reposition the starter INSIDE;**
        3. **Label the main subject;**
        4. **Label the (inside) companion verb.**

These are the SAME STEPS that you have been carrying out since you first learned the Main Subject Test—for Questions in Chapter 8.

● Do **_PRACTICE A_** (LABELING STARTER-VERB QUES-TIONS) in your *Skills Practice Book.*

Step III, B, 1

III. If YES, SEE IF IT IS A STARTER QUESTION:

A. If YES:

B. If NO:

    1. **Find the first starter—label it "MS".**

For this step, you carry out both verb tests until you are SURE that you have identified the FIRST starter.

Note that the rare kind of sentence in which the first starter is not the movable starter has been excluded from the practice work accompanying this text.

● Do **_PRACTICE B_** (LABELING THE MOVABLE STARTER IN QUESTION-WORD QUESTIONS) in your *Skills Practice Book.*

Step III, B, 2

III. If YES, SEE IF IT IS A STARTER QUESTION:

A. If YES:

B. If NO:

    2. **Test if the movable starter is shiftable** TO THE RIGHT.

This is the easiest way to tell whether the question-word wording is accompanied by question order (and therefore shifts elsewhere) or whether it is serving as main subject and belongs right there (because the rest of the sentence is the predicate).

● Do _PRACTICE C_ (TESTING WHETHER A STARTER CAN SHIFT TO THE RIGHT) in your *Skills Practice Book*.

Steps III, B, 2, a (ALL)

III. If YES, SEE IF IT IS A STARTER QUESTION:

   A. If YES:

   B. If NO:

      2. Test if MS is shiftable TO RIGHT:

         a. If YES:

            ① Reposition MS to right;

            ② Label main subject;

            ③ Label companion verb;

            ④ Label question-word wording (arrowheads).

These steps are exactly the same as the steps you carry out at Step III, A. You simply **also** add the special labeling for the question-word wording because this wording can shift to later in the sentence. Note this example.

⟨*If you <u>were building</u> a fire,*⟩⟨*what size branches*⟩

MS   Ⓢ **[would]**
<u>would</u> ⌐<u>you</u>⌐ₐ<u>choose</u>?

● Do _**PRACTICE D**_ (CARRYING OUT THE COMMA TEST AND THE MAIN SUBJECT TEST—FOR QUESTIONS (EXPANDED) THROUGH STEP III, B, 2, ④) in your *Skills Practice Book.*

● Do _**PRACTICE E**_ (MORE CARRYING OUT OF THE COMMA TEST AND THE MAIN SUBJECT TEST FOR QUESTIONS THROUGH STEP III, B, 2, A, ④) in your *Skills Practice Book.*

● Do _**PRACTICE F**_ (WRITING QUESTIONS WHOSE MOVABLE STARTER SHIFTS TO THE RIGHT) in your *Skills Practice Book.*

Step III, B, 2, b

III. If YES, SEE IF IT IS A STARTER QUESTION:

  A. If YES:

  B. If NO:

     2. **Test if the movable starter is shiftable** TO THE <u>RIGHT</u>**:**

        a. If YES:

        b. If NO: **Label question-word wording as "main subject."**

This is the easier of the question-word questions to label. You simply label the question-word wording by placing an overhead bracket over it with a circled *s* on top of the bracket. Note this example

FAV   [did vote]   Ⓢ   **MS**
                               [did become]

⟨*When you voted,*⟩ ⌐*who*⌐ *became president of the class?*

- Do *PRACTICE G* (CARRYING OUT ALL TESTS) in your *Skills Practice Book.*

- Do *PRACTICE H* (CARRYING OUT ALL TESTS) in your *Skills Practice Book.*

- Do *PRACTICE J* (CARRYING OUT ALL TESTS) in your *Skills Practice Book.*

- Do *PRACTICE K* (WRITING QUESTIONS WHOSE MOVABLE STARTER CAN <u>NOT</u> SHIFT TO THE RIGHT) in your *Skills Practice Book.*

Important Note: At this point, you should REVIEW Test 2 AS A WHOLE (see page 231). Then proceed to Practices L and M.

- Do *PRACTICE L* (CARRYING OUT ALL THE TESTS) in your *Skills Practice Book.*

- Do *PRACTICE M* (CARRYING OUT ALL THE TESTS) in your *Skills Practice Book.*

Endnote

Question Order after *Nor*: Another use of question order is after the (less common) conjunction *nor.* Here is an example.

                *He has not refused **NOR** <u>will</u> **HE.***

Note that no question resulted from question order in this sentence.

Review

Questions Words Listed: *HOW, WHAT, WHEN, WHERE, WHICH, WHO, WHOSE, WHOM, WHY.*

Question-Word Question: A question caused by a question-asking question word near its start.

Statement Order: A SUBJECT comes BEFORE ITS STARTER.

Question Order: A STARTER comes BEFORE ITS SUBJECT.

Question-Word Wording: The wording at the beginning of a question-word question that includes the question word and ends at the movable starter.

Labeling for Question-Word Wording That Can NOT Shift: Place an OVERHEAD BRACKET over it with a CIRCLED S on top of the bracket.

Labeling for Question-Word Wording That CAN Shift: Place an arrowhead on both sides of it. (Use NO other labeling for now.)

[continued]

TEST 2:   Main Subject Test—for Questions (Expanded):
I.   Note whether there is a <u>question mark</u>;
II.   <u>Cover</u> any front adverbial if "yes";
III.   If YES, SEE IF IT IS A <u>STARTER</u> QUESTION:
    A. If YES:
        1. Label the starter "MS;"
        2. Reposition the starter INSIDE;
        3. Label the main subject;
        4. Label the (inside) companion verb words;
    B. If NO:
        1. Find the first starter—label it "MS;"
        2. Test if MS is shiftable TO <u>RIGHT</u>:
           a. If YES:
              ① Reposition the MS to right;
              ② Label the main subject;
              ③ Label any (inside) companion verb words;
              ④ Label question-word wording with a pair of arrowheads;
           b. If NO: Label the question-word wording as the "main subject."
IV.   If A <u>PERIOD</u>: PROCEED TO TEST 3.

Chapter 14

Subjects versus Objects

You may recall that the job of nouns is second in importance in English—second to the job of verbs.

In this chapter, you will learn about these jobs in greater depth. The benefits for you should be greater self-confidence in both your writing and your reading.

Truths about Noun Jobs in Common

This section discusses several important truths that have a bearing on the most important noun jobs.

Truth A

The importance of the jobs of nouns is that they occupy those territories whose words alone supply the answers to the centrally important questions *who, whom,* and/or *what* when these are asked before a verb and after a verb or preposition.

Explanation: Each of these expressions (below) is INCOMPLETE. The blank spaces that stand in the noun-job territories raise those questions that only nouns or their replacers can answer. Note.

_____ *found* a toy. [WHO or WHAT *found a toy?*]

The boy *found* _____. [*The boy found* WHOM/WHAT?]

 The boy came with _____. [*The boy came with* WHOM/WHAT?]

NOUN-JOB WORDING ALONE can fill these blank spaces.

Truth B

The noun jobs take their names from the type of territory they occupy.

When nouns or their replacers occupy the territory IN FRONT OF a verb, they have the name SUBJECT.

When they occupy an AFTERWARD territory—that is, the territories after either a verb or a preposition—they have the name OBJECT.

Note: In grammar, the term "object" implies the carrying over of some IMPACT from the "force" of a verb or preposition onto whatever fills its "object" territory. See this illustrated.

Bill *broke* THE BAT.

He studies |*for* AN HOUR.

Though the impact from the verb *broke* on its object *the bat* is clear, the impact of the preposition *for* on its object *an hour* is far less clear. In fact, MANY VERBS AND PREPOSITIONS HAVE NO DETECTABLE IMPACT ON THEIR OBJECTS. Note.

Bill **lacks** THE TIME.

Bill came **with** FRIENDS.

Truth C

The primary jobs of nouns are to answer (or ask) *WHO, WHOM,* or *WHAT* when asked <u>before</u> a VERB or <u>after</u> a MAIN VERB or <u>after</u> a PREPOSITION.

Here is a diagram to illustrate this.

| Subject | { | *WHO* *WHAT* <u>*Verb*</u> | *WHOM* *WHAT* | } | Object of Verb |

| | *WHOM* | { | Object of |
| Preposition | *WHAT* | } | Preposition |

Study this chart to understand the different places and purposes for which you will now be asking *WHAT*.

TEST During Which You Ask *WHAT*	Where You Ask *WHAT*	Why You Ask *WHAT*
Helpers Subtest	AFTER HELPERS	To find word to test with ING Subtest
Noun Job Test— for Remaining Subjects	BEFORE HELPERS	To find the subject of a dependent clause
Noun Job Test—for Object of Verb	AFTER a MAIN VERB	To find an object of verb
Noun Job Test—for Objects of Prepositions	AFTER a PREPOSI- TION	To find an object of preposition

Terms to Know

There are terms that you must now know—a <u>NON</u>MOVABLE STARTER, a <u>NON</u>MAIN SUBJECT, an OBJECT OF VERB, a PREPOSITION, and an OBJECT OF PREPOSITION.

NONmovable Starter:
Any starter remaining after you have identified the movable starter.

NONmain Subject:
The wording before a NONmovable starter that answers *WHO* or *WHAT* when asked before the starter—in context.

Object of Verb:
The wording that answers *WHOM* or *WHAT* when asked after any verb (other than *be* or a verb *be* can replace—see endnotes in this and next chapter).

The Most Important Prepositions:

FROM	*WITH*	*IN*
ON	*BY*	*FOR*
AT	*TO*	*OF*

Object of Preposition:
The wording that answers *WHOM* or *WHAT* when asked after a preposition.

Truth D

The core of a dependent clause is its verb, and that verb must have a subject and may have an object of verb.

You remember that a dependent clause is wording that you can **not** turn into a question though it has a verb, a subject, and an introducer. The verb's <u>NON</u>MOVABLE STARTER is **both** the MARK OF ITS PRESENCE **and** the CORE OF THE CLAUSE. Note.

*[Because JOE **HAD MISPLACED** HIS WATCH]*

Notice how the side brackets ([ ]) mark the beginning and ending of the dependent clause. Notice, too, how the verb *had misplaced* has *JOE* for its subject and *HIS WATCH* for its object of verb.

You remember that *because* is one of the nine SUBORDINATING CONJUNCTIONS that help you begin sentences better. These are the other eight: *since, though/although, if, before, after, while,* and *until.* THE JOB OF THESE SUBORDINATING CONJUNCTIONS IS TO BE INTRODUCERS OF DEPENDENT CLAUSES. YOU MUST NOW RECOGNIZE THESE AS INTRODUCERS **ON SIGHT**.

You remember, too, that question words as well can have this role. Note.

WHEN the cold spell would pass couldn't be forecast.

YOU MUST NOW RECOGNIZE QUESTION WORDS TOO AS DEPENDENT CLAUSE INTRODUCERS **ON SIGHT**.

Truth E

Dependent clauses—plus their verbs and subjects—can come anywhere in a sentence.

You already know that extra verbs—and therefore dependent clauses—can appear inside a main subject and inside front adverbials. They can also appear inside an object of verb and inside an object of preposition. In addition, they can appear alongside either of these and/or alongside each other. In other words, they can appear ANYWHERE. See Chapter 17 for more details.

Labeling for Noun-Job Wording

This section contains important labeling advice.

Symbols for ALL Noun Jobs

This text has reserved the **OVERHEAD BRACKET** as the symbol to identify ANY/EVERY SORT OF NOUN-JOB WORD-ING. (You remember that you are already using it for main subjects, the most important of all the noun jobs.)

There are two reasons for this. First, the type of wording that can do a noun job is the same no matter what the job or where the "territory."

Second, the consistent use of these brackets will make it easier for you when you come to the next chapter because it will be under these "umbrellas" that you will first look for any noun, pronoun, adjective, or article (as well as for noun or adjective clauses—see Chapter 17).

Height of Bracket That You Must Use

In the next chapter, you will be placing lettering not only **over** each bracket (see below) but also **under** each bracket. YOU MUST RAISE YOUR BRACKETS HIGH ENOUGH SO THERE WILL BE ENOUGH ROOM.

Neatness Needed

If you draw the lines for the brackets too faintly or sloppily, this will hinder your successful finding and labeling of the elements that the bracket encloses when you come to Chapter 15. DRAW THESE OVERHEAD BRACKETS WITH CARE.

Labeling for Noun-Job Wording according to Job

Each noun job has as its label an ABBREVIATION which you place ON TOP OF THE OVERHEAD BRACKET. The labeling for the SUBJECT OF A DEPENDENT CLAUSE (all the subjects other than the main subject) is an UNCIRC-LED S. The labeling for an OBJECT OF VERB is *OV*. The labeling for an OBJECT OF PREPOSITION is *OP*.

Note that the label for a preposition (a word like *with* or *for*) is a RIGHT-ANGLE SYMBOL or "chair" that the preposition appears to "sit on."

Here is a sentence that demonstrates all these labels.

[is] Ⓢ MS · · · · · · · OP · Intro.
∧⌈Joe⌉ *is heading* |*for* ⌈*home*⌉ [*because*

S [did leave] · OV
⌈*he*⌉∧ *left* ⌈*his homework*⌉ *there*.]

Labeling for NONmain Subjects:
Use an OVERHEAD BRACKET with an UNCIRCLED *S* on top of the bracket.

Labeling for Object of Verb:
Use an OVERHEAD BRACKET with the the lettering *OV* on top of the bracket.

Labeling for Object of Preposition:
Use an OVERHEAD BRACKET with the the lettering *OP* on top of the bracket.

> ## Labeling for a Preposition:
> ### Use a RIGHT-ANGLE SYMBOL for the preposition to "sit on."

In the practice exercises, you will also see the label *INT*. This is the label for the INTRODUCER (of the dependent clause). You will find this label supplied for you but only on those introducers that you are still unfamiliar with.

Test 7:
The Noun Job Tests

Here is TEST 7 in full. Notice that it contains **all** of the Noun Job Tests as SUBTESTS. Explanations of the subtests will follow.

Test 7: The Noun Job Tests

Part A	Part B	Part C	Part D
NONmain Subject Subtest	Object of Verb Subtest	Preposition Subtest	Object of Preposition Subtest
Ask *WHO* or *WHAT* before all NONmovable starters.	Ask *WHOM* or *WHAT* after all MAIN verbs.	Know the NINE key prepositions ON SIGHT.	Ask *WHOM* or *WHAT* after all prepositions.

Note: You must observe that this is TEST 7. In other words, you carry out—in complete detail—every step of every test from Test 1 to Test 6 BEFORE you carry out Test 7.

ORDER IN WHICH TO CARRY OUT THE TESTS
1. Comma Test
2. Main Subject Test—for Questions
3. Helpers + WHAT/ING Word Verb Test
4. Do/does/did Test
5. Movable Starter Test
6. Main Subject Test—for Statements
7. NOUN JOB TESTS

You will now learn the SUBTESTS one at a time. The TRUTHS behind each subtest will come **first**; the SUBTEST itself, explanation, and practice **will follow.**

Part A
NONmain Subject
Subtest

Truths about Subjects

Truth A

Except in commands, every starter—visible or supplied—that is not a movable starter has a subject before it.

In English, there are AS MANY SUBJECTS AS THERE ARE VERBS that do not express a command. In addition, THERE ARE AS MANY NONMAIN SUBJECTS AS THERE ARE NONMOVABLE STARTERS.

Truth B

You find NONmain subjects by asking *WHO* or *WHAT* before all NONmovable starters.

Since these remaining starters are **not** movable starters, you can **not** shift them to find their accompanying subjects. Instead, you must ask *WHO* or *WHAT* before each and LOOK FOR THE ANSWER IN THE RIGHT PLACE—NAMELY, IN THE SUBJECT TERRITORY RIGHT BEFORE THE STARTER. Note.

FAV INT   S [does ring] [should] Ⓢ   MS
[⟨When ⌐the phone⌐ rings⟩⌐someone⌐ should answer it.

When you ask *WHAT rings*, the answer is *the phone*.

The Noun Job Tests			
Part A **NONmain Subject** **Subtest**	Part B Object of Verb Subtest	Part C Prepo- sition Subtest	Part D Object of Prepo- sition Subtest
Ask *WHO* or *WHAT* <u>before</u> all NONmov-able starters.	Ask *WHOM* or *WHAT* <u>after</u> all MAIN verbs.	Know the NINE key preposi- tions ON <u>SIGHT</u>.	Ask *WHOM* or *WHAT* <u>after</u> all preposi- tions.

Explanation: When you carry out the first subtest, the NONmain Subject Subtest, you **first** look for ALL STARTERS THAT ARE **NOT** MOVABLE. You **then** ask *WHO* or *WHAT* before each. **Finally,** you expect the answer—the starter's accompanying subject—to occupy the territory to its LEFT. Each subject stands BETWEEN the INTRODUCER (that usually starts the clause) and its NONMOVABLE STARTER. Note.

[will] Ⓢ   MS   INT ｓ

ᴧ⌐Pedro⌐ <u>will</u> <u>come</u>[⟨*if* ⌐he⌐ <u>is</u> able to⟩]

Important Note: For the practice work accompanying this text, you must KNOW ON SIGHT both ALL the EIGHT subordinating conjunctions **and** ALL the NINE question words that can serve as introducers to dependent clauses.

- **Do** *PRACTICE A* (CARRYING OUT TESTS 1-7 THROUGH THE NONMAIN SUBJECT SUBTEST) in your *Skills Practice Book.*

- **Do** *PRACTICE B* (CARRYING OUT TESTS 1-7 THROUGH THE NONMAIN SUBJECT SUBTEST) in your *Skills Practice Book.*

Part B
Object of Verb Subtest

Truths about Objects of Verbs

Truth A

OFTEN verbs do have an "object of verb" after them.

This happens so often—more than half the time possibly—that you must use your Object of Verb Subtest for every verb you meet.

Truth B

There is a special name both for verbs that have objects and for those that do not.

Grammarians have names for verbs according to whether they can or cannot have an object. VERBS THAT

CAN HAVE AN OBJECT have the name TRANSITIVE VERB. (In Latin, *trans-* means "across" and *it* means "to go.")

In contrast, VERBS THAT DO NOT OR CANNOT HAVE AN OBJECT have the name INTRANSITIVE VERB. Note that DICTIONARIES use the abbreviation *vt* for TRANSITIVE VERBS and *vi* for INTRANSITIVE VERBS.

Examples

TRANSITIVE VERB: *Sue BROKE HER NECKLACE.*

INTRANSITIVE VERB: *Cats MOVE quietly.*

> ## Transitive Verb:
> **A verb that can or must have an object of verb.**

> ## Intransitive Verb:
> **A verb that cannot or does not have an object of verb.**

Truth C

You find objects of verbs by asking *WHOM* or *WHAT* after a verb.

Notice that you do this for EVERY verb and that the wording that answers *WHOM* or *WHAT* can be OF ANY LENGTH.

FAV   INT   [did use]   OV   [did]Ⓢ   MS [did know]
[⟨Whenever Paul ᴧ used his favorite bat,⟩] he ᴧ knew

          OV
[INT S   OV
[that he could get a hit.]]

256

Notice that the object of the verb *knew* is the whole dependent clause *that he could get a hit*—whose verb *could get* ITSELF has an object of verb.

Note: Take note that when wording answers *WHAT* (or *WHO*) after the verb *be* or verbs that the verb *be* can replace you no longer have an object of verb. Instead, you have types of wording that you are not responsible for in this text—namely, a predicate noun or a predicate adjective. See the explanations of these in the endnotes in this chapter and the next.

Truth D

When wording after a verb answers *WHEN,* ***WHERE, HOW,* or *WHY,* it is NOT doing the job of object of verb.**

Sometimes wording after a verb does not answer *WHAT* or *WHOM.* Instead, it can answer *WHEN, WHERE, HOW,* or *WHY.* These are questions that adverbs answer (see Chapter 16). Note.

*Ed arrived **after the bell.***
[*After the bell* answers *WHEN.*]

*Who lives **on Houston Street?***
[*On Houston Street* answers *WHERE.*]

*Larry went **by car.***
[*By car* answers *HOW.*]

*We exercise **for our health.***
[*For our health* answers *WHY.*]

Truth E

When some wording answers *WHOM* or *WHAT* and OTHER wording answers *WHEN, WHERE, HOW,* and/or *WHY,* the object of verb is JUST THOSE WORDS THAT ANSWER <u>*WHOM*</u> or <u>*WHAT*</u>.

Sometimes wording of two or more sorts will follow a verb. Label as object of verb ONLY **those words that** answer *WHOM* or *WHAT*. Note.

MS
[did] Ⓢ [did put] OV
ᶺ ⌐He⌐ *put* ⌐his knapsack⌐ on the ground.
  ᶺ ‗‗‗

MS
[did] Ⓢ [did see]
OV
⌐Ed⌐ *saw* ⌐me⌐ in the corridor today.
ᶺ ᶺ‗‗‗

The Noun Job Tests			
Part A	Part B	Part C	Part D
NONmain Subject Subtest	**Object of Verb Subtest**	Preposition Subtest	Object of Preposition Subtest
Ask *WHO* or *WHAT* before all NONmovable starters.	**Ask *WHOM* or *WHAT* after all MAIN verbs.**	Know the NINE key prepositions ON SIGHT.	Ask *WHOM* or *WHAT* after all prepositions.

Explanation: Again, you carry out Tests 1-6 **before** you carry out Test 7. Inside Test 7, you should carry out the Subtests **in order.**

For this Object of Verb Subtest, you must be especially careful as to **where** you ask *WHAT*. You do **not** ask it after a helping verb. You ask it AFTER the **LAST WORD** IN THE VERB PHRASE or AFTER a **STAND-ALONE VERB.** You label as object of verb **just those words that answer *whom* or *what*—and NO others.**

If there is wording after the verb, it must answer *WHOM* or *WHAT* but **not** *WHEN, WHERE, HOW,* or *WHY*. Note.

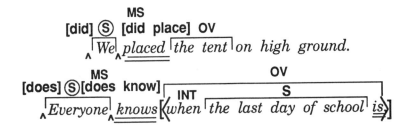

MS
[did] Ⓢ [did place] OV
We placed the tent on high ground.

MS   OV
[does] Ⓢ [does know] INT   S
Everyone knows when the last day of school is

- Do *PRACTICE C* (CARRYING OUT TESTS 1-7, THROUGH THE OBJECT OF VERB SUBTEST) in your *Skills Practice Book.*

- Do *PRACTICE D* (CARRYING OUT TESTS 1-7, THROUGH THE OBJECT OF VERB SUBTEST) in your *Skills Practice Book.*

- Do *PRACTICE E* (CARRYING OUT TESTS 1-7, THROUGH THE OBJECT OF VERB SUBTEST) in your *Skills Practice Book.*

Parts C and D
Preposition Subtest and Object of Preposition Subtest

Truths about Prepositions and Their Objects

Truth A

There are nine prepositions that occur over 92% of the time.

A grammarian studied usage of English and learned that nine prepositions do more than 92% of the work.

These nine are:

FROM	*WITH*	*IN*
ON	*BY*	*FOR*
AT	*TO*	*OF*

Truth B

Every preposition must have an "object" after it that answers *WHOM* or *WHAT*.

EXPECT an "object" to follow EVERY preposition.
In addition, this object answers the questions of an "object"—namely, WHOM or WHAT. Note.

Maria came WITH A FRIEND.
[*A friend* answers WHOM.]

George came WITH HIS TOOLS.
[*His tools* answers WHAT.]

Truth C

The preposition and its object form a tight-knit grammatical unit.

The preposition and its object form so tightly knit a unit that all its words—AS A UNIT—PERFORM A SINGLE GRAMMATICAL JOB. This unit of words has the name PREPOSITIONAL PHRASE. Note this sentence.

George went TO THE SHORE FOR A WEEK.

In this sentence, there are two prepositional phrases—namely, *to the shore* and *for a week*. The phrase *to the shore* answers WHERE after the verb *went* and the phrase *for a week* answers HOW LONG.

Prepositional Phrase:

A preposition plus its object.

Truth D

An object of preposition can include one or more WHOLE prepositional phrases.

When testing for an object of preposition, you must be careful to include all (and only) the words that answer *WHOM* or *WHAT*. Note.

Janice went TO THE STORE.

Janice went TO THE STORE BY THE GAS STATION.

Janice went TO THE STORE BY THE GAS STATION
WITH THE LOWEST PRICES.

Janice went TO THE STORE BY THE GAS STATION
WITH THE LOWEST PRICES yesterday.

When you ask *Janice went to WHAT*, the answer—for each sentence—is ALL THE DARKENED WORDING. Notice how for each sentence (except the last) the wording that answers *WHAT* **includes more and more words.**

Truth E

An object of verb can NEVER be just a prepositional phrase, but it can INCLUDE one.

Though prepositional phrases do perform grammatical jobs, they do **not** perform the job of object of verb. Note.

The deer disappeared in the woods.

When you ask *disappeared WHOM* or *disappeared WHAT*, there is NO ANSWER. The prepositional phrase *in the woods* answers *WHERE* and **not** *WHAT*.

An object of verb cannot **be** a prepositional phrase. However, an object of verb can INCLUDE a prepositional phrase. Note.

I found the book of my brother.

When you ask *found WHAT*, the **whole** answer is *THE BOOK OF MY BROTHER* (the prepositional phrase is *OF MY BROTHER*). Note this sentence with its labels.

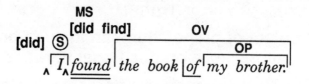

$$\overset{\text{MS}}{\underset{\text{[did find]}}{}}$$

[did] Ⓢ   OV

               OP

∧ ⌐I⌐ *found* the book ⌊*of*⌐ *my brother.*

The Noun Job Tests

Part A	Part B	Part C	Part D
NONmain Subject Subtest	Object of Verb Subtest	**Preposition Subtest**	Object of Preposition Subtest
Ask WHO or WHAT before all NONmovable starters.	Ask WHOM or WHAT after all MAIN verbs.	Know the NINE key prepositions ON SIGHT.	Ask WHOM or WHAT after all prepositions.

Explanation: There are close to 100 prepositions in English, but those that occur so frequently that you MUST know them ON SIGHT are these nine:

Prepositions That You MUST Know:

FROM	WITH	IN
ON	BY	FOR
AT	TO	OF

These words are the markers of the start of prepositional phrases just as the twenty starters are markers of the presence of a verb. KNOW THESE NINE WORDS BY HEART.

Here is a list of other prepositions and their uses for your information.

Other Prepositions Listed according to What They Indicate

Direction	Action	Position	
up	through	over	past
down	into	above	between
along	across	under	among
around	aboard	underneath	beside
about	off	outside	along-
past	onto	inside	side
by	upon	within	near
toward	against	beyond	around

Circumstance		Time Relationship	
besides	but	until	during
like	despite	after	through-
as	concerning	before	out
without	than	since	
except			

● Do **PRACTICE F** (IDENTIFYING PREPOSITIONS) in your *Skills Practice Book.*

● Do **_PRACTICE G_** (Carrying out Tests 1-7, through the Preposition Subtest) IN YOUR *SKILLS PRACTICE BOOK*.

The Noun Job Tests			
Part A	**Part B**	**Part C**	**Part D**
NONmain Subject Subtest	Object of Verb Subtest	Preposition Subtest	**Object of Preposition Subtest**
Ask *WHO* or *WHAT* <u>before</u> all NONmovable starters.	Ask *WHOM* or *WHAT* <u>after</u> all MAIN verbs.	Know the NINE key prepositions <u>ON SIGHT</u>.	**Ask *WHOM* or *WHAT* <u>after</u> all prepositions.**

Explanation: Since this is Test 7, you always carry out **both** all other tests **and** all the other subtests for this test **first**.

When you look for the answer to *WHOM* or *WHAT* after each preposition, you must include ALL those words—but ONLY those words—that answer *WHOM* or *WHAT*. You will often include additional **whole** prepositional phrases. Note.

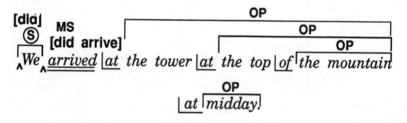

Notice that **all the words** *at the top of the mountain* answer *WHICH tower* and that the words *of the mountain* answer *WHOSE top*. On the other hand, the words *at midday* answer *WHEN* after the verb *arrived*—just as **all the words** *at the tower at the top of the mountain* answer *WHERE* after the verb *arrived*.

- Do *PRACTICE H* (Carrying out the Object of Preposition Subtest for Test 7) in your *Skills Practice Book.*

- Do *PRACTICE J* (Carrying out Tests 1-7 in their entirety) in your *Skills Practice Book.*

- Do *PRACTICE K* (Carrying out Tests 1-7 in their entirety) in your *Skills Practice Book.*

Writing Tips for Correct Choice of Pronoun Spelling

You know that you spell the personal pronouns differently according to whether you use them as subjects or as objects. Here is a review of these sets of spellings.

Spellings for Personal Pronoun Groups by Type	
As Subject	As Object
I	*me*
you	*you*
he	*him*
she	*her*
it	*it*
we	*us*
they	*them*

The name for such a choice of spelling in grammar is CASE.

Case:

The spelling you choose for a pronoun to indicate the type of noun job that it is performing.

There are two "cases" of special importance for writers, the NOMINATIVE CASE and the OBJECTIVE CASE. You use the NOMINATIVE CASE to indicate that the pronoun is doing the job of subject (or of predicate noun—see below). Note.

I know [that WE will succeed].
SHE asked [whether WE were coming].

Nominative Case:

The spelling you choose for a pronoun to indicate that it is doing the job of subject or predicate noun.

You use the OBJECTIVE CASE to indicate that the pronoun is doing the job of object of verb or object of preposition (primarily). Note.

Al said to Jane and ME [that the book was for HER].
When we throw sticks for our dog,
he brings THEM to US.

Objective Case:

The spelling you choose for a pronoun to indicate (usually) that it is doing the job of object of either verb or preposition.

Note: The question word WHO (in its use as a question

word **and** as introducer of a clause) has "case"—you use the spelling *WHO* when this "pronoun" does the job of subject and the spelling *WHOM* when it does the job of object. Note.

WHO knows [WHO is coming]?
Al asked [to WHOM he should send them].
[See Chapter 17 to learn more about the use of the word *WHO* as subject inside a dependent clause.]

● Do *PRACTICE L* (USING THE NOMINATIVE CASE IN SENTENCES OF YOUR OWN) in your *Skills Practice Book.*

● Do *PRACTICE M* (USING THE OBJECTIVE CASE IN SENTENCES OF YOUR OWN) in your *Skills Practice Book.*

Endnotes

Indirect Object: There is a less common noun job that you may want to know about. It is to answer *TO WHOM, TO WHAT, FOR WHOM,* or *FOR WHAT* after a verb. Note.

Harry gave THE DOG a bone.

When you ask *gave WHAT*, the answer is *a bone.* The words *the dog* answer *TO WHOM* after the verb *gave.*

Take note that there is another way to write this sentence in English. Observe.

Harry gave a bone TO THE DOG.

The clue that a verb has an indirect object is that it **appears** to have two objects right beside each other. You then test the first to see whether it is an indirect object instead of the true object.

Grammarians give the name INDIRECT OBJECT to this noun job and often call the object of the verb the DIRECT OBJECT.

This text does not use the name "direct object" and

does not include indirect objects in its practice material.

Predicate Nouns: The PREDICATE NOUN is wording after the verb (therefore, in the "predicate") that better identifies the subject—that is, it adds information about the subject. Note.

Brian was THE CAPTAIN.
Sheila was A CHEERLEADER.

The predicate nouns are *the captain* and *a cheerleader*. Notice that both of these predicate nouns answer WHAT when asked after the verb *was*. However, no "force" carries over from the verb as if to an object. Rather, the verb *was* serves to link the predicate nouns to their subjects. It identifies them as being the same.

The verb *be*—in all its spellings—can have a predicate noun follow it. However, other verbs also can have predicate nouns follow them. An example is the verb *become*. Note.

Joanne became THE PRESIDENT.

The test of whether wording that answers WHAT is a predicate noun is whether the verb *be* (in the same tense and agreement) could replace it. Note.

Joanne WAS THE PRESIDENT.

This text will not include predicate nouns in its practice material.

Noun in Apposition: There is still another noun job you may wish to know about. Observe this sentence.

[has]   Ⓢ   MS
⌐Fred, my brother,⌐ <u>has left</u>.

Notice that TWO nouns and/or noun replacers occupy the SAME noun job territory, the **subject territory**.

Whenever two nouns and/or noun replacers occupy the same noun-job territory (and have no coordinating conjunction "joining" them), the **second** noun or noun replacer has the name NOUN IN APPOSITION (meaning "in a nearby position"). The effect of such a noun in apposition is to add additional information about the noun or noun replacer to its immediate left.

It is helpful to know that a noun in apposition can stand beside a noun or noun replacer in practically all of the noun-job territories.

This text will not include nouns in apposition in its practice material.

Review

CONTENT IN DARKER LETTERING MUST BE REMEMBERED.

NONmovable Starter: Any starter that remains after you have identified the movable starter.

NONmain Subject: The wording before a NONmovable starter that answers *WHO* or *WHAT* when asked before the starter (and in context).

Object of Verb: The wording that answers *WHOM* or *WHAT* when asked after any verb (other than the verb *be* or a verb that the verb *be* can replace).

Prepositions (to Be Remembered) Listed: *FROM, WITH, IN, ON, BY, FOR, AT, TO, OF.*

Object of Preposition: The wording that answers *WHOM* or *WHAT* when asked after a preposition.

Prepositional Phrase: A preposition plus its object.

Case: The spelling you choose for a pronoun to indicate the type of noun job that it is performing.

Nominative Case: The spelling you choose for a pronoun to indicate that it is doing the job of subject or predicate noun.

Objective Case: The spelling you choose for a pronoun to indicate (usually) that it is doing the job of object of verb or object of preposition.

Transitive Verb: A verb that can or must have an object of verb.

Intransitive Verb: A verb that cannot or does not have an object of verb.

Labeling for NONmain Subjects: Use an OVERHEAD BRACKET with an UNCIRCLED *S* on top of the bracket.

Labeling for Objects of Verb: Use an OVERHEAD BRACKET with the lettering *OV* on top of the bracket.

Labeling for Prepositions: Use a RIGHT-ANGLE SYMBOL for the preposition to "sit on."

Labeling for Objects of Preposition: Use an OVER-HEAD BRACKET with the lettering *OP* on top of the bracket.

Order for the Tests:
1. Comma Test
2. Main Subject Test—for Questions
3. Helpers + WHAT/ING Word Verb Test
4. Do/does/did Test
5. Movable Starter Test
6. Main Subject Test—for Statements
7. Noun Job Tests

Test 7: The Noun Job Tests:
Part A—NONmain Subject Subtest: Ask *WHO* or *WHAT* before all NONmovable starters;
Part B—Object of Verb Subtest: Ask *WHOM* or *WHAT* after all MAIN verbs;
Part C—Preposition Subtest: Know the words *from, with, in, on, by, for, at, to, of* as prepositions ON SIGHT;
Part D—Object of Preposition Subtest: Ask *WHOM* or *WHAT* after all prepositions.

Chapter 15

Adjectives

You now have a picture of how the most important building blocks of the sentence work together to form a sentence. However, this picture is not complete until you examine how adjectives and adverbs fit into it.

The purpose of this chapter is to help you understand the jobs of the adjective and of its near relative the article, especially as you find these inside noun clusters.

This should give you richer choices in your writing and clearer understanding as you read.

Truths about Adjectives

These truths explain the nature and role of adjectives.

Truth A

The job of an adjective is to limit the meaning of (that is, "modify") a noun or pronoun.

Examples

TWO TREES
TALL TREES
MAPLE TREES
PRETTY TREES

In these expressions, the adjectives are the four words TWO, TALL, MAPLE, and PRETTY.

Truth B

Adjectives limit the meaning of a noun or pronoun by answering *WHICH, WHOSE, HOW MANY/MUCH,* **or** *WHAT KIND OF* **when asked BEFORE the noun or pronoun.**

Explanation: You would hesitate to say *Homeowners keep pets* because you have put no limitations on the word *homeowners.* These are the questions about "homeowners" that your reader wants to know the answer to:

> *WHICH homeowners?*
> *WHOSE homeowners?*
> *HOW MANY homeowners?*
> *WHAT KIND OF homeowners?*

As soon as you answer each question, you use an ADJECTIVE. Note.

> *NEARBY homeowners* [answers *WHICH*]
> *FAYETTEVILLE'S homeowners* [answers *WHOSE*]
> *COUNTLESS homeowners* [answers *HOW MANY*]
> *COUNTRY homeowners* [answers *WHAT KIND OF*]

Adjective:

A word that answers *WHICH, WHOSE, HOW MANY/MUCH,* or *WHAT KIND OF* when asked before a noun or pronoun.

● Do *PRACTICE A* (DETERMINING THE QUESTION ANSWERED BY AN ADJECTIVE) in your *Skills Practice Book.*

Truth C

Adjectives most commonly appear INSIDE A NOUN CLUSTER.

Examples

[are]   Ⓢ

‸*The* **TWO TALL PRETTY MAPLE** *trees*

          OP

MS

are ⌊*on* ⌐**MY** *property.*

The adjectives **TWO, TALL, PRETTY,** and **MAPLE** are inside the SUBJECT territory; the adjective **MY** is inside an OBJECT OF PREPOSITION territory.

You must now know the definition for a noun cluster that you learned in Chapter 2.

Noun Cluster:

All the words in a noun-job territory when the chief word is a noun or pronoun.

Important Note: For the work in this text, the ONLY PLACE TO LOOK FOR ADJECTIVES will be INSIDE A NOUN CLUSTER. Note that this is the territory where close to 90% of adjectives appear.

Truth D

Adjectives can appear on EITHER SIDE of the noun or pronoun that they belong with (modify).

Examples

LARGE **books**   **books** *AVAILABLE*

RED **ones**   **something** *NEW*

In these expressions, the adjectives *LARGE* and *RED* come **before** their noun or pronoun while the adjectives *AVAILABLE* and *NEW* come **after** theirs.

Truth E

Several adjectives can belong with (modify) the same noun or pronoun.

Example

ONE WORTHWHILE book MENTIONED was the <u>Bible</u>.

In this sentence, the adjectives *ONE, WORTHWHILE,* and *MENTIONED* all modify (answer some question about) the SAME NOUN—namely, *book.*

Notice that all FOUR words are part of the SAME MAIN SUBJECT—*Was ONE WORTHWHILE BOOK MENTIONED the* <u>Bible</u>.

Truth F

Adjectives that answer the question *WHAT KIND OF* can appear in a "string" with a comma taking the place of each possible *AND.*

Example

HIGH, RACING, FLEECY clouds passed overhead.

Notice that you could say *HIGH* **and** *RACING* **and** *FLEECY clouds passed overhead.*

Truth G

An easy proof that a word in a noun cluster is an adjective is that you can SAY IT TOGETHER WITH THE CLUSTER'S CHIEF NOUN OR PRONOUN.

Example

Beth owns **SEVERAL** *rather* **RARE** **STAMPS**.

In this sentence, you **can** say the adjectives **SEVERAL** and **RARE** with the noun STAMPS. Note.

SEVERAL STAMPS
RARE STAMPS

Note that you can **not** say ~~rather STAMPS~~. However, since you can say *rather* **RARE**, the word *rather* is an ADVERB—the kind of adverb that is sayable with an adjective (see Chapter 16).
See this more graphically presented.

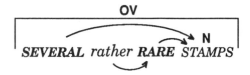

Important Note: This proof will become the main part of the ADJECTIVE TEST later in this chapter.

Labeling for Wording inside Noun Clusters

The labels that you will use for NOUNS, PRONOUNS, and ADJECTIVES will be abbreviations for the words.

Labeling for Nouns:
Place the letter *N* over each noun.

Labeling for Pronouns:
Place the lettering *PRN* over each pronoun.

● Do **_PRACTICE B_** (FINDING ADJECTIVES INSIDE NOUN CLUSTERS) in your **Skills Practice Book.**

Truth H

A prepositional phrase can do the job of an adjective.

Example

The ROOM WITH A CARPET has a beige tone.
The TOY OF THE CHILD has fallen.

Notice that the two prepositional phrase *with a carpet* and *of the child* have all these requirements for an adjective:

- They are INSIDE a noun cluster;
- They are AFTER a KEYWORD noun or pronoun;
- They are SAYABLE WITH the noun—*room with a carpet* and t*oy of the child*;
- They ANSWER THE QUESTION THAN AN ADJECTIVE ANSWERS—*WHICH carpet* and *WHOSE toy*.

You can even replace these prepositional phrases with a ONE-WORD ADJECTIVE—*CARPETED ROOM* and *CHILD'S TOY.*

Note: Prepositional phrases that do the job of an adjective have a FIXED LOCATION—they **must** come **AFTER** the CHIEF NOUN.

Labeling for Prepositional Phrases That Do the Job of an Adjective:
Place the lettering ADJ over the PREPOSITION ITSELF.

Note Also: Any prepositional phrase that is **not** inside a noun cluster—that is, **not** inside a noun-job territory—is **not** doing the job of an adjective (instead, it will be doing the job of an adverb—see Chapter 16).

● Do *PRACTICE C* (LABELING OF PREPOSITIONAL PHRASE THAT DO THE JOB OF AN ADJECTIVE) in your **Skills Practice Book.**

Truth J

A dependent clause can do the job of an adjective.

Examples

The ROOM [THAT IS CARPETED] has a beige tone.
The TOY [THAT THE CHILD OWNS] has fallen.

The dependent clauses are the wordings inside the side brackets—namely, *that is carpeted* and *that the child owns*. These dependent clauses have the POSITION of an adjective—AFTER A CHIEF NOUN and INSIDE A NOUN CLUSTER. In addition, they are SAYABLE WITH THE CHIEF NOUN. Moreover, each ANSWERS THE QUESTION OF AN ADJECTIVE—*WHICH ROOM* and *WHOSE TOY*. For a more detailed explanation, see Chapter 17.

Note: Dependent clauses that do the job of an adjective have a FIXED LOCATION—they **must** come AFTER the CHIEF NOUN.

Truths about Noun Clusters

These truths supply a fuller explanation of noun clusters.

Truth A

An ARTICLE often marks the start of a noun cluster.

Examples

AN UNEVEN SURFACE has drawbacks.
A SHORT ANSWER was requested.
THE SNOW fell heavily.

The three words AN, A, and THE are the only ARTICLES in English. They serve as ANNOUNCERS of the nouns or pronouns that follow them. Note that they are UNLIKE adjectives because you can **not** always say them with the noun or pronoun that they belong with. You **must** know these words as articles ON SIGHT.

Articles (Listed):

AN   A   THE

MEMORY AID FOR THE ARTICLES

Say: *AN•A•THE*—as if it were a word.

Labeling for Articles:

Place the lettering ART over each article.

● Do **_PRACTICE D_** (IDENTIFYING ARTICLES) in your *Skills Practice Book.*

Truth B

Noun clusters must contain a NOUN or PRO-NOUN that serves as nucleus or KEYWORD.

Explanation: A noun cluster **must** have a noun or pronoun as its KEYWORD or "chief word." The KEYWORD is the word that the other words either announce or answer some question about either directly or indirectly.

Keyword:

The noun or pronoun in a noun cluster that the article announces and/or that the adjectives answer some question about (modify).

Labeling for a KEYWORD Noun or Pronoun:

When a **KEYWORD** noun or pronoun has an adjective phrase or clause follow it, you must make the KEYWORD stand out more visibly. You do this by placing a broken-line overhead bracket over it and placing the *N* or *PRN* on top of this bracket. Note.

```
[can]  Ⓢ                              OV
  ┌──N──┐  MS          ┌ART  N  ADJ  OP┐
  ∧ January  can  bring    the ˈsongˈ⌊of ˈbirds.
```

Labeling for a KEYWORD followed by an adjective phrase or clause:

Place a broken-line overhead bracket over the keyword, and place the lettering *N* or *PRN* ON TOP OF THIS BRACKET.

Truth C

Noun Clusters usually occupy the
<u>WHOLE</u> NOUN-JOB TERRITORY.

Examples

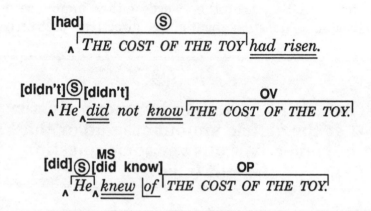

Notice that the noun cluster *the cost of the toy* occupies the **whole** of each of the noun-job territories—the WHOLE of the main subject, object of verb, and object of preposition territories.

Notice, too, how the SAME noun cluster wording can occupy ANY noun-job territory.

This next illustration shows how the entire noun cluster is under one noun-job overhead bracket.

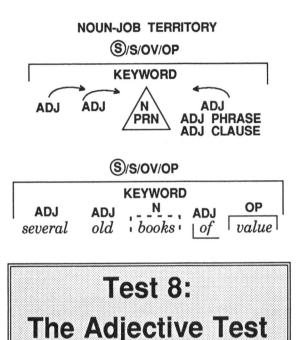

Test 8:
The Adjective Test

TEST 8 is the NEXT TO LAST TEST. Learn this new order for the tests.

ORDER IN WHICH TO CARRY OUT THE TESTS
1.   Comma Test
2.   Main Subject Test—for Questions
3.   Helpers + WHAT/ING Word Verb Test
4.   Do/does/did Test
5.   Movable Starter Test
6.   Main Subject Test—for Statements
7.   Noun Job Tests
8.   ADJECTIVE TEST

The Adjective Test has FIVE STEPS and no ground rules. Take great care that you carry out the steps in correct order. Here is an overview of the TEST.

Overview
Test 8: The Adjective Test
Steps

1. Apply the Capital Letter Test and the THE Test to WORDS INSIDE NOUN CLUSTERS, and label every KEYWORD <u>noun</u> a noun;
2. Label every KEYWORD <u>pronoun</u>;
3. Label every <u>article</u> (inside a noun cluster);
4. Label as an <u>adjective</u> every remaining word that is sayable with the KEYWORD;
5. Label as an <u>adjective</u> every <u>phrase</u> or <u>clause</u> that is sayable with the KEYWORD.

The FIRST STEP alone has SUBSTEPS. You will see all the substeps first. Then detailed explanations for each will follow.

Step 1

Apply the Capital Letter Test and the THE Test to WORDS INSIDE NOUN CLUSTERS, and label every KEYWORD noun a noun:

a. Label any keyword proper noun a noun;

b. Say *THE* before all other words—OUTSIDE THE SENTENCE;

c. Requirements (for the word after *the* to be a noun):

   - The two words must sound right together;
   - The word must keep the same dictionary meaning.

d. When two or more nouns stand beside each other, label the LAST ONE A NOUN and the others adjectives.

Step 1

Apply the Capital Letter Test and the THE Test to WORDS INSIDE NOUN CLUSTERS, and label every KEYWORD noun a noun.

Take careful note that you are looking SOLELY FOR A KEYWORD NOUN. Therefore, you apply this test ONLY TO WORDS THAT ARE UNDER AN OVERHEAD BRACKET—that is, TO WORDS <u>INSIDE</u> A NOUN-JOB TERRITORY.

Step 1a
Label any keyword proper noun a noun.

Examples

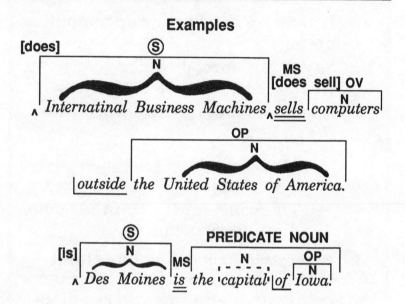

Remember that the words of a proper noun always begin with a capital letter.

● Do **_PRACTICE E_** (CARRYING OUT TESTS 1-8, THROUGH STEP 1A—LABELING PROPER NOUNS) in your *Skills Practice Book*.

Step 1b
Say the word THE before every remaining word—OUTSIDE THE SENTENCE.

This is the first stage of the THE Test. Remember that you must say *the* **plus** the word you are testing APART FROM THE SENTENCE. For the words *the friendly little kitten,* you say—**apart from the sentence:**

~~THE friendly~~
~~THE little~~
THE *kitten*

Notice that only the pair *the kitten* sound right together.

Step 1c

Requirements (for the word after *the* to be a noun):
- **The two words must sound right together;**
- **The word must keep the same dictionary meaning.**

First, you can easily tell which word you can say *the* in front of. You simply see whether you can make up a sentence with these two words as main subject. For the words *the kitten,* you can say *The kitten is playful.*

You must be careful, though. You often say *the* in front of an adjective but **not** in front of the adjective **alone.** For the test to be accurate, you must say *the* plus the word you are testing—just the TWO words—IN A SENTENCE OF YOUR OWN **and** as a MAIN SUBJECT. For example, you **can** say *THE OPEN DOOR should be closed,* but you can **not** make up a main subject with just the two words ~~the open~~.

● **Do _PRACTICE F_ (LABELING KEYWORD NOUNS) in your *Skills Practice Book.***

Second, the word you are testing must **not** have a different meaning with *the* in front of it than the meaning it carried in the sentence. For example, when you test the word *weak* in the expression *weak muscle,* you find that you **can** say *the weak*; BUT THIS *WEAK* HAS A DIFFERENT MEANING. In the expression *the weak, weak* means "PEOPLE with some weakness," whereas in *weak muscle* the word *weak* means "lacking strength."

● Do *PRACTICE G* (LABELING KEYWORD NOUNS) in your *Skills Practice Book.*

Step 1d

When two or more nouns stand beside each other, label the LAST ONE A NOUN and the others adjectives.

Modern English tends to use nouns to answer the question of an adjective and therefore do the job of an adjective. Always label ONLY THE LAST NOUN in a string of nouns with the *N*. Label any/all earlier ones as adjectives. Note.

ART   ADJ   ADJ   N
the Westbrook school building

● Do *PRACTICE H* (LABELING KEYWORD NOUNS) in your *Skills Practice Book.*

● Do *PRACTICE J* (CARRYING OUT TESTS 1-8, THROUGH STEP 1—LABELING KEYWORDS) in your *Skills Practice Book.*

Step 2

Label every KEYWORD pronoun.

Every noun cluster must have a KEYWORD. Therefore, when you can find NO KEYWORD **NOUN,** you simply search for either a PRONOUN YOU RECOGNIZE (see Chapter 2) or the word that the other word(s) modify. ANY

UNLABELED KEYWORD MUST BE A PRONOUN. Here are examples.

NOTHING particular
SOMEWHERE nearby

The pronouns are *NOTHING* and *SOMEWHERE*. Remember that there are a few **pronouns** that you **can** say *the* in front of. Try to remember to label these as pronouns and not as nouns. The most common of these are *ONE, ONES, OTHER,* and *OTHERS*.

●**Do _PRACTICE K_ (CARRYING OUT TESTS 1-8, THROUGH STEP 2—LABELING KEYWORD PRONOUNS) in your *Skills Practice Book*.**

Step 3
Label every <u>article</u>—inside a noun cluster.

You learned how to do this at Truth A of the Truths about Noun Clusters.

Step 4
Label as an adjective every word sayable with a KEYWORD.

You learned how to do this at Truth G of the Truths about Adjectives.

Step 5
Label as an adjective every phrase or clause sayable with the keyword.

You learned how to do this at Truths G and H of the Truths about Adjectives.

Here is the COMPLETE ADJECTIVE TEST.

Test 8: The Adjective Test
Steps
1. Apply the Capital Letter Test and the THE Test to WORDS INSIDE NOUN CLUSTERS, and label every KEYWORD noun a noun:
   a. Label any keyword proper noun a noun;
   b. Say *THE* before all other words—OUTSIDE THE SENTENCE;
   c. Requirements (for the word after *the* to be a noun):
      • The two words must sound right together;
      • The word must keep the same dictionary meaning.
   d. When two or more nouns stand beside each other, label the LAST ONE A NOUN and the others adjectives.
2. Label every KEYWORD pronoun;
3. Label every article (inside a noun cluster);
4. Label as an adjective every remaining word that is sayable with the KEYWORD;
5. Label as an adjective every phrase or clause that is sayable with the KEYWORD.

● Do *PRACTICE L* (CARRYING OUT TESTS 1-8) in your *Skills Practice Book.*

● Do *PRACTICE M* (CARRYING OUT TESTS 1-8) in your *Skills Practice Book.*

Spelling Rules

The purpose of this section is to make your writing something you can be proud of.

> ## Spelling Rule for *A/AN*:
> Use *A* when THE NEXT WORD begins with A CONSONANT SOUND but *AN* when THE NEXT WORD begins with A VOWEL SOUND.

Examples of Use of *A*

A Book
A Large apple
A Used book

Notice that the *U* at the start of the word *used* starts with the sound of the consonant *Y*.

● Do *PRACTICE N* (USING THE ARTICLE *A* CORRECTLY) in your *Skills Practice Book.*

Examples of Use of *AN*

AN Apple
AN Open book
AN Hour

Notice that the *H* at the start of *hour* is silent so that the first sound is a vowel sound.

● Do *PRACTICE P* (USING THE ARTICLE *AN* CORRECTLY) in your *Skills Practice Book.*

Spelling Rule for *ITS*:
**Use *ITS* before a noun
to mean *of it*—<u>not</u> *it's*.**

Examples of Use of *ITS*

ITS location
ITS meaning
ITS duration

The word *it's* can serve only as a contraction for either
it is or *it has*.

● Do <u>*PRACTICE Q*</u> (USING <u>*ITS*</u> CORRECTLY) in your
Skills Practice Book.

Spelling Rule for *THEIR/THEY'RE/THERE*:
**Use *THEIR* before a noun to mean *of
them*—<u>never</u> *they're* or *there*.**

Examples of Use of *THEIR*

THEIR pens
THEIR belongings
THEIR answers

The word *they're* can only mean *they are.* The word
there either carries the meaning *in that place* (in this
use, it contrasts with the word *here* that means *in this
place*), or it is serving as space-filler *there*.

● Do <u>*PRACTICE R*</u> (USING *THEIR, THEY'RE,* AND
THERE CORRECTLY) in your *Skills Practice Book.*

Spelling Rule for Using an Apostrophe plus *s* or Just an Apostrophe:

A word like *George's* before a noun means *belonging to George*. When you add *s* or *'s* to words like *George*, you must note the word's ending sound. When the word's ending <u>has</u> an *s* or *z* sound, add <u>just</u> an APOSTROPHE ('). When it has <u>no</u> *s* or *z* sound at the end (as is the case with *George*), you add an APOSTROPHE <u>plus *s*</u> ('S).

Examples of Adding Just an APOSTROPHE

FAMILIES' houses
WORKERS' union
SHIPS' sails

Examples of Adding an APOSTROPHE PLUS *S*

GEORGE'S
FAMILY'S
CHILDREN'S

● Do <u>*PRACTICE S*</u> (USING THE APOSTROPHE OR APOSTROPHE <u>+ *S*</u> FOR THE POSSESSIVE FORM OF NOUNS CORRECTLY) in your *Skills Practice Book*.

Spelling Rule for COMPARING <u>TWO</u> OF A KIND:

Use the *ER* ending when comparing ONLY TWO.

Examples

*Bill is FAST**ER** than Mike.*
*Volleyball is EAS**IER** than lacrosse.*
*The bus is LAT**ER** than usual today.*

● Do *PRACTICE T* (USING THE *ER* ENDING FOR ADJECTIVES CORRECTLY) in your *Skills Practice Book.*

Spelling Rule for COMPARING THREE OR MORE OF A KIND:
Use the *EST* ending when comparing THREE OR MORE.

Examples

*Bill is the FAST**EST** in his family.*
*English is my EAS**IEST** subject.*
*Summer is the WARM**EST** season.*

● Do *PRACTICE U* (USING THE *EST* ENDING FOR AN ADJECTIVE CORRECTLY) in your *Skills Practice Book.*

Spelling Rule for USING *MORE* OR *-ER*:
Both the word *MORE* before a word and the ending *ER* after a word carry the meaning *more*. Use either *MORE* or *ER*— NEVER both.

Examples

*That is pretti**ER**.* OR *That is MORE pretty.*
*He is happi**ER** now.* OR *He is MORE happy now.*

● Do **_PRACTICE V_** (WRITING SENTENCES THAT USE ONLY ONE COMPARATIVE FORM) in your *Skills Practice Book.*

Writing Tips for Using Hyphens and Irregular Comparisons

Using Hyphens When Two Words Do One Job: Writers use a hyphen (-) between two words that do the job of one adjective (or of one noun). **Example:** *This has* FAR-REACHING *importance.*

Adjectives with Special Spellings for Their "Comparative" Forms: These adjectives form their "more" and "most" spellings in special ways:

GOOD —	BETTER —	BEST
LITTLE —	LESS —	LEAST
MANY/MUCH —	MORE —	MOST
BAD —	WORSE —	WORST

Rules for Agreement of a Verb with Its Subject

You will find these in the Appendix, pages 327-29. Practice material accompanies the rules.

Endnotes

Predicate Adjectives: There is another place that adjectives can appear. It is right after the verb *be* or a verb that the verb *be* can replace. Note.

My brother is TALL.
My brother seems TALL.

Such adjectives have the name PREDICATE ADJECTIVE. They follow the verb *be* (or a replacer for it)—and therefore appear in the PREDICATE. The verb LINKS them to their subject, which they answer some question about (modify).

Note the similarity between the names PREDICATE ADJECTIVE and the PREDICATE NOUN. Remember that the predicate noun also follows the verb *be* (or a replacer for it).

Notice that the predicate adjective answers WHAT when asked after the verb.

For some sentences, you can test whether a word after a verb is an adjective BY SAYING IT WITH THE KEYWORD IN THE SUBJECT. Note.

> *My brother is TALL.* [Say TALL **BROTHER**.]

Other times, you must change a proper noun (like a person's name) or a pronoun (like *they* or *each*) to a NOUN THAT REPRESENTS ITS CLASS AS "PERSON" OR "THING." Note.

> *Bill is TALL.* [Say TALL **PERSON**.]
> *It is tall.* [Say TALL **THING**.]

Notice that though the PREDICATE ADJECTIVE answers the question WHAT when asked after a MAIN verb, it is **neither** a noun **nor** a pronoun.

Predicate adjectives will not be included in the practice material that accompanies this text.

Review

CONTENT IN DARKER LETTERING
MUST BE REMEMBERED.

Adjective: **A word that answers** WHICH, WHOSE, HOW MANY/MUCH, **or** WHAT KIND OF **when asked before a noun or pronoun.**

Noun Cluster: All the words in a noun-job territory when the chief word is a noun or pronoun.

Articles (Listed): *An, a, the.*

Keyword: The noun or pronoun in a noun cluster that all adjectives in the cluster answer some question about.

Labeling for Nouns: Place the letter N̲ over each noun.

Labeling for Pronouns: Place the lettering P̲R̲N̲ over each pronoun.

Labeling for Adjectives: Place the lettering *a̲d̲j̲* over each adjective.

Labeling for Prepositional Phrases That Do the Job of an Adjective: Place the lettering A̲D̲J̲ over the PREPOSITION ITSELF.

Labeling for Articles: Place the lettering A̲R̲T̲ over each article.

Labeling for a KEYWORD followed by an adjective phrase or clause: Place a broken-line overhead bracket over the keyword, and place the lettering N̲ or P̲R̲N̲ on top of this bracket.

Order for the Tests:

1. Comma Test
2. Main Subject Test—for Questions
3. Helpers + WHAT/ING Word Verb Test
4. Do/does/did Test
5. Movable Starter Test
6. Main Subject Test—for Statements
7. Noun Job Tests
8. Adjective Test

Test 8: The Adjective Test:

1. Apply the Capital Letter Test and the THE
   Test to WORDS INSIDE NOUN CLUSTERS,
   and <u>label every KEYWORD noun</u> a noun:
   a. Label any keyword proper noun a noun;
   b. Say *THE* before all other words—OUTSIDE
      THE SENTENCE;
   c. Requirements (for the word after *the* to
      be a noun):
      • The two words must sound right to-
        gether;
      • The word must keep the same dictio-
        nary meaning;
   d. When two or more nouns stand beside
      each other, label the LAST ONE A NOUN
      and the others adjectives.
2. Label every KEYWORD <u>pronoun</u>;
3. Label every <u>article</u> (inside a noun cluster);
4. Label as an <u>adjective</u> every remaining
   word that is sayable with the KEY-WORD;
5. Label as an <u>adjective</u> every <u>phrase</u> or
   <u>clause</u> that is sayable with the KEYWORD.

Spelling Rules:

For *A/AN:* Use <u>A</u> when THE NEXT WORD begins with
a CONSONANT <u>SOUND</u> but *AN* when the next word
begins with a VOWEL SOUND.

For *ITS:* Use *ITS* before noun to mean *of it*—<u>not</u>
it's.

For *THEIR/THERE/THEY'RE*: Use *THEIR* before a noun
to mean *of them*—<u>never</u> *they're* or *there.*

For USING AN APOSTROPHE PLUS *S* OR JUST AN APOSTRO-
PHE: Always add an APOSTROPHE <u>plus *S*</u> (*'s*)
whenever the word does NOT end in an *S* or *Z*
sound. Always add <u>just</u> an APOSTROPHE (')
whenever the word DOES end in an *S* or *Z*
sound.

For COMPARING TWO OF A KIND: Use the *ER* ending when comparing ONLY TWO.

For COMPARING THREE OR MORE OF A KIND: Use the *EST* ending when comparing AT LEAST THREE OR MORE.

For USING *MORE* OR *-ER*: Both the word *MORE* before a word and the ending *ER* after a word carry the meaning *more*. Use either *MORE* or *ER*—NEVER both.

Chapter 16

Adverbs

The purpose of this chapter is to explain the jobs of adverbs. Adverbs are another centrally important type of grammatical job.

Your benefits from this chapter should be more effective writing and better appreciation as you read.

Truths about Adverbs That Modify Verbs

These truths explain the nature of adverbs and the role of those that modify (answer specific questions after) the verb or the verb plus companion wording.

Companion Wording for a Verb:

Any wording (such as an object of verb) that answers
WHOM, WHAT, TO WHOM, or *TO WHAT*
when asked after a verb.

Truth A

One job of an adverb is to limit the meaning of ("modify") a verb or the verb plus its companion wording.

Examples

He walks SLOWLY.
He OFTEN takes a walk.
He does NOT KNOW THE ANSWER
HE FOUND THE BOOK QUICKLY.
SUDDENLY, the sun brightened everything.

In these sentences, the adverbs are the five words *SLOWLY, OFTEN, NOT, QUICKLY,* and *SUDDENLY.*

Notice how you **can** say together *walks SLOWLY, OFTEN takes,* and *does NOT know.* However, you can **not** say *found quickly*; instead, you must say the verb PLUS its companion wording TOGETHER. You must say *found the book QUICKLY.*

Notice, too, that the adverb *SUDDENLY* is a front adverbial.

Truth B

Adverbs limit the meaning of a verb by answering *HOW* (*HOW OFTEN, HOW LONG, HOW FAR, HOW SOON*), *WHEN, WHERE, WHY,* and *UNDER WHAT CIRCUMSTANCES* when asked after the verb or the verb plus companion wording.

Explanation: You can see from the "partial" sentences (below) that they leave questions unanswered—precisely those questions that it is the job of adverbs to answer:

he put it . . . [*WHERE?*]
he came . . . [*WHEN?*]
he left . . . [*WHY?*]
it moved . . . [*HOW?*]
it reappeared . . . [*UNDER WHAT CIRCUMSTANCES?*]
he wins . . . [*HOW OFTEN?*]
he will return . . . [*HOW SOON?*]

Now see how an adverb supplies an answer to each of these questions:

He put it **THERE**. [answers *WHERE*]
He came **LATE**. [answers *WHEN* or *HOW LATE*]
He left **DELIBERATELY**. [answers *WHY*]
It moved **RAPIDLY**. [answers *HOW*]
It reappeared **UNEXPECTEDLY**. [answers *UNDER WHAT CIRCUMSTANCES*]
He wins **OCCASIONALLY**. [answers *HOW OFTEN*]
He will return **SHORTLY**. [answers *HOW SOON*]

● **Do** *PRACTICE A* (DETERMINING THE QUESTION ANSWERED BY AN ADVERB) **in your** *Skills Practice Book.*

Adverb That Modifies a Verb:

A word that answers *HOW, HOW OFTEN, WHEN, WHERE, WHY,* **and** *UNDER WHAT CIRCUMSTANCES* **when asked after a verb or verb plus companion wording.**

Truth C

Adverbs that modify verbs can appear practically anywhere.

Examples

Now Al has lost his pen.
Al now has lost his pen.
Al has now lost his pen.
Al has lost his pen now.
Al has lost his pen again now.

Notice that the only place the adverb *now* does not appear is between the verb and its object. Notice, too, that it can also appear alongside another adverb—the adverb *again* in the last example.

Truth D

Many adverbs can modify the same verb (or verb plus companion words) AT THE SAME TIME.

Example

Undoubtedly, he did not stay long there yesterday deliberately.

In this sentence, the adverbs—*undoubtedly, not, long, there, yesterday,* and *deliberately*—all modify the verb *did stay.* Notice, too, that no comma separates adverbs when they are beside each other.

Truth E

A helpful indicator that a word is an adverb is that it is a still UNLABELED WORD that you can say with the verb or with the verb plus companion wording.

Example

FAV   [couldn't] $\overset{MS}{\underset{PRN}{\textcircled{S}}}$ [couldn't]   OV

⟨*Unfortunately,*⟩ *he* ˄ *could*   not   *put* | *the note* | *there*

       ART N

immediately   yesterday.

In this sentence, all the unlabeled words **and** the front adverbial are adverbs. Here is the full labeling for the sentence.

FAV   [couldn't] $\overset{MS}{\underset{PRN}{\textcircled{S}}}$ [couldn't]   OV

⟨*Unfortunately,*⟩ *he* ˄ *could*   ADV   *not*   *put* | ART N | ADV

the note   there

ADV   ADV

immediately   yesterday.

Note that the front adverbial does **not** need an added label.

Take note, too, of the use of the lettering *ADV* as a label for an adverb.

Labeling for an Adverb:

Place the lettering *ADV* over each adverb.

Important Note: The fact that adverbs are the still UNLABELED words will be the most important clue to help you find them in the ADVERB TEST that will come later in this chapter.

Note Again: As in the earlier chapter, you **must** recognize on sight all the clause introducers that you have learned—the eight subordinate conjunctions and the nine question words.

● Do *PRACTICE B* (FINDING ADVERBS THAT MODIFY VERBS OR VERBS PLUS THEIR COMPANION WORDING) in your *Skills Practice Book.*

Truth F

A prepositional phrase can do the job of an adverb.

Prepositional phrases too can answer the questions of an adverb. Note how they can complete the sense of the partial sentences you saw under Truth B:

He put it *ON THE SHELF.* [answers *WHERE*]
He came *AT NOON.* [answers *WHEN*]
It moved *WITH GREAT SPEED.* [answers *HOW*]
It reappeared *WITH NO WARNING.* [answers *UNDER
WHAT CIRCUMSTANCES*]
He wins *ON OCCASION.* [answers *HOW OFTEN*]
He will return *IN NO TIME.* [answers *HOW SOON*]

Notice that these prepositional phrases not only answer the questions of an adverb and appear in one of the positions of an adverb but also will be STILL UNLABELED after you carry out Tests 1-8 because they do **not** appear inside a noun cluster.

Labeling for Prepositional Phrases That Do the Job of an Adverb:

Place the lettering *ADV* over the preposition itself.

● Do *PRACTICE C* (LABELING ADVERBS AND ADVERBIAL PREPOSITIONAL PHRASES) in your *Skills Practice Book.*

Truth G
A dependent clause can do the job of an adverb.

Not only a prepositional phrase but also a dependent clause can answer the questions of an adverb. Note.

*He put it **WHERE HE COULD FIND IT**.* [answers *WHERE*]
*He came **WHEN HE COULD GET FREE**.* [answers *WHEN*]
*He left **BECAUSE HE WAS LATE**.* [answers *WHY*]
*It moved **AS A STEAM ROLLER WOULD**.* [answers *HOW*]
*It reappeared **THOUGH IT HAD NOT BEEN EXPECTED**.*
[answers *UNDER WHAT CIRCUMSTANCES*]
*He wins **WHENEVER HE GETS LUCKY**.* [answers *HOW OFTEN*]
*He will return **WHEN HE HAS FINISHED LUNCH**.*
[answers *HOW SOON*]

Just like prepositional phrases, these dependent clauses answer the questions of adverbs, fill the positions of adverbs, and will be still UNlabeled when you reach the Adverb Test.

You will get a chance to work with adverb dependent clauses in Chapter 17.

Truths about Adverbs That Modify Adjectives or Other Adverbs

These truths explain the role of the adverbs that modify adjectives and other adverbs.

Truth A
Another job of an adverb is to limit the meaning of ("modify") an adjective or another adverb.

Examples	
Modifying an Adjective	**Modifying an Adverb**
RATHER DISTANT rumble *ESPECIALLY STRONG magnet*	*drives TOO QUICKLY* *visits FAIRLY OFTEN*

In the expressions on the left, *RATHER* modifies the adjective *DISTANT* and *ESPECIALLY* modifies the adjective *STRONG*. In the expressions on the right, *TOO* modifies the adverb *QUICKLY* and *FAIRLY* modifies the adverb *OFTEN*.

Truth B

These adverbs MUST appear IMMEDIATELY TO THE LEFT OF the adjective or other adverb and can be said together with it.

You saw in the above examples how the ADVERB took the position IMMEDIATELY IN FRONT OF the adjective or adverb modified.

Notice how you **can** say together all the pairs of words that begin with the adverb. You can say *rather distant, especially strong, too quickly,* and *fairly often.*

Truth C

These adverbs answer the question HOW when asked in front of the adjective or adverb modified.

For the examples in Truth C, you ask *how* before the adjective or adverb. Note these examples.

HOW distant a rumble? [The answer is *RATHER*.]
HOW strong a magnet? [The answer is *ESPECIALLY*.]
drives HOW quickly? [The answer is *TOO*.]
visits HOW often? [The answer is *FAIRLY*.]

Adverb That Modifies an Adjective or Another Adverb:

A word that answers *HOW* when asked before an adjective or another adverb.

Note: Occasionally, these adverbs will modify a prepositional phrase (or a clause) that follows them. Note.

```
                  ADV    ADV        OP
  That put me SOMEWHAT |at |an advantage|
```

Notice that *SOMEWHAT* stands before the prepositional phrase *at an advantage* and answers *HOW* when asked there.

Note, finally, that these adverbs, like the ones discussed earlier, will be UNlabeled when you come to the Adverb Test.

Adverb:

A word that limits the meaning of a verb, a <u>verb plus companion wording</u>, an adjective, or another adverb and can be said with it.

● Do *PRACTICE D* (LABELING ADVERBS THAT MODIFY AN ADJECTIVE OR ANOTHER ADVERB) in your Skills Practice Book.

TEST 9, the Adverb Test, FOLLOWS the Adjective Test. Note the order for the tests now.

ORDER IN WHICH TO CARRY OUT THE TESTS

1. Comma Test
2. Main Subject Test—for Questions
3. Helpers + WHAT/ING Word Verb Test
4. Do/does/did Test
5. Movable Starter Test
6. Main Subject Test—for Statements
7. Noun Job Tests
8. Adjective Test
9. ADVERB TEST

Test 9: The Adverb Test

This test has no ground rules and consists of a single STEP.

Test 9: The Adverb Test

Label all UNLABELED words, phrases, and clauses as adverbs.

● Do *PRACTICE E* (CARRYING OUT ALL THE TESTS) in your *Skills Practice Book.*

Spelling Rules

The purpose of this section is to make your writing something you can be proud of.

Spelling Rule FOR USING *TOO* RIGHT:

Use the spelling *TOO* just for adverbs.
As a modifier of a verb, it means *also*.
As a modifier of an adjective or
adverb, it means *overly*.

Examples as a Modifier of a Verb

Louise came TOO.
She writes neatly TOO.

Examples as Modifier of an Adverb

Everyone arrived TOO early.
He speaks TOO quickly.

Examples as Modifier of an Adjective

We have TOO little time.
You cannot have TOO many spare pens.

● Do <u>PRACTICE F</u> (USING THE ADVERB *TOO* COR-
RECTLY) in your *Skills Practice Book*.

Spelling Rule FOR USING ADVERBS THAT END IN *LY* RIGHT:

Some words have TWO SPELLINGS. One
spelling is for use as an adjective—the
spelling <u>without</u> an *LY* ending. The
other spelling is for use as an
adverb—the spelling <u>with</u> the *LY*
ending. Use the word <u>WITHOUT THE *LY*</u>
SPELLING to do the job of an ADJECTIVE.
Use the word <u>WITH</u> THE *LY* ENDING to do
the job of an ADVERB.

Examples	
Adjective Use	**Adverb Use**
He has a LOUD laugh.	*He laughs LOUDLY.*
He has a REGULAR job.	*He wears jeans REGULARLY.*
He has a RAPID gait.	*He walks RAPIDLY.*

Spelling Rule FOR USING THE ADVERB *WELL* RIGHT:

Use the word *GOOD* to do the job of an ADJECTIVE and the word *WELL* (meaning *in a good manner*) to do the job of an ADVERB.

Examples	
Adjective Use	**Adverb Use**
Dan is a GOOD student.	*Dan studies WELL.*
Juan has a GOOD bat.	*Juan bats WELL.*
Emily has GOOD clothes.	*Emily dresses WELL.*

● Do *PRACTICE G* (WRITING SENTENCES USING ADVERBS CORRECTLY) in your *Skills Practice Book.*

● Do *PRACTICE H* (WRITING SENTENCES USING ADJECTIVES CORRECTLY) in your *Skills Practice Book.*

Endnotes

Adverbs That Look like Prepositions: It is not exceptional for words to have two or more uses in English. For example, you know that the word *there* has the meaning *in that place* as an adverb but functions simply as a space filler with no meaning of its own when it occupies a subject position.

Some of the nine words in your list of key prepositions can have two uses too. Some of them can have uses AS **ADVERBS** instead of as prepositions. Note.

> *No one went IN.* [means *inside*]
> *We just stood BY.* [means *to the side*]
> *He just went ON.* [means *onwards*]
> *He then came TO.* [means *to consciousness*]

When you find one of these words AND IT HAS NO OBJECT, the author must be using it as an adverb instead of as a preposition.

Adverbs as Modifiers of Sentence Units: Though you can say an adverb with the verb or verb plus companion wording that it modifies, the reality seems to be that adverbs modify the entire sentence unit (or predicate) that you place them in. For example, when you add *not* to the sentence *The phone rings often*, you are contradicting the entire statement. Note.

> *The phone does NOT ring often.*

It seems that other adverbs modify the whole sentence unit (or predicate) in exactly the same way.

An Adverb in the Front Position That Cannot Shift: There is one important adverb that can appear in the front position, that can serve as a transitional adverbial, and that does **not** shift to the end of the unit with grammatical fit. It is the word *yet*.

Note that the words *yes* and *no* can appear in the front position and also be unable to shift.

Review

CONTENT IN DARKER LETTERING MUST BE REMEMBERED.

Companion Wording for a Verb: Any wording (such as an object of verb) that answers *WHOM, WHAT, TO WHOM,* or *TO WHAT* when asked after a verb.

Adverb That Modifies a Verb: A word that answers *HOW, HOW OFTEN, WHEN, WHERE, WHY,* and *UNDER WHAT CIRCUMSTANCES* when asked after a verb or verb plus companion wording.

Adverb That Modifies an Adjective or Another Adverb: A word that answers *HOW* when asked before an adjective or another adverb.

Adverb: A word that limits the meaning of a verb, a <u>verb plus companion wording</u>, an adjective, or another adverb and can be said with it.

Labeling for an Adverb: Place the lettering *ADV* over each adverb.

Labeling Prepositional Phrases That Do the Job of an Adverb: Place the lettering *ADV* over the preposition itself.

[continued]

Order for the Tests:
1. Comma Test
2. Main Subject Test—for Questions
3. Helpers + WHAT/ING Word Verb Test
4. Do/does/did Test
5. Movable Starter Test
6. Main Subject Test—for Statements
7. Noun Job Tests
8. Adjective Test
9. Adverb Test

Test 9: The Adverb Test—Label all UNLABELED words, phrases, and clauses as adverbs.

Spelling Rules:

For USING *TOO* RIGHT: Use the spelling *TOO* just for adverbs. As a modifier of a verb, it means *also*. As a modifier of an adjective or adverb, it means *overly*.

For USING ADVERBS THAT END IN *LY* RIGHT: For words that can have an *LY* ending, use the word WITHOUT THE *LY* SPELLING to do the job of an ADJECTIVE. Use the word WITH THE *LY* ENDING to do the job of an ADVERB.

For USING THE ADVERB *WELL* RIGHT: Use the word *GOOD* to do the job of an ADJECTIVE and the word WELL (meaning *in a good manner*) to do the job of an ADVERB.

Chapter 17

Introduction to Dependent Clauses

You know how words—and groups of words like a noun cluster or a prepositional phrase—can do the job of a noun, adjective, or adverb.

The goal of this chapter is to explain in some detail how dependent clauses too can do each of these jobs.

Your benefits from this chapter should be greater variety in the way you write and clearer understanding as you read.

Truths about Dependent Clauses

These truths consolidate the knowledge about dependent clauses that you already have and will give the foundation you need to understand the Dependent Clause Test, which comes later in the chapter.

Truth A

You find a dependent clause wherever you find a NONmovable starter, a NONmain subject, and (usually) an accompanying clause introducer.

Examples

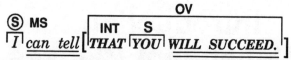

[The dependent clause is the object of verb *THAT YOU WILL SUCCEED.*]

[The dependent clause is doing the job of an adverb. It is the wording *WHEN THEY STUDY RIGHT.*]

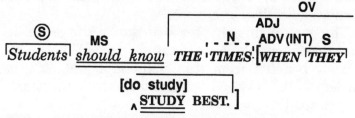

[*WHEN THEY STUDY BEST* is a dependent clause doing the job of an adjective because it answers *WHICH* when asked before the noun *times*.]

Note: These examples will have only partial labeling to help you concentrate on the point under discussion.

Truth B

The words of a dependent clause do the job of a noun, adjective, or adverb AS A UNIT.

This means that ALL THE WORDS OF A CLAUSE ACT TOGETHER—as if they were a SINGLE WORD—TO ANSWER THE QUESTION OF THE NOUN, ADJECTIVE, OR ADVERB. Note.

I can tell **[*THAT YOU WILL SUCCEED.*]**   { [answers *can tell* **WHAT** ?] }

Students learn best **[*WHEN THEY STUDY RIGHT.*]**   { [answers *learns best* **WHEN** ?] }

Students should know **[*THE TIMES*]** **[*WHEN THEY STUDY BEST.*]**   { [answers **WHICH** *times* ?] }

Truth C

You must recognize the chief introducers
ON SIGHT.

The chief introducers are easy to remember.

THAT AS INTRODUCER

The most important introducer is the word *THAT*. This word is the most commonly used introducer, especially of noun clauses and adjective clauses. Note these examples.

The birds knew [*THAT SPRING WAS NEAR*].
[The dependent clause *that spring was near* is doing the noun job of object of verb.]

The birds [*THAT WE HEARD*] *had just arrived.*
[The dependent clause *that we heard* is doing the adjective job of answering *WHICH* birds.]

SUBORDINATING CONJUNCTIONS AS INTRODUCERS

Besides the word *THAT*, subordinating conjunctions serve as introducers. The most common of these are the eight that you have already learned. Note this review.

Subordinating Conjunctions That Do the Job of Introducer of a Dependent Clause	
BECAUSE	*BEFORE*
SINCE	*AFTER*
THOUGH/ALTHOUGH	*WHILE*
IF	*UNTIL*

Example

We must finish this [BEFORE THE BUSES LEAVE].
[The dependent clause ***before the buses leave*** answers the adverb question *WHEN* when asked after *must finish this.*]

QUESTION WORDS AS INTRODUCERS

Another group of commonly used introducers of dependent clauses are the nine question words that you have already learned. Here is a review of these.

Questions Words Listed Alphabetically					
Non-wh.. Word	Wh.. Words (Alphabetically)				
HOW	*WHAT*	*WHEN* *WHERE*	*WHICH*	*WHO* *WHOM* *WHOSE*	*WHY*

We asked [WHAT KIND OF BREAD WAS THE MOST WHOLESOME].
[The dependent clause **what kind of bread was the most wholesome** does the noun job of object of verb.]

Note: As in the earlier chapters, you only need to **recognize** these words. They appear either alone or as part of a group of words and either RIGHT BEFORE or AS BELONGING TO a NONMAIN SUBJECT.

Truth D

Introducers of adverb clauses and some noun clauses have no grammatical job to do
OTHER THAN to be clause introducers.

Examples

We finished the dishes [BEFORE the evening news starter].
He knew [THAT he would be late].

In these sentences, both *BEFORE* and *THAT* are introducers that are independent of any grammatical job inside their clauses.

Note that SUBORDINATING CONJUNCTIONS ARE GENERALLY OF THIS SORT but that the introducer *THAT* is of this sort only **part of the time.**

Important Note: The END of a dependent clause will OFTEN COINCIDE WITH THE END OF A SENTENCE OR A FRONT ADVERBIAL OR A MAIN SUBJECT.

Labeling for Dependent Clauses

You are already familiar with the labeling for dependent clauses. You ENCLOSE the dependent clause in SIDE BRACKETS ([ ]) just as this has been done for you in the practices until now. You also add the LETTERING *INT* over the introducer.

In addition, you must PLACE THE LETTERING *ADJ* OR *ADV*—according to whether it is doing the job of an adjective or adverb—OVER THE FIRST SIDE BRACKET **whenever it is NOT doing the job of a noun.** Note that noun dependent clauses do not need a label other than the overhead bracket that you will have already placed over them.

Labeling for a Dependent Clause:

Enclose the dependent clause between SIDE BRACKETS; place the lettering *INT* over its introducer; and, when appropriate, place *ADJ* or *ADV* over the first bracket.

Dependent Clause:

All the wording that has a NONmovable starter plus subject plus introducer AS ITS BASE and that—AS A UNIT—can do the job of a noun, adjective, or adverb.

● Do *PRACTICE A* (CARRYING OUT ALL TESTS) in your *Skills Practice Book*.

Truth E

Most introducers of noun clauses do an additional job AS PART OF THE CLAUSE.

Question words always have a grammatical job to do inside the clause when you use them to introduce noun

*I remember [**WHO** IS COMING].*
[**WHO** does the job of **SUBJECT** of the verb *is coming*.]

*I remember [**WHOM** I HAVE PHONED].*
[**WHOM** does the job of **OBJECT OF THE VERB**
have phoned.]

*I remember [**WHOSE** BOOK I HAVE BORROWED].*
[**WHOSE** does the job of **ADJECTIVE**
before the noun *book*.]

*I remember [**WHOM** I SENT IT TO].*
[**WHOM** does the job of **OBJECT**
OF THE PREPOSITION *to*.]

*I remember [TO **WHOM** I SENT IT].*
[**WHOM** does the job of **OBJECT**
OF THE PREPOSITION *to*.]

*I remember [**WHERE** I HAVE PUT MY WATCH].*
[**WHERE** does the job of **ADVERB** after
the predicate *have put my watch*.]

All of these dependent clauses do the job of object of
the verb *remember* because they answer WHAT when
asked after this verb.

Notice the labeling for the words INSIDE each of these object-of-verb clauses.

```
S (INT)
 ┌PRN┐
[WHO  IS COMING]
```

```
OV (INT)   S
 ┌ PRN ┐ ┌PRN┐
[WHOM   I   HAVE PHONED]
```

```
        OV          S
 ┌ADJ(INT)    N ┐ ┌PRN┐
[WHOSE   BOOK   I   HAVE BORROWED]
```

```
OP (INT)  S          OV
 ┌ PRN ┐ ┌PRN┐     ┌PRN┐
[WHOM   I   SENT   IT ⌞TO]
```

```
OP (INT)  S          OV
 ┌ PRN ┐ ┌PRN┐     ┌PRN┐
⌞TO WHOM   I   SENT   IT]
```

```
              S              OV
ADV(INT) ┌PRN┐          ┌ADJ    N ┐
[WHERE   I   HAVE PUT   MY WATCH]
```

Notice in the wording **WHO** IS COMING (in the first example) that the word **WHO** does TWO JOBS SIMULTANE-OUSLY—it does the jobs of **INTRODUCER** OF THE CLAUSE **and** of **SUBJECT** OF THE VERB IS COMING **INSIDE** THE CLAUSE.

Second, notice that in ALL these sentences the intro-ducers have an additional grammatical label **to indi-cate the job they are doing** INSIDE **the clause.** Because the job each does INSIDE its clause is of the greatest importance, you yourself may omit the INT label whenever you have no room for it.

Be sure, however, to correctly mark the starting point of the clause (with an opening side bracket). This will always be BEFORE at least the question word. As a matter of fact, for the next-to-last sentence, it would be

BEFORE THE PREPOSITION *TO* as well.

Added Labeling for Introducers That Have Other Grammatical Jobs:

First, always include the label for the "other" grammatical job, whatever it is. Second, also add the lettering *INT* in parentheses if there is space.

● Do **_PRACTICE B_** (CARRYING OUT ALL TESTS AND LABELING NOUN CLAUSES) in your *Skills Practice Book*.

● Do **_PRACTICE C_** (CARRYING OUT ALL TESTS AND LABELING NOUN CLAUSES AND ADVERB CLAUSES) in your *Skills Practice Book*.

Truth F

Introducers of adjective clauses also do an additional job AS PART OF THE CLAUSE.

Here are examples of question words used as introducers of adjective clauses. Remember that adjective clauses ALWAYS come INSIDE A NOUN CLUSTER and TO THE RIGHT OF THE KEYWORD NOUN OR PRONOUN.

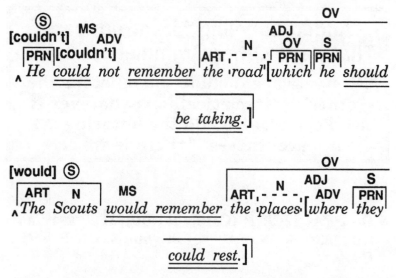

Notice the internal structure of the clause [*which he should be taking*] in the FIRST sentence. First, you can easily identify the subject, verb, and introducer (*which*). Second, note that the verb *should be taking* is a TRANSITIVE VERB and therefore **must** have an object. Consequently, the word *which* must be that object (note that *which* is a PRONOUN that replaces the noun cluster *the road*).

For your information, this sentence is a short-cut expression for these two "source" sentences:

> *He should be taking a road.*
> *He could not remember the road.*

Notice the internal structure of the clause [*where they could rest*] in the SECOND sentence. Again, you can easily identify the subject, verb, and introducer (*where*). Note that the verb *could rest* is an INTRANSITIVE VERB. In this sentence, therefore, the introducer *where* (which takes the place of the words *the places*) answers the question of an ADVERB; it means *at which / what place.*

Here are the "source" sentences for this sentence:

The Scouts could rest at places.
They would remember the places.

- Do ***PRACTICE D*** (CARRYING OUT ALL TESTS AND LABELING ADJECTIVE CLAUSES) in your *Skills Practice Book.*

- Do ***PRACTICE E*** (CARRYING OUT ALL TESTS) in your *Skills Practice Book.*

NEW Test 8: The Dependent Clause Test

Because the Adjective and Adverb Tests are ALWAYS THE LAST TWO TESTS TO BE CARRIED OUT, the Dependent Clause Test **must** become TEST 8. The Adjective Test, then, is bumped into the Test 9 position; and the Adverb Test is bumped into the Test 10 position.

Note the NEW order for the tests.

ORDER IN WHICH TO CARRY OUT THE TESTS
1. Comma Test
2. Main Subject Test—for Questions
3. Helpers + WHAT/ING Word Verb Test
4. Do/does/did Test
5. Movable Starter Test
6. Main Subject Test—for Statements
7. Noun Job Tests
8. INDEPENDENT CLAUSE TEST
9. Adjective Test
10. Adverb Test

This test has THREE steps. Carry them out with care.

(NEW) Test 8: The Dependent Clause Test

1. For each NONmovable starter and its NONmain subject, find and label the clause introducer.

2. Place the opening side bracket for the clause before the introducer itself (or before the unit of words it is part of).

3. Place the closing side bracket after the last adverb or companion word that belongs with the CLAUSE'S verb.

● Do **_PRACTICE F_** (CARRYING OUT ALL TESTS) in your *Skills Practice Book*.

● Do **_PRACTICE G_** (CARRYING OUT ALL TESTS) in your *Skills Practice Book*.

Endnotes

THAT as **Introducer of Adjective Clauses:** The word *that* is also an introducer of adjective clauses. It carries the meaning of the word *which*. Note.

I do not remember the day **THAT** *you mentioned.*
I do not remember the day **WHICH** *you mentioned.*

THAT as **Omitted Introducer of Adjective Clauses:** When you cannot find an introducer, the reason will usually be that the introducer *THAT* has been omitted.

You can omit introducer *that* in the sentence you just saw. Note.

I do not remember the day ... you mentioned.
[The reader can—and does—easily supply the word *that* where it has been omitted.]

THAT as Omitted Introducer of Noun Clauses: The word THAT can also be omitted in noun clauses. Note these two sentences.

*I know **that** you will do well.*
I know ... you will do well.

One More Noun Clause Introducer: There is one more noun clause introducer that might be helpful for you to know about. It is the word WHETHER. Note.

He did not say WHETHER he would join us.

Several More Adverb Clause Introducers: There are quite a few more adverb clause introducers that you may find yourself using. The more common of these are *as, than, lest, provided, unless,* and *whereas.*

Review

CONTENT IN DARKER LETTERING
MUST BE REMEMBERED.

Dependent Clause: All the wording that has a NONmovable starter plus subject plus introducer AS ITS BASE and that—AS A UNIT—can do the job of a noun, adjective, or adverb.

Clause Introducers (Listed): *THAT; BECAUSE, SINCE, THOUGH/ALTHOUGH, IF, BEFORE, AFTER, WHILE, UNTIL; HOW, WHAT, WHEN, WHERE, WHICH, WHO, WHOM, WHOSE, WHY.*

Labeling for a Dependent Clause: Enclose the dependent clause between SIDE BRACKETS; place the lettering *INT* over its introducer; and, as necessary, place *ADJ* or *ADV* over the first bracket.

Labeling for Introducers That Have Other Grammatical Jobs: First, always include the label for the "other" grammatical job, whatever it is. Second, add the lettering *INT* in parentheses if you can.

Order for the Tests:
1. Comma Test
2. Main Subject Test—for Questions
3. Helpers + WHAT/ING Word Verb Test
4. Do/does/did Test
5. Movable Starter Test
6. Main Subject Test—for Statements
7. Noun Job Tests
8. Dependent Clause Test
9. Adjective Test
10. Adverb Test

(NEW) Test 8: The Dependent Clause Test:
1. For each NONmovable starter and its NON-main subject, find and label the clause introducer.
2. Place the opening side bracket for the clause before the introducer itself (or before the unit of words it is part of).
3. Place the closing side bracket after the last adverb or companion word that belongs with the CLAUSE'S verb.

Appendix A

Rules for Agreement of a Verb with Its Subject

Rule for KEYWORDS:

Make the number and person of the verb agree with the number and person of the keyword in its subject.

Examples

JUNGLES ARE rich in vegetation.
A BIKE_ NEEDS a lock.
I WAS not listening.
YOU WERE an asset.

● Do **PRACTICE A** (MAKING VERBS AGREE WITH THE KEYWORD IN THE SUBJECT) in your *Skills Practice Book.*

Rule for SUBJECTS THAT FOLLOW SPACE-FILLER *THERE*:

When space-filler *there* fills the subject territory, make the verb AGREE WITH THE SUBJECT (after it), NOT with *there*.

Examples

THERE were ten COOKIES on the plate.
There IS no HURRY.

● Do <u>*PRACTICE B*</u> (WRITING SENTENCES WITH SPACE-FILLER *THERE* AND WITH CORRECT AGREEMENT) in your *Skills Practice Book.*

Rule for a Few INDEFINITE PRONOUNS:

As subjects, these indefinite pronouns require SINGULAR agreement— *EACH, EITHER, NEITHER, MUCH,* AND the -ONE/-THING/-BODY GROUP.

Examples

EVERYONE HAS worked hard.
EVERYBODY WANTS second helpings.
EACH of us KNOWS what to do.

Important Note: A nearby pronoun must also have singular agreement. Note.

EVERYBODY HAS raised HIS/HER hand.

● Do <u>*PRACTICE C*</u> (WRITING SENTENCES USING INDEFINITE PRONOUNS WITH SINGULAR AGREEMENT) in your *Skills Practice Book.*

Rule for SUBJECTS MODIFIED BY PREPOSITIONAL PHRASES:

You make a verb AGREE IN NUMBER with the KEYWORD, <u>never</u> with wording at the end of a prepositional phrase.

Examples

*The **REASONS** for that decision **WERE** convincing.*
*The **GUIDE** for the hikers **HAS** chosen a difficult trail.*

● Do **PRACTICE D** (WRITING SENTENCES WITH PREP-
OSITIONAL PHRASES IN THE SUBJECT TERRITORY) in
your *Skills Practice Book.*

Rule for SUBJECTS JOINED BY *AND*:

**When the conjunction *AND* joins sub-
jects, use PLURAL agreement.**

Examples

*TREES AND SHRUBS **ADD** value to a person's property.*
*BILL, JOAN, AND I **ARE** in the band.*

● Do **PRACTICE E** (WRITING SENTENCES WITH
SUBJECTS JOINED BY *AND*) in your *Skills Practice
Book.*

Rule for SUBJECTS JOINED BY *OR*, *EITHER ... OR*, OR *NEITHER ... NOR*:

**When you join subjects by *OR*, *EITHER ...
OR*, or *NEITHER ... NOR*, you make the
verb agree with the NEAREST keyword.**

Examples

*Light snow **OR FLURRIES ARE** predicted.*
*Either Pedro **OR TWO** of his friends **ARE** coming.*

● Do **PRACTICE F** (WRITING SENTENCES WITH SUB-
JECTS JOINED BY *OR*, *EITHER ... OR*, OR *NEITHER ...
NOR*) in your *Skills Practice Book.*

Index

A

A/an spelling rule, 289
-Body group, 28
Adjective, 271-297
 comparisons using, 291-93
 defined, 272, 294
 diagram for, 275, 281
 dependent clause as, 311-15,
  318, 321-26
 introducer as, 319
 job of, 271-72
 modified by adverb, 304-9,
  311-12
 noun clusters and, 273-88
 overhead bracket and, 250
 personal pronouns as, 25
 positions for, 273-74, 276-77,
  280-81
 prepositional phrase as, 276-
  77
 questions answered/asked by,
  25, 272, 274, 276-77, 279,
  286, 293-94, 315
 "state of being" and, 58
 test for. See Adjective Test.
 truths, 271-77, 287, 293-94
Adjective clause, 311-15, 318,
 321-26
Adjective Test, 271-97. See also
 Adjective.
 adjective clauses and, 274-77,
  287
 adjective phrases and, 274-76,
  287
 adjectives and, 271-75, 279,
  287
 articles and, 278, 287
 Capital Letter Test and, 283-
  84
 endnotes, 293-94
 keyword nouns and, 273-77,
  279, 281, 283-86
 keyword pronouns and, 273-
  77, 279, 281
 labeling, 275-76, 278-79, 318
 order for tests, 281
 review, 294-97
 spelling rules (related), 289-93
 steps, 288
 terms, 272-73, 278-79
 test, whole, 288
 THE Test, 284-86
 writing tips (related), 293
Adverb clause, 219, 249, 304,
 313-25. See also Subordinating conjunction.
Adverb, 96, 123, 170, 182, 195,
 212, 257-58, 264, 271, 298-
 318. See also Front adverbial.
 defined, 300, 306
 dependent clause as, 219, 249,
  304, 313-25
 front adverbial as, 178-205.
 See also Front adverbial.
 ing spelling as lacking, 123
 introducer as, 319, 322
 job of, 271, 298-312
 labeling for, 302
 modifier of adjective, 275,
  304-6
 modifier of adverb, 304-6
 modifier of predicate, 310
 modifier of verb, 298-302
 noun cluster and, 275, 303-6
 positions for, 170, 195, 300,
  301, 305
 preposition, as different from,
  310
 prepositional phrase as, 277,
  303
 questions answered by, 96,
  257-59, 264, 299-301, 305-6

spelling rules, related, 307-9
test for, 275, 298-312
truths about, 298-306
Adverbial, 182. *See also* Adverb,
    Front adverbial, Transitional
    Adverbial.
Adverb Test, 298-312. *See also*
    Adverb.
    adverbs and, 298-302, 304-7
    adverb clauses and, 304
    adverb phrases and, 303
    endnotes, 310-11
    labeling, 302-3, 318
    order for tests, 307
    spelling rules (related), 307-9
    terms, 300, 306
    test, whole, 307
    truths about adverbs that
        modify verbs, 298-304
    truths about adverbs that
        modify adjectives or other
        adverbs, 304
After-had spelling of a verb, 11-
    12, 14, 46-52, 60, 69, 71-72,
    88-89, 91-93. *See also* Basic
    components for a verb.
    defined, 11-12
    helper before and matching,
        69, 75, 89-90
    Helpers plus WHAT/ING Verb
        Test, finding in, 91-93
    irregular verbs and, 12, 46-52,
        60, 91-93
    main verb and, 88-89
    regular verbs and, 12, 47, 60
    requirement of, due to type
        helping verb, 69, 75
    verb *be* and, 71-72
Afterward territory, 246
Agreement of a verb with its
    subject, 34-45, 327-29
    as "match," 34
    Do/does/did Test and, 100, 116
    keyword and, 327
    number, in, 34-36, 39-45, 327-
        29
    of nouns with verbs, 34-36
    of verbs with nouns, 34, 36,
        40-45, 327-29
    person, in, 34, 37-45, 116,
        327-29
    replacer for the verb *be* and,
        268
    rules for, 40-41, 176, 294, 327-
        29
    space-filler *there* and, 171,
        328
And, 207-11, 213-17, 223, 329
Announcer, 278
Answering *how. See How.*
Answering *what. See What.*
Answering *when. See When.*
Answering *where. See Where.*
Answering *which. See Which.*
Answering *who. See Who.*
Answering *whom. See Whom.*
Answering *whose. See Whose.*
Answering *why. See Why.*
Article, 21, 32, 250, 271, 278-79,
    282, 287-89, 295-96
    a/an, 289
    adjective, relation to, 271, 278
    Adjective Test and, 278-89,
        295-96
    announcer of keyword, 279
    job of, 278
    labeling for, 278, 295
    list of, 32, 278, 295
    marker of noun cluster, 21,
        278
    memory aid for, 278
    noun and, 278
    position in a noun territory,
        250
    pronoun and, 278
    spelling rule for A/AN, 289
    THE Test for nouns. *See* THE
        Test for Nouns.
Apostrophe, 67, 76, 118, 291,
    297

for possession, 118, 291, 297
for contractions, 67, 76, 118.
See also Contractions.

B

Basic components for a verb, 10-12, 14, 40-44, 46-52, 55-57, 60, 68-69, 74-75, 90, 100-101, 108-9, 113, 116, 119-21. *See also* After-had component of a verb, Basic spelling of a verb, *Ing* spelling of a verb, Past tense spelling of a verb, *S/es* spelling of a verb.
do/does/did substitution and, 100-102, 108-9
future tense and, 57
jobs of. *See* Agreement of a verb with its subject, After-had/Basic/*Ing*/Past tense/*S/es* spelling of a verb, Commands, Movable starter, *Not/n't*, Tense.
list of, 11
matching required, 68-69, 74-75, 90, 101, 108
names for, descriptive, 10-11, 14
names for, traditional, 10-12
number of, 11-12
past tense and, 43-45, 55-56, 113, 119-21
present tense and, 40-44, 55-56, 116, 120-21
spelling changes for, 12, 46-52. *See* Regular verb, Irregular verb.
verb *be*, 10, 51-52, 60
verb *have*, 52
Basic components for personal pronouns, 22-24
groups for, 23-27, 37-39
jobs of, 23. *See also* Case.
list of, 22
Basic spelling of a verb, 5, 10-14,

41-44, 46-52, 55-57, 60, 69, 71-72, 74-75, 87-94, 99-102, 106, 108, 112, 119-20. *See also* Basiccomponents for a verb.
agreement and, 40-44
commands and, 99. *See* Commands.
defined, 11-12
Do/does/did Test and, 101-2, 106, 108, 112, 120
listed, 11
future tense and, 5, 10, 14, 57, 60, 74
helpers before and matching, 68-69, 72, 74-75, 90, 101, 108
helpers, without, 99-100
irregular verbs and, 46-52, 92-93, 119-20
main verb and, 88-89, 99-101
present tense and, 40-41
regular verbs and, 12, 47
verb *be* and, 71-72
Basic spellings for personal pronouns, 22-24
-*Body* (indefinite pronoun ending), 28, 33
Building blocks
for sentences: adjective as, 271; adverb as, 271; noun as, 15
for tenses: components of main verb as, 55; helping verbs as, 55
for verb phrases: starters as, 61; followers as, 61
But, 208-11, 215-16, 223

C

Cannot/can't, 86
Capital letter
Adjective Test and, 282-86, 288, 296
Capital Letter Test, 16, 20,

32, 282-84, 288, 296
proper noun with, 19-20, 284.
See also Proper noun.
reading and, 220
sentence's first word with, 19,
207, 217-18, 220
Case, 23-25, 33, 265-67, 269
Check mark, 88-96
Chief word in a noun
cluster/territory
Capital Letter Test and, 32
defined, 21. *See* Keyword.
keyword as, 279. *See* Keyword.
noun as, 16, 21, 31-2, 147,
273-75, 295
noun clause as lacking, 31
noun cluster having, 21
phrase that does the job of a
noun as lacking, 30
pronoun as, 21-22, 32, 273-75,
295
proper noun as, 32
Chief verb, 127-28. *See* Core
verb.
Clearness, 202
Code by which you know a
command, 53
Coherence, 202
Comma
adjectives in string with, 274
adverbs in string without, 301
comma for front adverbials,
204. *See* Front adverbial.
Comma Test (to Find Front
Adverbials), 183-205. *See*
Comma Test.
capitalization, without, 207
city with, 20
end wording without, 180
front adverbial, after, 179-92,
197-201, 204-5. *See also*
Comma Test.
front wording and omission of,
180-81, 190, 192-97

jobs of, 207-9
marker for elements other
than front adverbials, 181-
82, 188-90
minor series and, 216-17, 224
predicates joined without,
214-15,
replacers of *and* or *or*, 207
rule for use after front
adverbials, 203-4
Comma splice, 220-22, 224
Commands, 53-54
front adverbial with, 178-80,
182, 186
helping verb in, 141
helping verb omitted in, 99
punctuation and, 220, 224
sentence and, 2, 53-54, 60,
178
sentence unit and, 132, 142
starter (movable) and, 126-27
subjects and, 53-54, 253
verb position in, 108
Comma Test (to Find Front
Adverbials), 178-205
commas and, 188
covering required, 186-87, 189
direction of shifting, 179, 186
editing required, 197-200
endnote, 204
grammatical fit and, 189-90,
197-201
ground rules, 185-87
order of tests, 184-86
position to shift to, 179, 186
review, 204-205
shifting and, 186, 189-90
steps, 188
test, whole, 188
uncovering required, 187-88
See also Front adverbial,
Comma, Front wording.
Companion test (to the THE
Test), 20
Companion wording (after Main

Verb), 298-302, 306, 310-11

Companion main verb (after Helpers)

identification helps, 77-90, 133, 137, 139-40, 143

ING Subtest and, 81-83, 86-95

order of tests for, 107, 134, 137, 139-40, 143, 191-92, 235-40, 244

position, 6, 133, 137, 139-40, 143, 191-92, 235-40, 244

spelling controlled by helpers, 68-69, 74, 90, 108

starters as markers for, 77

WHAT Subtest and, 81-87, 95, 130

Components. *See* Basic components for a verb, Basic components for a personal pronoun.

Conjunctions, 206-18, 221-24

Coordinating conjunction, 206-11, 213-18, 221-24, 242, 329

Subordinating conjunction, 210-12, 219, 223, 249, 255, 316-17

Comparisons, 291-93

Connectedness, 202, 219

Contraction, 66-69, 76

defined, 66-67, 76

explained, 67

not and, 66-68, 85-86, 155-56, 160-62

subjects and, 68-69, 118, 290

Coordinating conjunction, 206-24, 242, 329

agreement and , 329

and as, 207-8, 210-11, 216, 329

but as, 210-11, 216

comma and, 207, 215-17, 221-24

defined, 210, 223

job of, 212-14

joined elements, finding, 214

listed, 211, 223

nor as, 242, 329

or as, 207-8, 210-11, 216, 329

predicates and, 215, 224

punctuation and, 207-9, 215-17

semi-colon and, 208-9, 218, 223

sentence combining and, 215-18, 221-22

sentence units and, 215-16, 221-22, 224

series and, 207-9, 218, 223

Core verb, 127-29, 131-32, 142, 148

chief verb as, 129

definition, 127, 131, 142

dependent clause and, 147-48, 211

front adverbial and, 186, 193

higher order unit and, 211, 223

importance, 131

labeling for, 128, 142

lower order unit and, 211, 224

main subject and, 129, 131, 146

movable starter and, 127, 142, 148, 159, 161-62, 164, 166, 194

predicate and, 213

sentence unit and, 132, 142

See Movable starter.

Counterpart subject, 141

Covering of front adverbials, 184-94, 205, 237-38, 244

Covering of words as you test for a movable starter, 138, 150-51, 154, 159-64, 166, 168, 184-94, 205-6, 237-38, 244

D

Demonstrative pronoun, 29-30, 33

Dependent clause, 313-26
  adjective clause, 250, 277, 279, 282, 287, 318-19, 321, 324-25
  adjective inside as introducer, 319
  adverb clause, 304, 306-7, 311, 315, 317-18
  adverb inside as introducer, 319, 322-23
  defined, 2, 60, 249, 318, 325
  Dependent Clause Test, 323-26
  end of, 317, 324, 326
  endnotes, 324-35
  front adverbial and, 219, 249, 317
  introducer of, 54, 211-13, 219, 223, 228, 249, 252, 254, 302, 314-21, 325-26
  labeling, 318-20, 326
  main clause, versus, 131
  main subject and, 317
  NONmain subject and, 247, 314, 317-26
  NONmovable starter and, 141-42, 147-48, 249, 314-26
  noun clause, 19, 30-31, 33, 97, 250, 256-57, 266-67, 315, 317-21, 325
  noun clause, 30-31, 33, 96-97, 250, 318-21, 325
  object of inside preposition as introducer, 319
  object of inside verb as introducer, 319, 322
  object of verb, versus, 96-97
  order for tests, 323
  position, 249-50, 321-22
  predicate and, 212-13, 224
  question words as introducers, 228, 249, 255, 266-67, 302, 316-18
  review, 325-26
  sentence combining and, 219
  sentence, versus, 1-3, 46, 54
  start of, 320-21, 324, 326
  steps, 324
  subject inside as introducer of, 318-21
  subject inside of, 252-55, 267, 318-20
  subordinating conjunction as introducer, 210-12, 219, 223, 249, 255, 302, 316-17. *See* Introducer.
  test, whole, 324
  that as introducer, 315, 317, 324-25
  truths about, 313-17
  verb and, 1, 3, 52, 54-55, 60, 249. *See also* NONmovable starter.
Descriptive names for components of verb, 10-11
Do, 62, 75, 101, 117-18, 121-23
Do/does/did substitute spellings, 100-101, 111. *See* Do/does/did Test.
Did, 62, 75, 102, 113-16, 119-20, 123
Direct object, 267
Do/does/did Test, 99-124, 136, 149, 156-58. *See also* Order for the Tests.
  basic spelling of verb and, 100-101, 108-9, 117-18, 120-21
  did as choice, 113-16, 119-20
  did substitution defined, 102, 123
  do as choice, 117-18, 120-21
  do substitution defined, 101, 123
  does as choice, 116-18
  does substitution defined, 102, 123
  endnote, 123
  ground rules, 105-11
  Helpers plus WHAT/ING Word

Verb Test and, 105-8
helping verbs and, 99-100
ing double check with, 123
Movable Starter Test and, 154, 156-59, 161-62, 164, 166, 194
past tense spelling and, 100-102, 113-16, 119-20
proof that a word is/is not a verb, 102-3, 109-21
question-asking and, 149
review, 123-24
s/es spelling and, 100-102, 116-18
spelling rules as background, 114, 117
spelling tips, 114-16, 118-19, 124
steps, 105, 111-21
tense and, 99-100
test, 122, 124
truths (related), 99-104
two "verbs" together and *ing* double check, 123
Does, 62, 75, 102, 116-18, 123

E

Echoing, 203
Ed Exception, 89-90
End of
    dependent clause, 317, 324, 326
    front adverbial, comma as marker of, 179-80, 188-89, 203-5
    question-word wording, verb word as marker of, 232
    sentence, period as marker of, 207, 209
    sentence, question mark as marker of, 207, 209
    statement, period as marker of, 228
End wording, 180
Either...or, 329

-*Er* (OR *more*) spelling rule, 292

F

First person, 37, 39-45
Follower (helping verb), 5-9, 13-14, 61-76, 78-79, 81-98
    as bridge to main verb, 13, 61, 71, 78
    as dictator of spelling of accompanying verb word, 74-75
    as main verb, 13, 61, 72, 79
    as separated from main verb, 73-74, 78
    helper set and, 82, 97
    defined, 9, 14
    Helpers plus WHAT/ING Word Verb Test and, 81-98
    labeling for, 79
    listed, 71-72, 76
    memory aid for, 73
    sounding right with starters, 73
    truths about, 73-75
    verb *be* and, 71-72
    verb *have* and, 72
    verb phrases and, 5-9, 61
For *what*, 267-68
For *whom*, 267-68
Fragment, 220-21, 224
Front adverbial, 178-205, 232, 299. *See also* Adverb.
    absence, 201
    advantage, 201-2
    adverb as, 299, 302, 317
    characteristics, 179-81
    coherence, by means of, 202
    comma as marker for, 179-81, 195-97, 204
    commas as marker for, 204
    comma missing for, 180-81, 195-97, 310
    covering of, 184-94, 205, 237-38, 244
    defined, 182, 204

dependent clause as, 219, 249, 317

"echoing," by means of, 203

editorial changes required for, 197-201

end of, 180-81, 195-97, 317. *See also* Comma.

labeling for, 182-83, 205, 302

Main Subject Test—for Questions and, 190-92, 205, 237-38, 244

Movable Starter Test and, 192-95, 205

order for tests, 184, 205

paragraphs, inside, 200-201

position, 178-82, 204

punctuation for, 203-5

questions and, 178-82, 185, 190-94

repetition, by means of, 203

sentence combining and, 219

test for, 183-90, 197-201, 205

transitional adverbial, as, 201-4, 218-19

truths about, 178-82, 201

variety by means of, 203

uncovering of, 185, 187-88, 205

words that do not shift and, 310

yet and, 310

Front position/section/word-ing, 178-79, 181-82, 185-86, 189-90, 310. *See also* Front adverbial.

Future tense, 5, 10, 14, 57

G

Grammatical element, 207-8

coordinating conjunction and, 210-11, 213, 216-17, 223-24

defined, 208, 223

front position and, 186

higher order of, 211, 223

lower order of, 211, 216-17, 224

series of, 207-8, 210-11, 216-17, 224

tests and, 80

Grammatical fit, 103-4, 133-43, 149, 182-205

Ground rule

defined, 105

tests and, 80

See Do/does/did Test, Main Subject Test—for Questions, Movable Starter Test, Comma Test (for Front Adverbials).

Groups of personal pronouns, 37-39

H

Have. See Verb *have.*

Helping verb, 5-11. *See* Starter, Movable starter, NONmovable starter, Follower.

Helper set, 82-84, 87, 97

Helpers plus WHAT/ING Word Verb Test, 77-98, 130, 134, 136, 142, 183-88

asking *what* right, 84-86

contractions with *not*, 85

ed exception, 89-90

endnotes, 96-97

helper set, 82, 97

Helpers Subtest, 81-82, 247

importance, 77, 80

ing exception, 90-91

ING Subtest, 84, 86-94, 191, 247

irregular verb exception, 91-92

order for testing, 102-3, 106-7, 122-24, 134, 142, 183-86

positions of main verb and, 77-79

position of movable starter for testing, 134

positions of helpers in

sentence, 136, 187-88
requirement for *what*-answering word, 83-84
review, 97-98
sameness of dictionary meaning requirement, 93-94
test, whole, 95
test for sameness of dictionary meaning, 93-94
tests to follow to succeed and, 80
truths about main verbs, 78-79, 99-104, 113
WHAT Subtest, 83-86, 96-97, 191
Helpers Subtest, 81-82, 247
How
  introducer of clause, 228, 254-55, 316, 325
  question answered by adverbs, 257-58, 299-300, 303-6, 311
  question word, 225-26, 243, 255, 316-17
How far, 299
How long, 260, 299
How many/much, 272, 295
How often, 299, 300, 305, 311
How soon, 299
Hyphen, 28, 293

I

Indefinite pronoun, 27-29, 33, 328
Indirect object, 267-68
Infinitive, 11
Ing component, 11, 14
Ing spelling of a verb, 11-12, 14, 46-52, 60, 69, 75, 87-94, 123
  defined, 11-12
  Do/does/did Test and, 109, 123
  helpers before and matching, 69, 75
  Helpers plus WHAT/ING Word

Verb Test and, 89-98
  irregular verbs and, 46-52, 92
  main verb and, 90-91
  mark of verb, 11, 81-84, 86-98, 109, 123
  meaning change and, 93-94
  requirement of, due to type of helper, 69, 75
  regular verbs and, 12, 47
  verb *be* and, 71-72
ING Subtest, 84, 86-94, 191, 247. *See* Helpers plus WHAT/ING Word Verb Test.
Intensive pronoun, 26
Intransitive verb, 256, 270, 322
Introducer (of a dependent clause), 54, 60, 141-42, 212, 219, 228, 249, 252, 254-55, 266, 302, 313-26
  invisible, 141
  job of—inside a clause, 317-23
  labeling for, 252, 317-18, 320, 326
  list of, 315-17, 325
  question word and period as sign of, 228
  question words as, 228, 249, 255, 266-67, 302, 316-23
  sign of presence of clause, 54, 60, 141-42, 314
  subjects and, 254
  subordinating conjunctions as, 212, 219, 249, 255, 302, 316-17, 325
  suppliable, 141
  that as, 315, 317, 324-25
  visible, 54, 60, 141
Invisible starter, 125
Irregular verb, 12, 47-52, 60, 91-92, 98, 102, 109, 112, 119-24
  defined, 48, 60
  Do/does/did Test and, 102, 109, 112, 119-24
  Helpers plus WHAT/ING Word Verb Test and, 87, 91-92, 98

ing spelling and, 91-92
verb *be* as, 11, 41, 43-45, 51-52
verb *have* as, 11, 52
with five spellings, 49
with four spellings, 49-50
with three spellings, 50-51
Its spelling rule, 290

J

Job of adjective, 319
Job of noun, 17-18, 30-32, 245-70. *See* Noun job.
Job of object of preposition, 17-18, 25. *See* Object of preposition.
Job of object of verb, 17-18, 31, 232, 261-62, 266-67, 269, 315, 317. *See* Object of verb.
Job of subject, 16-18, 20-21, 29, 31, 128-29, 132, 246-49, 252-55, 266-67, 319. *See* Main subject, NONmain subject.

K

Keyword, 279, 281-288, 294-296, 321-22
agreement with verb and, 327
adjective clause and, 321-22
adjectives and, 274-75
Adjective Test and, 282-88, 296
defined, 279, 295
diagram for, 281
labeling for (when followed by an adjective phrase or clause), 279
noun as, 283-86
noun cluster and, 279, 282-88
pronoun as, 286-87

L

-Ly spelling rule, 308-9

M

Main clause, 132
Main subject, 128-34, 137, 139-47, 150, 152, 165, 167-70, 174, 176-77, 184, 186, 190-93, 195-97, 205, 211, 213, 223-24, 230, 233-38, 240-41, 244, 249-51, 274, 280, 285, 317.
adverb and, 169-70, 195-97
belonging together requirement, 168-70, 174, 177, 195-97
core verb and, 129, 131-32, 142, 146
defined, 128-29, 131-32, 143, 145-47
dependent clause and, 211, 249, 317
front adverbial and, 186, 193, 195-97
higher order unit and, 211
grammatical fit and, 149
labeling for, 130, 139
lower order unit and, 211
movable starter and, 131-32, 149-52. *See* Movable starter test.
NONmain subject, versus, 249, 251
position, 128-32, 139, 141-44, 234
predicate and, 213
sentence unit and, 132, 142
tests for, 177, 192
THE Test and, 285
truths about, 145-47
See also Main Subject Test—for Questions, Movable Starter Test, Main Subject Test—for Statements.
Main Subject Test—for Questions, 132-43, 225-35, 236-44
companion verb to movable

starter and, 134, 139-40, 191, 235
covering of front adverbial while testing, 191
covering of movable starter in original location, 138
endnotes, 141-42
grammatical fit, 135, 138-39
ground rules, 133-37
Helpers plus WHAT/ING Word Verb Test and, 134
importance, 125
main subject and, 139, 141, 143, 229-32, 134-37, 240-44
movable starter and, 134-40, 191, 229-33, 235-37, 240-41
order for the tests, 134, 142
question mark and, 133, 137-38, 190, 227
question-word question and, 225-44
review, 142-43
starter-verb question and, 70-71, 76, 101, 126, 226-27
starting word, 226-28, 238-40
steps, 133, 137-40
test, revised whole, 192
test, whole, 140, 143, 192, 244
undoing a question and, 135, 138-39
verb tests and, 134
Main Subject Test—for Statements, 145-77, 195-97
advantages, 145-47
belonging together requirement, 169-70, 195-97
endnotes, 175-76
movable starter and, 167-70, 174-75, 177, 180
order for tests, 167-68, 177
review, 176-77
steps, 168-73
subject territory and, 170
test, whole, 168, 174, 177

there and, 168-77
writing tips for using there, 174-75
Main verb, 6-14, 46-52, 55-57, 59-66, 69, 71-73, 83-124, 126-30, 154, 157-59, 161, 164, 213, 247, 252-54, 258-59, 262, 264, 276, 294
agreement and, 34-45. See also Agreement of a verb with its subject.
be set as, 64, 66
commands and, 53-54. See also Commands.
components, 10-12, 14
component/spelling dictated by helper, 68-69, 74-75, 90, 101, 108
contractions and, 69
coordinating conjunctions and, 213-16, 223
defined, 7, 14
do/does/did substitution and, 100-104, 123
do set as, 62, 66, 154, 157-58, 164, 194
ed ending and, 89-90, 113-15
e/es ending and, 116-18
followers as, 13, 61, 72, 79
have set as, 63-64, 66, 71-73, 154, 157-58, 164, 194
helping verbs and, 6, 99-100, 125-26. See also Starter, Follower, Movable starter, Companion main verb, Do/does/did Test.
helping verbs as markers of, 77-98. See Basic components for a verb.
ing ending and, 90-91, 93-94, 121
ing spelling as part of English and, 87-94, 123
Ing Subtest for, 86-94
irregular verbs as, 91-92, 119.

See Irregular verb.
labeling for, 79
number in a sentence, 104-5
object of verb and, 130, 247.
    See also Object of verb.
position in sentence, 104, 249
predicate adjective and, 294
predicate noun and, 268
proof for, 87, 102-3, 109-10.
    See also Helpers plus
    WHAT/ING Word Verb Test,
    Do/does/did Test.
reason for name, 7
spelling changes for, 12, 46-
    52. *See also* Regular verb,
    Irregular verb.
stand-alone/one-word, 7, 126,
    258
starters as, 12-13, 61-64, 78-
    79, 126, 157-58
tense and, 4-5, 10-13, 41-45,
    55-57, 59-60. *See* Tense.
tests for. *See* Helpers plus
    WHAT/ING Word Verb Test,
    Do/does/did Test
truths about, 77-79, 99-104,
    113
verb phrase and, 6-9, 12, 14,
    77-98, 100-104, 258
What Subtest for, 83-86
See also Verb *be*, Verb *do*,
    Verb *have*.
Major series, 208, 210, 224
Matching required
    for agreement with subject,
        34, 41-42, 44-45
    for components with starters,
        68-69, 74-75, 90
    for wording before *and* with
        wording after, 214
    in dictionary meaning for ING
        Test, 93-94
Memory aids, 23, 28, 62-66, 73,
    80, 263, 278
Minor series, 216-17, 224

Miscellaneous indefinite
    pronoun, 28-29
Modifying, 271, 273-74, 279, 286,
    293-94, 298-301, 303-6, 308,
    310
More (versus *-er*) spelling rule,
    292
Movable starter, 125-32, 134-42,
    144-80, 185-86, 190-96, 229-
    44, 252-54, 269
    companion verb for, 134, 139-
        40, 191, 235, 237, 240-41
    core verb and, 127, 142, 148,
        159, 161-62, 164, 166, 194
    covering of, 149, 160
    defined, 128, 131, 142
    Do/does/did Test and, 156-58
    editing and, 148-49
    front adverbial and, 192-94
    importance, 127
    inside-the-sentence position,
        126-27, 134-35, 138-39, 191
    labeling for, 128, 142
    main subject and, 128-29, 139,
        141-42, 151-52, 167-70,
        174, 185-86, 190-94, 229-
        32, 234-37, 240-44
    Main Subject Test—for
        Questions and. *See* Main
        Subject Test—for
        Questions.
    Main Subject Test—for
        Statements and. *See* Main
        Subject Test—for
        Statements.
    NONmovable starter, versus,
        127, 136, 141-42, 147-48,
        152-53, 248-49, 252-54,
        269-70, 314, 318, 324-26
    not addition/deletion and, 135
    n't and, 155-56
    number of per statement, 147
    pausing and, 156, 163
    positions, 70-71, 126-27, 134-
        35, 138-39, 144, 191. *See*

also Movable Starter Test, Main Subject Test—for Statements.
    proof for, in question-word questions, 231-32
    proof for, in statements, 148
    question order and, 229-33, 234-36, 240-43
    requirements for finding, 190-94
    sentence unit and, 132, 142
    statement order and, 229-32
    See Do/does/did Test.
Movable Starter Test, 149-67, 180, 185-86, 190, 192-96, 205
    covering and, 159-62, 192-93
    do/does/did substitution and, 156-58
    do set and, 157-58
    ground rules, 150, 154-63
    have set and, 157-58
    importance, 144-45, 150, 165
    n't and, 155-56
    order for tests, 150, 165
    pausing and, 156, 163
    pitch, rising and, 162-63
    review, 165-66
    steps, 150-54
    test, whole, 164, 166, 194
    test, whole revised, 194
    See also Movable starter.

N

Neatness and labeling, 250
Neither...nor, 327
No, 311
Nominative case, 266-67, 269
NONmain subject, 31, 56, 136, 141-2, 147-48, 248, 251-54, 258, 262, 264, 269-70, 314, 317, 324
    defined, 248, 269
    dependent clause and, 14, 141, 249, 314, 317-18, 324
    introducers as, 318

introducers as before, 254, 317
    labeling for, 251, 269
    marker of dependent clause, 141
    NONmovable starter and, 141-42, 247-48, 252-4
    noun-job test for, 252-54, 270
    truths about, 253-54
NONmovable starter, 127, 131, 141-42, 147-48, 152-53, 247-49, 252-54, 258, 262, 264, 269-70, 314, 318, 324-26
    defined, 248, 269
    dependent clause and, 314-15, 318, 324-26
    job of, 141-42, 249, 252-54, 314-15
    noun-job tests and, 252-54, 270
    NONmain subject and, 141-42, 247-48, 252-54
Not, 66-67, 85-86, 100-101, 135-36, 159-60, 162
    addition/deletion as editor for sense, 135-36
    covering of, 159-60
    do/does/did substitution and need for, 100-101
    position when negator of predicate, 66
    starter and, 66-67, 85-86, 155
N't, 66-67, 70, 85-86, 135, 155, 159-60, 162. *See also Not.*
    addition/deletion as editor, 135-36
    contraction, as, 66-67
    covering of, 159-60, 162
    starter and, 66-67, 70, 85-86, 155
Noun Job Tests, 245-70. *See* NONmain subject, NONmovable starter, Object of verb, Object of preposition, Preposition.

endnotes, 267-69
labeling, 250-52
memory aid, 263
order of tests, 253
review, 269-70
steps, 253
terms, 248
test, whole, 252
truths (related), 245-50, 253-54, 255-57, 259-61
writing tips for correct choice of pronoun spelling, 265-67
Noun, 1, 15-22, 30-33, 35-36, 38-41, 45, 58, 118, 129, 197-98, 213, 245-47, 250-54, 258, 262, 264, 266-88, 291, 293-97, 303, 307, 311, 313-15, 317-19, 321-22, 325-26
adjective clauses and, 321-22
Adjective Test and, 283-88
adjectives and, 271-75, 294, 319
agreement of with a verb, 40-42
articles and, 278
as adjective, 286
Capital Letter Test for, 16, 20, 32, 282-84, 288, 296
chief word in cluster/territory, 16, 21, 31-32, 147, 273-75, 295. See Keyword.
"class" regarding, 294
coordinating conjunctions and, 213
defined, 16, 31
dependent clause and, 277
hyphens for, 293
importance, 1, 15
its before, 290
jobs of, 17-18, 30-32, 245-70. See Noun job, Subject, Object of verbs, Object of prepositions, Indirect object, Noun in apposition, Predicate noun, Main subject, NONmain subject.
keyword as, 279, 283-86
noun clusters and, 21. See Noun cluster.
nouns in apposition, 268-69
noun territory and, 16-17, 19, 21, 245-46
number and, 35-36
person and, 38-40
positions, 16, 18, 249-50, 273-74, 276-77, 280-81
plural, 36, 40-41
possessive pronouns as adjectives before, 25
predicate nouns, 266, 268, 293-94
prepositional phrase and, 276
present tense and, 41-42
proper nouns, 19-21, 32, 283-84, 294
pronoun, versus, 21-22, 197-98, 286-87
questions answered, 16-17. See also Subject, Object of Preposition, Object of verb.
replacers, 19-33, 245-46, 268-69. See also Proper noun, Noun cluster, Pronoun, Phrase that can do the job of a noun, Noun clause.
s'/' ending for, 118, 291
s/es ending for, 35-36, 40-41
singular, 36
"state of being words" and, 58
territories of, 16-17, 170-73, 246, 273
their before, 290
THE Test for, 15-16, 282-86
writing rule and, 197-98
See also Noun job.
Noun clause, 30-31, 33, 96-97, 250, 315, 317-21, 325
introducers of with an additional job, 325
labeling for, 250

that as introducer of, 315, 317, 325
whether as introducer of, 325
Noun cluster, 19, 21-22, 31-32, 271, 273-80, 282-83, 286-88, 294-96, 303, 313, 321-22
  adjective clauses and, 277, 287, 321-22
  adjectives and, 273-77, 282-88, 294
  Adjective Test and, 282-88
  adverbs and, 274-75, 277, 303
  article as marker of, 21, 278, 287
  defined, 21, 32, 273, 295
  keyword in, 279, 282-88
  labeling for, 250-52, 280-81
  noun clause, versus, 31
  prepositional phrases and, 276-77
  pronouns in, 21-22, 282, 286-87
  territory of, 280-81
  truths, 278-81, 287
Noun in apposition, 268-69
Noun job, 17-18, 30-32, 245-70, 315, 317
  case for, 266-67, 269
  defined, 17, 32
  diagram for, 18
  labeling for, 250-51
  listed, 17, 267-69
  noun clauses as doers of, 31
  noun replacers and, 15-33, 245-46, 268-69
  order for tests, 253
  phrases as doers of, 30
  territory and, 16-18, 170-73, 246, 273
  tests for, 252-70
  truths about, in common, 245-47
  See also Subject, Object of verbs, Object of prepositions, Indirect object, Noun in apposition, Predicate noun, Main subject, NONmain subject, NONmovable starter.
Noun Job Tests, 245-70. *See also* Noun job, Subject, NONmain subject, NONmovable starter, Object of verbs, Object of prepositions, Indirect object, Noun in apposition, Predicate noun, Main subject.
  endnotes, 267-69
  labeling for, 250-52
  object of preposition test, 247, 264
  object of verb test, 247, 258
  order for tests, 253
  preposition test, 262-63
  review, 269-70
  steps, 253
  terms, 248
  test, whole, 252
  truths about noun jobs, 245-47
  truths about objects of prepositions, 259-60
  truths about objects of verbs, 255-57
  truths about prepositional phrases, 260-61
  truths about prepositions, 259-60
  truths about subjects, 253-54
  writing tips for pronoun choice, 265-67
Noun replacer, 15-33, 245-46, 268-69
Noun in apposition, 268-69
Number, 34-36, 39-45

O

"Object," 246
Object of preposition, 17, 24-25, 32, 130, 246-48, 250-51, 252-

54, 258-61, 266-67, 269-70,
273, 280, 310, 319
  adverb versus, 310
  afterward territory and, 246
  coordinating conjunctions and,
    214
  defined, 249
  dependent clause and, 248-50
  diagram for, 18
  frequency of occurrence, 259
  impact on, 246
  introducer as, 319
  job of, 17-18, 32, 247
  labeling for, 250-52
  noun cluster and, 280
  noun job and, 17-18
  Noun-job Test for, 252, 261-65
  noun replacers and, 19
  objective case and, 266
  personal pronouns as, 24-25,
    265-66
  prepositional phrases inside
    of, 260
  territory of, 17, 273
  test for, 130, 247, 264
  truths about, 259-61
  whom as, 266-67
Object of verb, 17, 21, 24, 26, 31-
  32, 130, 212, 232, 246-51, 252-
  58, 261-62, 264, 266-67, 269-
  70, 280, 298, 301, 311, 315,
  317, 319-20, 322
  adverbs and, 298, 301
  afterward territory and, 246
  companion wording for verb
    and, 298
  defined, 248
  dependent clause and, 248-50,
    258, 319-20
  dependent clause as, 31
  diagram for, 18
  frequency of occurrence, 249,
    255
  impact on, 246
  indirect object and, 267-68

  introducer as, 319, 322
  job of, 17-18, 32, 247
  labeling for, 250-52
  noun cluster and, 280
  noun job and, 17-18, 247
  noun job test for, 258
  noun replacers and, 19
  objective case and, 266
  personal pronouns as, 24, 26,
    265-66
  predicate and, 212-14
  prepositional phrase, versus,
    261
  question-word questions and,
    232
  territory of, 17
  test for, 130, 247, 256-59
  truths about, 255-57
  whom as, 266-67
Objective case, 266-67, 269
On-goingness, 91
-One/*-thing*/*-body* indefinite
  pronouns, 28, 33
Or, 207-9, 211, 215-16, 223, 329
Order for the tests, 107, 134,
  150, 168, 184, 253, 281, 307,
  323
Overhead bracket, 250-51. *See*
  Noun job.

P

Past participle, 11
Past tense. *See* Past tense
  spelling of a verb.
Past tense spelling of a verb, 11-
  12, 14, 43, 46-52, 55-56, 59,
  62-64, 72, 75, 99-100, 102,
  112-13, 119-24
  agreement and, 43-45
  defined, 11-12
  Do/does/did Test and, 99-100,
    102, 112-13, 119-24
  helpers versus, 75, 99-100
  helpers from, 62-64, 72
  irregular verbs and, 42-52,

102, 112, 119-21. *See* Do/does/did Test.
  main verb and, 99-101
  past tense and, 55-57, 59-60
  regular verbs and, 12, 47, 60
  verb *be* and, 42-45, 51-52
Pause
  comma and, 207
  front adverbial with no comma and, 181, 195
  Movable Starter Test and, 154, 156, 163-64, 166, 194
  semi-colon and, 208-9
Period, 1-2, 138, 206-7, 209, 220-22, 224, 228, 237, 244
  capital letter after, 207, 218, 220
  fragment and, 220-21
  marker of end of statement (vs. question), 137-38, 237
  marker of end of sentence, 1-2, 207, 209
  question-word wording without, 228
  separator of sentence units and, 222
Person, 11, 19, 37-45, 116, 294
  agreement in, 37-45, 116
  class, as, 294
  defined, 37
  first, 27, 39-45
  personal pronouns with, 23. *See* Personal pronoun.
  proper noun as the name of a, 19-20, 30
  second, 37-45
  third, 11, 38-45, 116
Personal pronoun, 22-27, 33, 35-45, 68, 97, 265-67, 269
  agreement and, 35-45
  case and, 265-67
  contractions and, 68
  groups, 37-39
  list of, 27
  number and, 36, 39-45

object and, 24-25, 33, 265-67, 269
  ownership and, 25-26, 33
  person and, 27-45
  self-indicating use of, 26-27, 33
  spellings for, 22-27, 33
  subject and, 23-24, 33, 265-67, 269
Phrase that can do the job of a noun, 30, 97
Pitch, 162, 181
Place, name for as proper noun, 19-20, 30
Plural in number, 35-36, 39-45
Possessive pronoun, 25
Predicate, 212-15, 224, 235, 240, 266, 268-69, 293-94, 310, 319
  adverb and, 310
  coordinating conjunction and, 214
  defined, 211-12, 224
  predicate adjective and, 293-94
  predicate noun and, 266, 268-69, 293-94
  punctuation when two are joined, 214-15, 224
  question-word question and, 125, 129-40
Predicate adjective, 257, 293-94
Predicate noun, 257, 266, 268, 293-94
Preposition, 17-18, 22, 24-25, 32, 130, 228, 245-48, 250-54, 258-64, 266, 269-70, 273
  adverbs, versus, 310
  asking *what* after, 130, 245, 247, 260, 264, 266
  asking *whom* after, 245, 247, 264, 266
  coordinating conjunction and, 214
  defined, 18, 32
  diagram of, 18

"force" from, 246
labeling for, 18, 251-52, 270
listed, 260, 262-63, 269
markers of prepositional phrases, 262
memory aid for, 263
objects and, 259. *See* Object of preposition.
position, 246
test for, 262, 270
truths about, 259-61
See also Object of preposition, Prepositional phrase.
Prepositional phrase, 18, 25, 214, 228, 232-33, 260-62, 269, 276-77, 295, 303-4, 306, 311, 313
adjective job and, 276
adverb job and, 303
adverbs and, 306
components, 260, 264
coordinating conjunctions and, 214
defined, 18, 260, 269
diagram of, 18
labeling for, 277, 295, 303, 311
location in sentence, 18, 276, 303
object of preposition and, 260, 264
object of verb including, 261
of them, 25
question-word question and, 228, 232-33
test for, 262
truths about, 259-61
See also Preposition, Object of Preposition
Present participle, 11
Present tense, 4-5, 10-13, 41-44, 51, 55-57, 59-60, 62-64, 72, 99-100, 116, 121
basic spelling and, 41-42, 51, 55-56, 121

defined, 4-5, 13, 51, 56, 60
do/does substitute for, 59, 100-101, 116
formation, 55-56
future tense, versus, 4-5, 10, 56-67
helping verbs as lacking, 99
number and, 41-44
past tense, versus, 4-5, 55-56
person and, 41-44
s/es ending and, 41-42, 51, 55-56, 116, 121. *See* Third person singular.
third person singular for, 11, 42, 51-52, 116. *See S/es* spelling of a verb.
verb *be* and, 43-44, 51, 63-64, 72
verb *do* and, 62
verb *have* and 63
Principal parts of a verb, 12
Pronoun, 21-33, 37-38, 45, 118, 197-98, 250, 265-67, 269, 271-75, 278-79, 281-83, 286-96, 322
adjective and, 271-96
adjective, as, 25
agreement and, 35-45
articles and, 278
basic spelling for personal pronouns, 22-24
case of, 23-25, 33, 265-67, 269
contractions and, 68-69, 118
defined, 21-22, 32
demonstrative type, 29-30, 33
groups (of personal pronouns), 23-27, 37-38
indefinite type, 27-29, 33
its as adjective, 25, 290
its as pronoun, 25-27, 33
keyword, as, 279, 286-87, 294, 296
labeling for, 275
noun, versus, 197-98
noun replacer and, 19

number and, 36, 39-45
object (use as), 24-25, 33, 265-67, 269
one(s), 29, 33, 287
other(s), 29, 33, 287
ownership type, 25-26, 33
personal type, 22-27, 33, 37-45
person and, 37-39, 42-45
position for, 250, 273, 275, 277
self-indicating type, 26-27, 33
spellings for (personal pronouns), 22-27, 33
subject (use as), 23-24, 33, 265-67, 269
THE Test and, 287
Proper noun, 19-21, 32, 283-84, 294
   Adjective Test and, 282-86, 288, 296
   Capital Letter Test and, 16, 19-20, 32, 282-84, 288, 296
   city with, 20
   defined, 19-20, 32
   keyword and, 283-84
   many-word, 20
   noun cluster and, 21
   noun replacer, as, 19
   noun, as, 19
   predicate adjective as modifier of, 294
   state with, 20
   two-/three-word, 20
Punctuation fault, 219-22, 224
Punctuation marks, 206, 209, 220, 238
Punctuation rules, 57, 203-5, 214-17, 223-24
   for comma after front adverbials, 203-5
   for comma plus conjunction to separate sentence units, 214-16
   for commas in series, 216-17
   for no comma between predicates, 214-15
   for semi-colons in series, 223

Q

Question order, 229-32, 234-35, 239, 242
   defined, 230, 243
   diagram for, 229
   questions with, 231-32, 234-35, 239
   nor followed by, 242
Question mark, 1-2, 70, 133, 137, 140, 143, 190, 192, 206, 209, 220-21, 224, 227-28, 238, 244
   capital letter after, 207, 220
   fragment with, 220-21
   Main Subject Test—for Questions and, 137-38, 237-38
   marker of end of question (versus statement), 137-38
   marker of end of sentence, 1-2, 207, 209
   marker of a question, 70, 227-28
   question-asking tone of voice and, 207
Question order, 225-28, 234, 266
Question, 2, 32, 70-71, 76, 101. 108, 110, 125-44, 147-66, 168-69, 175-76, 190-92, 195-97, 205, 207, 214, 220-22, 224-43, 281, 296, 307, 311, 323, 326
   answered by nouns/adjectives/adverbs. See Questions answered/asked by nouns/adjectives/adverbs.
   capital letter for, 207
   causing a question, 2, 147-49, 214. See Movable Starter Test.
   Do/does/did Test and, 101,

108, 110

fragment and, 220-21, 224

front adverbials and, 178-82, 185, 190-94, 238

fully worded, 2, 220

Main Subject Test and, 168-69, 175-76, 195-97

movable starter and. *See* Movable starter.

question mark and, 2-3, 137, 206-7, 209, 227, 237-38

question order and, 225-28, 234, 266

question words and, 225-28, 231-32

question-word type of, 70-71, 138, 225-44

question-word wording in, 232-36

run-ons and, 222

sentence type, as, 2-3, 53-54

space-filler *there* and, 175-76

starter-verb type of, 70-71, 101, 125-44, 226-27

tone of voice and, 162-63, 207

WHAT Subtest and. *See* Helpers plus WHAT/ING Word Verb Test.

Questions answered/asked by adjectives, 25, 272, 274, 276-77, 279, 286, 293-94, 315. *See also Which, Whose, How much/many, What kind of.*

Questions answered/asked by adverbs, 96, 257-60, 298-301, 303-6, 315, 322. *See also How, When, Where, Why.*

Questions answered/asked by nouns, 16-19, 32, 128-29, 146-67, 245, 254, 256-62, 264, 267-68, 270. *See also Who, Whom, What.*

Question-asking tone of voice, 154, 162-64, 166, 194, 207

Question-word question, 70-71, 138, 225-44

answering and, 230-32

first word and, 226-28, 238-39

front adverbial and, 238

helps for answering questions, 231-32

jobs of question word in, 233

labeling help, 230-31

labeling for, 232, 235-36, 243

main subject and, 229-32, 234-37, 240-44

movable starters and, 229-33, 235-37, 240-41

question mark and, 133, 137-38, 190, 227, 237-38

question order and, 229, 231

question word and, 225-26, 243

question-word wording and, 232-33

starting word and, 227-28

statement order and, 229-30

Question-word wording, 232-237, 239-243

Question word

as introducer (of dependent clauses), 228, 249, 255, 266-67, 302, 316-23

as question-asking word, 70-71, 138, 225-44

R

Regular verb, 12, 47, 60, 119

Repetition, 203

Rules for agreement of a verb with its subject, 327-29

Run-on sentence, 220, 222, 224

S

'S, 64, 68-69, 118, 124, 291, 297

Do/does/did Test and, 118, 124

meaning *belonging to*, 291, 297

meaning *has* or *is*, 68-69, 118

memory aid (for verb *be*

helpers) and, 64
spelling rule for, 291, 297
Second person, 37-45
S/es spelling for a noun, 35-36, 40-41
S/es spelling of a verb, 11-12, 14, 40-44, 46-52, 55-56, 60, 75, 88-89, 99-101, 109, 112, 116-21
  agreement and, 40-44
  defined, 11-12
  Do/does/did Test and, 99-104, 109, 112, 116, 120, 122-24
  Helpers plus WHAT/ING Word Verb Test, 88-89
  helpers versus, 75, 99-100
  irregular verbs and, 12, 47, 60
  main verb and, 99-101
  regular verbs and, 12, 47, 60
  present tense and, 40-41, 55-56, 60
Same meaning, as verb test requirement, 87-88, 91, 93-95, 98
Same meaning, as noun test requirement, 283, 285-86, 288
Same word twice as testing (not allowed), 2, 70, 159-61, 187
Second person, 37-45
Secondary role of verb, 3, 55
Semi-colon, 206, 208, 209, 218, 219, 222-23
  jobs of , 208-9
  replacer of *and* or *or* in a series, 208
  replacer of a period between sentence units, 209, 218, 222
  sentence combining and, 218
Sentence combining, 214-16, 217-19
Series, 207-8, 210, 216-17, 223-24
  comma and, 207-8, 210, 216-17, 223-24

defined, 208, 224
major, 208-10, 223-24
minor, 216-17, 224
semi-colon and, 208-9, 223
Singular (in number), 11, 35-36, 39-45, 116
Sounding right together, 15, 73, 96, 169, 283, 285, 288
Space-filler *there*, 170-77, 290, 327-28
  agreement of subject with verb and, 327-28
  defined, 171, 177
  labeling for, 172, 177
  questions and, 175-76
  verb *be* changes with, 171-73
  writing with, 174-75
Spelling rules, 114, 117, 289-93, 296-97, 308-9, 312
  for changing *Y* to *I*, 114
  for changing *Y* to *IE*, 114
  for choosing *an* or *a*, 289
  for choosing *its*, 290
  for choosing *their*, 290
  for choosing *-ly*, 308-9
  for choosing *more* OR *-er*, 292
  for choosing *'s/'*, 291
  for choosing *too*, 308
  for choosing *well*, 309
  for comparing TWO of a kind, 291-92
  for comparing THREE OR MORE of a kind, 292
  for doubling a final consonant, 114
  for dropping final silent *E*, 114
  for irregular comparisons, 293
Starter (helping verb), 8-9, 12-14, 59, 61-76, 77-79, 81-83, 96, 99-125
  as dictator of spelling of accompanying verb word, 69, 72, 74-75
  as main verb, 12-13, 61-64,

78-79, 126, 157-58
as verb word, 79
be set, 63-64, 72, 75
   as helper, 63-64, 71-72, 75-76
   as main verb, 12-13, 64, 72, 171
contractions of, 68-69
core verb and, 127-29, 131-32, 142, 148
defined, 8-9, 14
do / does / did substitutions and, 100-103. *See* Do/does/did Test.
Do/does/did Test and, 99-124
do set, 62, 75
   as helper, 62, 76, 99-124
   as main verb, 12-13, 62
follower and, 9
future tense and, 5, 10, 14, 57, 60
have set, 63, 75
   as helper, 63, 71-73, 76
   as main verb, 12-13, 63, 72-73
Helpers plus WHAT/ING Word Verb Test and, 77-98
helper set and, 82, 97
invisible, 125-26, 253
job of, 61-62
labeling for, 79
listed, 62-65, 72, 76
main subject and, 128-32. *See* Movable starter, Main Subject Test—for Questions, Movable Starter Test, Main Subject. Test—for Statements.
main verb after, 6-9, 78-79, 81-83, 130, 156. *See* Helpers plus WHAT/ING Word Verb Test, Companion main verb.
memory aids for, 62-66
marker of verb, 8, 12, 59, 61, 77, 125, 141
marker of verb phrase, 8, 12, 61-62, 77, 125
movable starter, 126-32, 142. *See also* Movable starter, Main Subject Test—for Questions, Movable Starter Test, Main Subject Test—for Statements.
NONmain subject and, 136
NONmovable starter, 141-42. *See also* NONmovable starter.
not and, 66-67, 135, 159-60
n't and, 66-67, 85-86
questions and, 70
question-word questions and, 226-27
sentence unit and, 132, 142
sets, 62-66, 72
sounding right with followers, 73
starter-verb question, 70-71, 76, 101, 125-43, 185, 226-27, 238. *See* Main Subject Test—for Questions, Main Subject Test—for Statements.
supplied, 125-26, 253
truths about, 66-70, 73-75, 77-79, 96, 125-26, 147-48
verb phrase and, 5-9, 61, 77-79, 96, 126
will set, 65, 74-75
See Helpers plus WHAT/ING Word Verb Test, Do/does/did Test.
Starter-verb question, 70-71, 76, 101, 125-43, 185, 226-27, 238. *See* Helpers plus WHAT/ING Word Verb Test.
Statement, 2, 53-54, 66, 70-71, 101, 126-27, 131, 134-35, 142, 144-77, 182, 184, 186-87, 229-30, 243

changing to a question, 3, 70-71, 101, 126-27, 144-77, 187, 249

core verb and, 127

defined, 2, 53

front adverbial and, 180, 182, 186

main subject and. *See* Movable Starter Test, Main Subject Test — for Statements.

movable starter and, 126-27. *See* Movable Starter Test, Main Subject Test—for Statements.

NONmovable starter and, 127. *See* NONmovable starter.

Not as adding denial to, 66

question turned to, 126-27. *See* Main Subject Test—for Questions.

sentence type, as, 2, 53-54

Statement order, 229-31, 235, 243

defined, 229, 243

diagram for, 229

questions with, 230-31, 235

Steps to Follow to Succeed, 80. *See also* Tests to Follow to Succeed.

Subject, 4, 13, 16-17, 20-21, 23-27, 29, 31-34, 36, 40-44, 53-55, 60, 68-69, 128-47, 150-52. 167-74, 176-77,184, 186, 190-93, 195-97, 210-13, 223-24, 229-31, 233-38, 240-55, 265-70, 273-74, 280-81, 285, 292-94, 296, 307, 310-11, 314, 317-20, 322-26. *See also* Main subject, NONmain subject.

adjectives and. *See* Adjective, Noun.

agreement of verb with, 34, 36, 40, 171, Appendix.

as core of dependent clause, 54

chief word in, 21, 30-31

commands and, 53-54

contractions of with starters, 68

coordinating conjunctions and, 210, 213

counterpart, 141

defined, 4, 13

dependent clause as, 31

diagram for, 18

job of, 16-17, 32, 129, 141, 247

match with verb for, 34

movable starter and, 128. *See* Main subject.

nominative case and, 266

NONmovable starter and, 252-53. *See* NONmovable starter.

nouns and, 16

noun job and, 17-18

noun replacers and, 19-31

number in, 35-36, 39-44

personal pronoun as, 23, 24, 265-66

person in, 37-44

positions, 54. *See also* Main subject, NONmain subject.

predicate and, 212-13

predicate adjective and, 293-94

predicate noun and, 268

questions and. *See* Main Subject Test — for Questions.

questions asked/answered, 16

question order and, 229-30

rules for agreement of verb with, 40-44, Appendix.

starter and, 252-53

statement order and, 229

territory of, 16, 170-73, 246

test for, 128-30, 247

there as space-filler for, 170-73, 176-77

truths about, 145-47, 253-54
verbal phrase as lacking, 55
who as having nominative case, 266-67
word order and, 176, 229-30
Subordinating conjunction, 210-12, 219, 223, 249, 255, 316-17, 325
defined, 212, 223
dependent clause and, 249
introducers of dependent clauses and, 249, 255, 316-17. *See* Introducer (of Dependent Clause).
job of, 211
listed, 212, 316, 325
sentence combining and, 219

T

Tense, 4-5, 10-13, 40-57, 59-60, 72, 99-100, 176, 268
agreement and, 40-52
defined, 5, 13
future tense, 5, 10, 13, 57, 59-60
past tense, 4-5, 11-13, 43-45, 55-56, 59-60, 62-64, 72, 99-100, 113
present tense, 4-5, 10, 12, 41-44, 55-57, 59-60, 62-64, 72, 99-100, 116, 121
starters and, 62-64
Tests to Follow to Succeed, 80. *See also* Comma Test, Main Subject Test—for Questions, Helpers plus WHAT/ING Word Verb Test, Do/does/did Test, Movable Starter Test, Main Subject Test—for Statements, Noun Job Tests, Dependent Clause Test, Adjective Test, Adverb Test.
That as introducer, 315, 324
THE Test for Nouns, 15-16, 282-86

Their spelling rule, 290
There as space-filler, 168, 170, 174, 176-77
Thing, as a class, 294
-Thing (indefinite pronoun ending), 28, 33
Thing, name for as proper pronoun, 19-20, 30
Third person, 11, 38-45, 116
Tone of voice, 100, 207. *See* Movable Starter Test.
Too spelling rule, 308
Topic sentence, 175
Tour guide, 202
Transitive verb, 255-56, 270, 322

U

Uncovering of front adverbials, 185, 187-88, 205
Under what circumstances, 299-300, 303-4, 311

V

Variety, 174, 203, 219
Verb. *See* Agreement of a verb with its subject, After-had spelling of a verb, Basic spelling of a verb, Basic components for a verb, Commands, Core verb, Follower (helping verb), *Ing* spelling of a verb, Intransitive verb, Irregular verb, Main subject, Main verb, Movable starter, NONmain subject, NONmovable starter, *Not/n't*, Object of verb, Past tense spelling of a verb, Regular verb, *S/es* spelling of a verb, Sentence unit, Starter (helping verb), Subject, Tense, Transitive verb, Verb phrase, Verbal phrase.
as core of dependent clause, 3, 52-55, 147-48, 213, 224

as core of English, 53, 57-58
as core of sentence, 3, 52-55, 213, 224
as core of verbal phrase, 3, 55
jobs of, 3-4
number of in sentence, 104
positions in sentence, 104
primary role of, 3, 53-55, 100
secondary role of, 3, 55
truths about, 66-0, 73-75, 77-79, 96, 125-26, 147-48
Verb *be*, 10-11, 14, 41, 43-45, 51-52, 55-57, 60, 71-72, 171, 268-69, 293-94
  agreement of with subject, 43-45
  components for, 10-11, 14, 60, 72
  component spellings of a verb after, 68-69, 74-75
  contractions of with subjects, 68-69
  followers and, 71-72, 75-76
  irregular verb, a, 11, 41, 43-45, 51-52, 55-57
  main verb, as, 12-13, 64, 72, 171
  meanings of with *there*, 171-72
  memory aids for, 64, 66, 73
  past tense and, 43-45, 56-67, 72
  predicate adjective and, 293-94
  predicate noun and, 268-69
  present tense and, 43-44, 55, 72
  replacer for, 168, 293
  s/es spelling for, 11
  starters and, 63-64, 72, 75-76
  there, with, 171-72
Verb *do*, 62, 74-76, 99-124
  component spellings of a verb after, 74-75
  main verb, as, 12-13, 62

memory aids for, 62, 66
starters and, 62, 76, 99-124. *See* Do/does/did Test.
Verb *have*, 11, 52, 62-63, 66, 68-69, 71-76
  component spellings of a verb after, 68-69, 74-75
  contractions of with subjects, 68-69
  followers and, 71-73, 76
  irregular verb, as, 52
  main verb, as, 12-13, 63, 72-73
  memory aids for, 63, 66, 73
  s/es spelling for, 11, 52
  starters and, 63, 73, 76
Verbal phrase, 3, 30, 55, 97
Verb phrase, 5-9, 12, 14, 59 61, 73, 77, 79, 85, 89-91, 96-97, 126, 140-41, 158
  definition, 5-6, 14
  do/does/did substitution and, 59. *See* Do/does/did Test.
  helping verbs and, 6-9, 12, 14, 59, 61, 73, 79, 96, 140-41. *See* Starter, Follower.
  ingredients, 5-9
  length, 8
  main verb and, 6-9, 14, 77-98, 258. *See* Helpers plus WHAT/ING Word Verb Test, Core verb, Companion main verb.
  number in a sentence, 85
  object of verb and, 258
  order of words, 79. *See* Starter, Follower.
  sounding right together requirement, 96-97
  truths about, 77-79, 96-97
Voice change after front adverbials, 181, 195-96

W

Well spelling rule, 309

What

    introducer of clause, 255, 316, 325

    question asked by noun-job wording, 247

    question asked by object of preposition, 16

    question asked by object of verb, 16

    question asked by subject, 16, 129

    question answered by companion wording to a verb, 298, 311

    question answered by noun clauses, 96-97

    question answered by noun-job wording, 245-47

    question answered by objects of prepositions, 24, 130, 247-48, 252, 258-70

    question answered by objects of verbs, 24, 130, 247-48, 252, 256-59, 269-70, 319-20

    question answered by phrases doing the job of a noun, 96-97

    question answered by predicate adjectives, 294

    question answered by predicate nouns, 268

    question answered by subjects, 16, 23, 32, 129-30, 146-47, 195-96, 247-48, 252-55, 269-70

    questions answered by subjects as a unit, 147

    question answered by words to be also tested by the ING Subtest, 81-87, 95-98, 130, 134, 247

    question word, 225-26, 243, 255, 316-17

What kind of, 272, 274-75, 295

WHAT Subtest, 81-87, 95-98, 134

Which

    introducer of dependent clause, 249, 255, 316, 325. *See also* Introducer of a dependent clause.

    question answered by adjectives, 264, 272, 276-77, 295, 315

    question word, 225-26, 232-33, 235, 242, 255, 316

    pronoun, 322

    that, meaning same as, 324

When

    doing job of adverb inside a clause, 318-19

    introducer of clause, 31, 228, 249, 255, 316. *See* Introducer of a Dependent Clause.

    question answered by adverbs, 96, 257-58, 299-300, 303-4, 311, 316, 325

    question word, 225-26, 235, 243, 255

Where

    introducer of clause, 255, 316, 319, 322. *See* Introducer of a dependent clause.

    meaning as introducer, 322

    question answered by an adverb, 96, 257-58, 264, 299-300, 303-4, 311, 316, 322-23, 325

    question word, 225-26, 235, 243, 255

Who

    as subject inside a clause, 266-67, 318-20

    case of, 266-67

    introducer of clause, 228, 255, 266-67, 316, 319, 325

    pronoun with case, 267

    question asked by noun-job wording, 245-47

    question asked by subjects,

16, 129
question answered by noun-
job wording, 245-47
question answered by
subjects, 16, 23-24, 32, 129,
134, 146-47, 170, 195-96,
233, 248, 252-55, 269-70
question word, 225-26, 232-33,
243, 255, 316-17
Whom
as object of preposition inside
a clause, 318-19
as object of verb inside a
clause, 266-67, 318-19
case of, 266-67
introducer of clause, 228, 255,
266-67, 316, 325
pronoun with case, 267
question asked by noun-job
wording, 247
question asked by objects of
prepositions, 17, 248, 252,
258-64
question asked by objects of
verbs, 17, 248, 252, 256-59
question answered by com-
panion wording to a verb,
298, 311
question answered by noun-
job wording, 245-57
question answered by objects
of preposition, 17, 24, 32,
264-70
question answered by objects
of verb, 17, 24, 26, 32, 256-
58, 269-70

question word, 225-26, 243,
255, 316-17
Whose
as adjective inside a clause,
318-19
introducer of clause, 228, 255,
316, 325
question answered by
adjectives, 25, 264, 272,
276-77, 295,315
question word, 225-26, 232,
243, 255, 316-17
Why
introducer of clause, 228, 255,
316, 325
question answered by
adverbs, 257-58, 299-300,
303-4, 311
question word, 225-26, 243,
255, 316-17
Won't, 67, 86
Word order reversal, 176
Writing tips
for correct choice of pronoun
spelling, 265
for using front adverbials, 201
for using hyphens and irregular comparisons, 293
for using space-filler *there*,
174
See also Punctuation rules,
Spelling rules.

Y

Yes, 311
Yet, 310-11
You (when omitted), 53-54